The WHOLE GOLF CATALOG

The WHOLE GOLF CATALOG

Rhonda Glenn
and Robert R. McCord

A PERIGEE BOOK

Perigee Books
are published by
The Putnam Publishing Group
200 Madison Avenue
New York, NY 10016

A Golf Ink Book

Library of Congress Cataloging-in-Publication Data

Glenn, Rhonda.
   The whole golf catalog / Rhonda Glenn and Robert R. McCord.
    p. cm.
   ISBN 0-399-51623-9
   1. Golf—Miscellanea. I. Title.
GV965.G49   1990   89-49241 CIP
796.352—dc20

Printed in the United States of America
1 2 3 4 5 6 7 8 9 10

This book is printed on acid-free paper.

∞

CONTENTS

The WHOLE GOLF CATALOG

INTRODUCTION

G OLF, AT its lyrical best, remains the course, the elements, the golfer, the game. Nothing more. In its most pure state, golf's mystique is intact. It has even kept its silence, the quiet crunch of spikes in turf and the occasional swish and pop of the club head through the ball. In that classic sense, golf seemingly defies evolution and today, centuries after the Scots first paced their ancient windswept links, the golfer still lopes down the fairway in the early-morning damp, weapons slung in a bag across the shoulder. The golfer— intrigued by the old battle, the humbling pursuit of the flawless swing, the perfect shot, the lower score. These qualities endure.

And yet, the game isn't trend resistant. Its evolution may be glacierlike, but it has changed in the last decade. For one thing, golf has grown. More people play it, on more courses, than ever before. In 1988, 23.4 million golfers teed it up in this country alone, up from 15.1 million in 1980. Since 1985, the number of American golfers has jumped 30 percent.

Even more startling, of the two million new golfers in 1988, 40 percent were women. If that trend continues, women will make up one-third of the American golfing population by the year 2000, which is only ten years away. The National Golf Foundation, which keeps track of such things, reports that senior golfers, those at least sixty years old, also have a growing influence in the game. Seniors played 31 percent of all

> "... golf seemingly defies evolution and today, centuries after the Scots first paced their ancient windswept links, the golfer still lopes down the fairway in the early-morning damp, weapons slung in a bag across the shoulder."

rounds of golf in 1987. Junior golfers represent 11 percent of the American golfing population.

In the last thirty years, the number of golf courses has more than doubled. In 1959, there were about 6,000 courses in the United States. In 1988, the number of layouts had leaped to 13,626. However staggering those statistics, golf course development isn't keeping pace with demand. David B. Heuber, president and CEO of the National Golf Foundation, sees a need for some 4,500 new golf courses between now and the turn of the century; that's about 375 new courses per year, or one a day for the next twelve years. The current rate of golf-course development is closer to 120 new courses a year, not nearly enough for America's growing enthusiasm for the game.

Worldwide, golf is booming. New courses

> "The golfer—intrigued by the old battle: the humbling pursuit of the flawless swing, the perfect shot, the lower score. These qualities endure."

THE GROWTH OF U.S. GOLF

	1970	1975	1978	1979	1980	1981	1982	1983
Golfers (millions)	11.2	13.0	14.0	14.6	15.1	15.6	16.0	16.5
Rounds Played (millions)	266	309	337	346	358	368	379	391
Golf Facilities	10,188	11,370	11,885	11,966	12,005	12,035	12,140	12,197
Private	4,619	4,770	4,872	4,848	4,839	4,789	4,798	4,809
Daily Fee	4,248	5,014	5,271	5,340	5,372	5,428	5,494	5,528
Municipal	1,321	1,586	1,742	1,778	1,794	1,818	1,848	1,860

in Europe and the Far East are producing hot young players, the best of whom threaten to dominate the game in the international arena. It boggles the mind to think that Russians are learning to play and that the Chung-shan Hot Springs Golf Club is an Arnold Palmer–designed layout in China.

Second only to the United States, Japan now has 1,441 golf courses. That's more layouts than in Canada, more even than in England. There are 13.2 million golfers in Japan, nearly two-thirds the number of Americans who play, and only roughly 10 percent of our total courses.

Japanese golfers pay up to $3,600 for a set of irons, about $60 for a dozen top-grade balls. Membership in a private club can cost up to a staggering $1 million!

In frosty old Sweden, there are 123,000 golfers, one of whom, Liselotte Neumann, won the U.S. Women's Open in 1988. Korea has 40 layouts, India has 150, Egypt boasts 5. Even Yugoslavia and Sri Lanka boast two golf courses. There's a golf course in Israel, and Costa Rica, Tahiti, Antigua, Cayman, and the tiny isle of St. Martin all have one.

Golf has gone global.

"Golf seems destined to be the game for the 1990s," *Time* magazine said in May 1989.

This growth is ongoing and flashy. Go to any PGA or LPGA Tour event, golf's showcases, and you'll see innovations that Harry Vardon and Glenna Collett Vare never dreamed of in their playing days:

Fairways and greens are a study in symmetrical perfection. Television towers and radio antennae poke above the crowds. Scoreboards are computerized. Flash cameras pop in the dusk.

The golfers themselves glitter with advertising. They are genuine stars now, bolstered by armies of agents, sports psychologists, medical trainers, security guards, media consultants, and manufacturer's reps. "Team golf" is upon us and golf, as a career, offers new and intriguing positions. Today, an estimated 450,000 people earn their liv-

> "... the game isn't trend resistant. Its evolution may be glacierlike but it has changed in the last decade. For one thing, golf has grown. More people play it, on more courses, than ever before."

> "Worldwide, golf is booming. New courses in Europe and the Far East are producing hot young players, the best of whom threaten to dominate the game in the international arena."

1984	1985	1986	1987	1988
17.0	17.5	20.2	21.7	23.4
403	415	421	434	487
12,278	12,346	12,384	12,407	12,582
4,831	4,861	4,887	4,898	4,897
5,566	5,573	5,585	5,583	5,748
1,881	1,912	1,912	1,926	1,937

ing in some way connected to the game of golf.

In the last decade, the monarchs of space-age technology have been tempted by the pursuit of the perfect shot. Golf shafts flash gold in the sunlight and locker-room banter sounds like the conversation at a chemist's convention. Gone are the old caddie anecdotes—today's golfers compare the qualities of balata, Surlyn, lithium, titanium, boron, beryllium, and graphite. They argue shaft torque, perimeter weighting, grooves, and dimple patterns.

Ben Hogan, who with idyllic grace swung golf clubs and now manufactures them, is one who maintains that the game has changed.

"Everything is better now," said Hogan, "I don't know of one thing that isn't better than it used to be. Everything is better, especially in golf."

The golf industry now tops $20 billion a year, a gross that will more than double by the year 2000, predicts Paul Hencke, a Wall Street business editor.

"Golf is on the verge of becoming a national mania, a sport reshaping life-styles, spending habits, real estate development, and investment patterns," wrote Hencke, editor-in-chief of the National Institute of Business Management newsletter.

Hencke's evidence supports the golf boom.

- Sales of clubs, balls, and clothing top $2 billion per year.
- Golfers spend $7.8 billion annually on golf travel and lodging.
- Golf-related real estate generates $4 billion in yearly sales.

Even conservative forecasts, like that of Terry Williams, director of McKinsey & Co., a business-planning and consulting firm used by the National Golf Foundation, predict that the golf industry will gross $31 billion by the turn of the century. This is a 50 percent growth in the number of rounds played, demand, and in spending patterns. McKinsey & Co.'s best-case scenario, with the introduction of the right programs, is $40.7 billion in the year 2000, a figure which represents a doubling of the game.

The demand for golf videos, golf art, and golf books is keeping pace with this growing interest in the game. In the literary department, *Publishers Weekly* reported in February 1989 that major publishers believe golf books are the best-selling of all sports how-to books. Simon & Schuster has sold 300,000 copies of *Golf My Way*, by Jack Nicklaus, while Random House has sold 100,000 copies of *The New Rules of Golf,* by Tom Watson and Frank Hannigan.

In the last decade, golf's giant strides can be measured by the popularity of its literature, equipment, art, resorts, careers, tech-

"Gone are the old caddie anecdotes—today's golfers compare the qualities of balata, Surlyn, and lithium, titanium, boron, beryllium, and graphite. They argue shaft torque, perimeter weighting, grooves, and dimple patterns. Golf has gone space age."

" 'Everything is better now,' said [Ben] Hogan. 'I don't know of one thing that isn't better than it used to be. Everything is better, especially in golf.' "

DEMOGRAPHIC PROFILE OF ALL GOLFERS

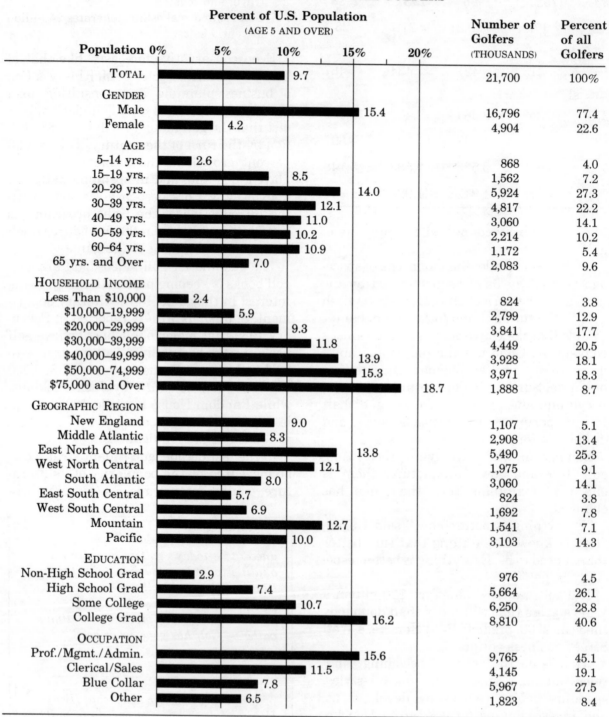

Population	Percent of U.S. Population (AGE 5 AND OVER)	Number of Golfers (THOUSANDS)	Percent of all Golfers
TOTAL	9.7	21,700	100%
GENDER			
Male	15.4	16,796	77.4
Female	4.2	4,904	22.6
AGE			
5–14 yrs.	2.6	868	4.0
15–19 yrs.	8.5	1,562	7.2
20–29 yrs.	14.0	5,924	27.3
30–39 yrs.	12.1	4,817	22.2
40–49 yrs.	11.0	3,060	14.1
50–59 yrs.	10.2	2,214	10.2
60–64 yrs.	10.9	1,172	5.4
65 yrs. and Over	7.0	2,083	9.6
HOUSEHOLD INCOME			
Less Than $10,000	2.4	824	3.8
$10,000–19,999	5.9	2,799	12.9
$20,000–29,999	9.3	3,841	17.7
$30,000–39,999	11.8	4,449	20.5
$40,000–49,999	13.9	3,928	18.1
$50,000–74,999	15.3	3,971	18.3
$75,000 and Over	18.7	1,888	8.7
GEOGRAPHIC REGION			
New England	9.0	1,107	5.1
Middle Atlantic	8.3	2,908	13.4
East North Central	13.8	5,490	25.3
West North Central	12.1	1,975	9.1
South Atlantic	8.0	3,060	14.1
East South Central	5.7	824	3.8
West South Central	6.9	1,692	7.8
Mountain	12.7	1,541	7.1
Pacific	10.0	3,103	14.3
EDUCATION			
Non-High School Grad	2.9	976	4.5
High School Grad	7.4	5,664	26.1
Some College	10.7	6,250	28.8
College Grad	16.2	8,810	40.6
OCCUPATION			
Prof./Mgmt./Admin.	15.6	9,765	45.1
Clerical/Sales	11.5	4,145	19.1
Blue Collar	7.8	5,967	27.5
Other	6.5	1,823	8.4

Courtesy of The National Golf Foundation

nology, services, instruction, and related games and events. The sheer volume of golf information can be overwhelming. That's why we produced *The Whole Golf Catalog*—to help today's golfer sort out new services and products.

Many of us are addicted to the game. We sneak behind a file cabinet to surreptitiously recheck the "V's" of our grip. We wait for elevators, and daydream about the hills and hidden hollows of our home course. We putt on the carpet and pose before our living-room mirror in what we believe to be a flatter swing plane. And yet, we are unable to define golf's greatest lure. We know only that we love it and, as in all great passions, love is enough. Because we love the game, we also find comfort in the knowledge that the elemental ingredients of it go unchanged.

". . . essentially, golf has remained the same strange, elusive, maddening, beckoning, wonderful game it has always been," wrote Herbert Warren Wind, the game's premier modern scribe.

Golf has challenged and charmed many of us for much of our lives and, frankly, we're not surprised that the passion is bewitching a new generation. Whether this newcomer is a junior in scuffed sneakers swinging his father's old persimmon brassie, a career woman plumb-bobbing a center-shafted putter, a senior flailing a new graphite iron, or a strapping young executive wielding a titanium driver, they are golfers. Gifted with that newly acquired status, they too share the knowledge that in its purest and best sense golf remains—the course, the elements, the golfer, the game.

> *"In the last decade, golf's giant strides can be measured by the popularity of its literature, equipment, art, resorts, careers, technology, services, instruction, and related games and events."*

> *". . . in its purest and best sense golf remains—the course, the elements, the golfer, the game."*

1
ORGANIZATION OFFICES

Golf's current upbeat status in the sports world is due, in large part, to the efforts of ten key organizations. One of these organizations, the American Junior Golf Association, which was born in 1977, is a relative newcomer. The other nine have long been working for the good of the game.

The United States Golf Association:

The United States Golf Association is the oldest of these key organizations. Founded in 1894, the USGA is approaching its centennial. The very fact that it has managed to reign as golf's ruling body—the one organization honored by amateurs and professionals alike—is a tribute to the USGA's integrity and its reputation as a nonprofit group working solely for the good of the game.

The USGA's number-one goal is preserving the integrity and values of golf, a role in which it has had great success for nearly 100 years.

A key to that success is that the USGA runs virtually because of the efforts of dedicated volunteers. The paid staff at Golf House, the USGA's headquarters, numbers around 200. The remainder of USGA workers, and there are a thousand, are all volunteers who donate their services and pay their own expenses, no small matter since they travel around the nation and the world doing the work of the USGA.

They conduct the national championships, select the international teams, decide policy on amateur status and equipment standards, raise funds, write The Rules of Golf, oversee the USGA's almost universally used handicapping and course-rating systems, and promote the USGA's efforts in developing new and better turf grasses, preserving the game's history, and encouraging fair play.

The sixteen-member USGA Executive Committee decides policy and oversees all other committees. There's a committee for every facet of USGA interest: from the intricacies of handicapping and equipment standards, to running the United States national championships for everyone from junior girls to seniors.

Summer and fall are whirlwind seasons. That's when the USGA conducts the following championships: the U.S. Amateur, the

"The USGA's number-one goal is preserving the integrity and values of the game, a role in which it has had great success for nearly 100 years."

15

Golf House, USGA headquarters.

U.S. Open, the U.S. Women's Amateur, the U.S. Amateur Public Links, the U.S. Women's Amateur Public Links, the U.S. Junior Amateur, the U.S. Girls' Junior Amateur, the U.S. Women's Open, the U.S. Senior Amateur, the U.S. Senior Women's Amateur, the U.S. Senior Open, the U.S. Mid-Amateur, and the U.S. Women's Mid-Amateur.

Helping golf clubs develop high standards of course maintenance is another USGA role. In 1988, USGA staff members made 1,380 visits to the nation's golf courses under the unique program called the turf advisory service to help golfers learn how to improve their fairways and greens. Any USGA member club may subscribe.

The organization sponsors two annual awards:

The Green Section Award is given annually in recognition of distinguished service to golf through work with turf grass. The Bob Jones Award has been presented annually since 1955 in commemoration of the vast contribution by Jones to the cause of fair play during and after his distinguished playing career.

The USGA's influence is widespread. In the United States, 6,122 golf clubs and courses and 65 foreign courses are USGA member clubs. Additionally, about 250,000 golfers belong to the USGA's Associates Program.

Add to that the fact that almost every golfer plays by The Rules of Golf (written by the USGA with the Royal and Ancient Golf Club of St. Andrews), and the USGA surely represents the most golfers and has the most far-flung influence in the game in the United States.

The United States Golf Association
Golf House
Far Hills, NJ 07931
(201) 234–2300

KEY STAFF MEMBERS

Senior Executive Director:
  David B. Fay

Executive Director, Rules and Competitions:
  P.J. Boatwright, Jr.

Manager, Championship Administration:
  Larry L. Adamson

Director, Communications:
  Robert Sommers

Museum Curator/Librarian:
  Karen Bednarski

Director, Public Golf:
  Eric G. Shiel

Director, Handicapping & GHIN:
  Dean L. Knuth

USGA OFFICERS

President:
  C. Grant Spaeth
  915 Waverly St., Palo Alto, CA 94301

Vice-President:
  Stuart F. Bloch
  P.O. Box 1372, Wheeling, WV 26003

Vice-President:
  Reg Murphy
  P.O. Box 1377, Baltimore, MD 21202

USGA EXECUTIVE COMMITTEE

THE ABOVE OFFICERS AND:
Raymond B. Anderson
  1506 Park Ave., River Forest, IL 60305

Miss Judy Bell
  15 El Encanto, Colorado Springs, CO 80906

Thomas W. Chisholm
  26101 Northwestern Hwy, Southfield, MI
  48037

D. Ronald Daniel
  55 East 52nd St., 21st Floor, New York,
  NY 10022

Director, Rules and Competitions:
  Thomas J. Meeks

Director, USGA Foundation:
  Donald L. Spencer

Technical Director:
  Frank W. Thomas

Director, Merchandising:
  Chris Johnson

Director, Operations:
  John K. Matheny

Director, Regional Affairs and Amateur
Status:
  Anthony J. Zirpoli, Jr.

Director, Broadcasting:
  Mark Carlson

Secretary:
  B. P. Russel
  305 Madison Ave, Morristown, NJ 07960

Treasurer:
  Eugene M. Howerdd, Jr.
  Overlook III, 2859
  Paces Ferry Rd. #1900, Atlanta, GA 30339

J.P. Diesel
  P.O. Box 2511, Houston, TX 77252

M.J. Mastalir, Jr.
  6950 E. Belleview Ave, #202 Englewood,
  CO 80111

John D. Reynolds, III
  One Highgate South, Augusta, GA 30909

Richard F. Runkle
  1350 Comstock Ave., Los Angeles, CA
  90024

Gerald A. Stahl
  8 Whitney Lane, Rochester, NY 14610

F. Morgan Taylor, Jr.
  215 South Beach Road, Hobe Sound, FL
  33475

Peter T. Trenchard
  1116 Little Road, Sister Bay, WI 54234

USGA COMMITTEES

Executive Committee	Women's Committee	Handicap Committee	Associates Committee
Championship Committee	Senior Amateur Championship	Intercollegiate Relations	Museum & Library Committee
Junior Championship	Girls' Junior Championship	Public Golf Committee	Bob Jones Award Committee
Women's Public Links	Amateur Public Links	Public Information Committee	Regional Association Committee
Women's Mid-Amateur	Mid-Amateur Championship	Sectional Affairs Committee	Green Section Committee
Amateur Status and Conduct	Equipment Standards	Green Section Award Committee	
Rules of Golf Committee	Development Committee		Finance Committee

THE NATIONAL GOLF FOUNDATION

With the growth of the game, the importance of the National Golf Foundation has leaped forward in the last decade. Like the USGA, the National Golf Foundation is a nonprofit organization.

Serving as the national clearinghouse for information about the game, the NGF truly keeps its finger on the pulse of golf. Major manufacturers formed the NGF in 1936, but the organization has grown well beyond the manufacturers: Members include golf-course architects, professionals, managers, construction engineers, golf associations, golf clubs, schools and colleges, teachers, and golf-course superintendents, among others.

Information collected by the NGF is invaluable. For example, it was the NGF that put together the famous survey saying that the demand for golf courses in the United States is so great that one golf course per day would have to be built for the next eleven years to satisfy the growing number of golfers in the year 2000.

Golf-course development is a key area of concern, and the NGF offers assistance to would-be developers in identifying geographic trends in golf's growth, along with key contacts in course design and clubhouse architecture and books on all phases of building and operating golf courses.

The NGF also promotes instruction, offering information about learning how to play golf to groups such as schools, colleges, facilities for the handicapped, as well as to individuals.

One of the NGF's most notable achievements was its sponsorship of the 1988 Golf

Summit. This three-day meeting in Ponte Vedra, Florida, pulled together a far-reaching collection of 400 of golf's movers and shakers under the theme "Strategic Plan for the Growth of Golf."

The summit gave golf's leaders a chance to plan strategic initiatives, both to promote the game and to handle the boom effectively.

Industry speakers addressed subjects near and dear to the NGF's goals: course development; instruction for juniors, seniors, and women, as well as men; equipment development; marketing the game; and media relations and golf.

This first summit was widely hailed as a boost to the game, and plans are under way for a 1990 Golf Summit.

The National Golf Foundation offers numerous publications pinpointing needs and trends in the game. NGF consultants are also available for course planning, marketing, and instructional programs.

The NGF sponsors two annual awards, the Herb Graffis Award and the Joe Graffis Award. The Herb Graffis Award is presented annually to an individual for preserving the spirit of the game—specifically for keeping golf as it was meant to be: for recreation, good fellowship, and health. The Joe Graffis Award is given to an individual for outstanding service and dedication to the educational advancement of golf.

> *"The [National Golf Foundation's] summit gave golf's leaders a chance to plan strategic initiatives, both to promote the game and to effectively handle the boom."*

National Golf Foundation
1150 South U.S. Highway One
Jupiter, FL 33477
(407) 744–6006

KEY STAFF MEMBERS

President & CEO:
  David B. Hueber

Executive Vice President:
  Joseph Beditz, Ph.D.

Vice President, Administration:
  Gary Treater

Controller:
  David Claude

Vice President, Communications:
  William A. Burbaum

Vice President, Research:
  Gordon Benson, Ph.D.

Vice President, Marketing, Golf Course
  Development:
  Al Bechtel

Vice President, Membership Services:
  South T. Smith

THE WESTERN GOLF ASSOCIATION

The Western Golf Association conducts four important championships: The Beatrice Western Open has been played since 1899, and its long list of champions include the greats of the game: Hagen, Sarazen, Armour, Nelson, Hogan, Snead, Palmer, Nicklaus, and Watson, among others.

The WGA has also sponsored the Western Amateur, one of the key amateur events for men, since 1899. The Western Junior, for junior boys, was inaugurated in 1914. The Ameritech Senior Open started in 1989. The Western Women's Golf Association conducts the Women's Western Amateur and the Western Girls' Junior Championship.

Included in the services provided by the Western Golf Association is a fine scholarship program which began in 1930. The Evans Scholars Foundation named the scholarship in honor of Chick Evans, the golfing great who was also the father of the scholarship program.

More than 5,000 alumni have graduated from college as Evans Scholars. The Evans Scholars program is the largest scholarship operation in the nation funded by individual contributions. Sources of contributions include the WGA's Par Club, dedicated golfers who contribute $100 or more. Another source is the Evans Bag Tag program in which some 100,000 golfers in 500 WGA member clubs buy a bag tag to support the scholarship.

All WGA proceeds from its championships go to the Evans Scholars programs,

> *"More than 5,000 alumni have graduated from college as Evans Scholars. The Evans Scholars program is the largest scholarship operation in the nation funded by individual contributions."*

and alumni contribute to the championships by serving as volunteers during the tournaments. There's also the annual alumni fund-raising drive, which has raised more than $4 million from past scholars.

The Evans Scholars Program has houses at fourteen major midwestern universities. Each year, more than 200 tuition and housing grants are awarded to deserving, qualified caddies. To qualify, caddies must be nominated by their club with letters of recommendation. There are also strict requirements for academic standing and the need for financial aid.

Nineteen state and regional golf associations help cosponsor the Evans Scholars Program with the WGA.

For information about Western Golf Association championships or the Evans Scholars Foundation, write:

The Western Golf Association
1 Briar Road
Golf, Illinois 60029
(312) 724-4600

KEY STAFF MEMBERS:

Executive Director:
  Donald D. Johnson

Public Information Director:
  Tracey Mendree

Education Director:
  Roland F. McGuigan

Tournament Director:
  Peter de Young

GOLF COURSE SUPERINTENDENTS ASSOCIATION OF AMERICA

Its slogan is "We keep golf green." The members of this association are key behind-the-scenes members of the golf community. Sixty pioneer golf-course superintendents formed the GCSAA in 1926 to advance the art and science of golf-course management. The group also sought to form closer relations between American and Canadian superintendents, and to spread practical knowledge about the problems of course management.

The group—first known as the National Association of Greenkeepers of America—today has more than 8,500 members worldwide. The GCSAA's professional journal, Golf Course Management, has a circulation of more than 22,000.

One of the key events sponsored by the GCSAA is the International Golf Course Conference and Show, attracting more than 13,000 representatives each winter.

This is another organization sponsoring a scholarship program. Theirs is the Robert Trent Jones, Sr., scholarship, named for the veteran course architect, and the program has raised and distributed a little over $600,-000 since its inception in 1956.

Golf Course Superintendents Association of America (GCSAA)
1617 St. Andrews Drive
Lawrence, Kansas 66047–1707
(800) 472–7878 or (913) 841–2240

KEY STAFF MEMBERS

Executive Director:
  John M. Schilling

Director, Headquarters Operations:
  Diana B. Green

Director, Sales and Marketing:
  Karyn Zarley Davis

Director, Communications:
  Pat Jones

Perhaps the association's most dramatic contribution to the golf industry is its Certification Program, which began in 1970. The program encourages superintendents to raise the standards of their field by demonstrating ability in golf-course and turf-grass maintenance and development. More than 1,000 members are today Certified Golf Course Superintendents.

The GCSAA annually sponsors Distinguished Service Awards and the Old Tom Morris Award, honoring one of golf's first greenkeepers and golf professionals who presided at the Royal and Ancient Golf Club in St. Andrews, Scotland. Throughout his life, Morris demonstrated selfless commitment to golf and promoted the game.

"Sixty pioneer golf-course superintendents formed the Golf Course Superintendents Association of America in 1926 to advance the art and science of golf-course management."

Director, Publications:
  Clay Loyd

Director, Education:
  Colleen Smalter Pederson

Director, Membership:
  Janet Rose

AMERICAN SOCIETY OF GOLF COURSE ARCHITECTS

This is an elite group with only 102 members. The organization was born in 1947 when thirteen charter members met in New York City. Two of the founding members were Donald Ross, the premier designer whose masterpieces include Pinehurst #2, and a young Robert Trent Jones.

Ross, the father of golf architecture in America, who is credited with designing 600 courses in his fifty-year career, hosted another meeting late in 1947 where the group adopted a constitution, bylaws, and a code of ethics.

While the membership of the society does not include a number of well-known golf-course architects, many of those nonmembers can be found in the listings of The Business of Golf section of our catalog.

The society roster today includes eighty-four Regular Members (including fourteen Fellows), and eighteen Associate members, representing about 80 percent of the full-time golf-course architects in North America.

Applicants for membership must demonstrate an established ability to design representative golf courses and are reviewed regarding their ethics and methods of professional practice.

The society has a number of interests. The

Donald Ross, the father of golf architecture in America (Courtesy American Society of Golf Course Architects)

ASGCA recently sponsored a project on the "Chemical Impact of Golf Courses on Groundwater Resources," at Cornell University. In a cooperative project with the USGA, the GCSAA, and the University of Florida, the group also participated in a study on sewage effluent for irrigation. Alone, the society produced a white paper on the golf course and the environment.

The architects' group offers literature for those interested in building or remodeling a golf course. The literature is designed to help individuals or groups approach a project with a plan that will save money over the long run.

Each year, the society presents the Donald Ross award to a member of the golf industry who has made a significant contribution to golf in general and golf-course architecture specifically.

Incidentally, members of the society wear a blazer designed in the Ross tartan, honoring their famous founding member.

> *"Two of the founding members were Donald Ross, the premier designer whose masterpieces include Pinehurst #2, and a young Robert Trent Jones."*

The American Society of Golf Course Architects
221 N. LaSalle St.
Chicago, IL 60601
(312) 372–7090

KEY STAFF AND OFFICERS

Executive Secretary:
Paul Fullmer
221 N. LaSalle St.
Chicago, IL 60601
(312) 372–7090

President:
Robert Trent Jones, Jr.
705 Forest Ave.
Palo Alto, CA 94301

Vice President:
Dan Maples
P.O. Box 3014
Pinehurst, NC 28374

Secretary:
Thomas E. Clark
2311 University Blvd. W.
Wheaton, MD 20902

Treasurer:
Arthur Hills
7351 W. Bancroft
Toledo, OH 43617

AVAILABLE PUBLICATIONS FROM ASGCA

*Planning the Real Estate Development Golf Course

*Master Planning: The Vital First Steps in Golf Course Construction

*Planning the Municipal Golf Course
*Selecting Your Golf Course Architect
Evolution of the Modern Green ($5 per copy).

*No charge. To order brochures, please write to the ASGCA at the Chicago address listed above.

THE PROFESSIONAL GOLFERS ASSOCIATION OF AMERICA

In sheer numbers and range of activities, the Professional Golfers Association of America joins the United States Golf Association as one of the most far-reaching golf groups in the nation.

In 1916, 82 men attended the PGA's first formal meeting, in New York City, and created this far-reaching organization. Today the PGA oversees a membership of over 16,000 certified golf professionals in all fifty states.

The PGA sponsors some of golf's most important awards and also sponsors seventeen golf tournaments. Most notable are the PGA Championship and the PGA Ryder Cup Matches, but just as important are tournaments like the Foot-Joy PGA Assistants'

Championship, the Wilson PGA Club Professional Classic, and the United Van Lines PGA Junior Championship. These events are representative of the PGA's role at the grass roots of the golf business—while the touring player gets the most press, it is the home club professional, the assistant, and the teaching pro who most have their fingers on the pulse of the game.

The PGA seeks to provide golfers with direction and leadership at the grass-roots level, through 41 geographical sections. The organization seeks to help the club professional become a well-educated and well-rounded businessman, as well as a good player of the game.

PGA club professionals must complete a

1939 Ryder Cup Team. Standing: *Horton Smith, incoming PGA President Tom Walsh, nonplaying captain Walter Hagen, Vic Ghezzi, Sam Snead, and Henry Picard.* In front: *Byron Nelson, Jug McSpaden, Ralph Guldahl, Paul Runyan, Dick Metz, and Jimmy Hines.* (Courtesy PGA of America)

The 1959 Ryder Cup Team Match featured (left to right) Joe Novack, Sam Snead, U.S. captain Robert Hudson, Sr., Lord Brabazon of Tara, president of British PGA Jimmy Hines, Great Britain captain Dai Rees.

formal apprenticeship, which lasts from four to seven years. They're trained in a vast number of facets of the golf business, learning everything from accounting procedures and merchandising to conducting tournaments.

The PGA's eighty national staff members also provide member services, including: Education, Information, Junior Golf, PGA Section Offices, National Golf Day (which has raised $5 million for a number of golf-related charities since 1952), PGA Awards, Marketing and Promotion, Grass Roots Program, PGA Merchandise Show, Communications, PGA Magazine, PGA Club Operations, and PGA Credit Union, in addition to running the group's tournaments and championships.

While the PGA is separate from the PGA Tour, most touring professionals are also PGA members.

The Professional Golfers' Association of America
P.O. Box 109601
Palm Beach Gardens, FL 33410–9601
(407) 626–3600

KEY OFFICERS AND STAFF MEMBERS

President:
  Patrick J. Rielly

Vice President:
  Dick Smith

Secretary:
  Gary L. Schaal

Executive Director and CEO:
  Jim L. Awtrey

Honorary President:
  James Ray Carpenter

Deputy Executive Director:
  Jesse Holshouser

Senior Director, Administration:
  Paul Bogin

Senior Director, Strategic Planning:
  Joe O'Brien

Senior Director, Marketing & Promotions:
  Joe Steranka

Director, Education:
  Jan Gilpin

Director, Sales & Licensing:
  Steve Nazaruk

Manager, Junior Golf:
  Mike Peterson

Director, Section Affairs:
  Greg Shreaves

Director, Research & Information:
  Henry Thrower

Director, PGA Merchandise Show:
  John Zurek

THE PGA TOUR

The most well-known showcase for golf's best players is the PGA Tour.

Officially, the association in its present form got its start in 1968 when the touring professionals first branched off from the PGA to control their own organization. The group was first known as the Tournament Players Division. Joseph C. Dey, former executive director of the United States Golf Association, was the first tour commissioner. Dey served until 1974. The PGA Tour then selected one of its own players, former Walker Cup team member and insurance executive, Deane Beman, to head their organization and Beman still holds the reins today.

For all practical purposes, the tour began before the turn of the century when professionals first teed it up for prize money in American tournaments. The first such event, the U.S. Open, began in 1895. The Western Open was first staged in 1899. Golf, of course, was a new game in this country and these first championships attracted only a handful of players.

For the next forty years, professional tournament players hopscotched to an assortment of events. The major championships held steady and the remaining events were a collection of tournaments sponsored by clothing companies, automobile manufacturers, resort hotels, and the like.

Three great players began to attract new fans in the 1940's—Ben Hogan, Sam Snead, and Byron Nelson. The popularity of professional golf began to take off. Television and Arnold Palmer gave the game a great boost in the late 1950s and early 1960s, then Jack Nicklaus was there to pick up the torch. The pro-golf explosion had begun.

Today, the PGA Tour has a variety of interests: Besides scheduling and conducting its own round of tournaments, the PGA Tour initiated the successful Senior PGA Tour. The tour is also involved in golf-course

> *"Television and Arnold Palmer gave the game a great boost in the late 1950s and early 1960s, then Jack Nicklaus was there to pick up the torch. The pro-golf explosion had begun."*

Many of the older stars of professional golf, like Al Geiberger, have found that they don't have to retire. They just tee it up on the PGA Senior tour. (Dost & Evans)

development (with its TPC courses), operating Family Golf Centers, marketing and licensing, youth clinics, and even video production. The association reported in 1988 that its assets had leaped from $730,-000 in 1974 to more than $62 million.

The PGA Tour annually presents the Card Walker Award to the person who has made significant contributions to the support of junior golf. The award has been given since 1981.

The heart of the PGA Tour's appeal to the public, however, remains the players and their ability to play the game well.

> *"For all practical purposes, the tour began before the turn of the century when professionals first teed it up for prize money in American tournaments."*

AWARDS SPONSORED BY THE PGA OF AMERICA

PGA Golf Professional of the Year
Vardon Trophy
PGA Player of the Year
Horton Smith Trophy
Bill Strausbaugh Award
PGA Club Professional Player of the Year
President's Plaque

Herb Graffis Award
PGA/World Golf Hall of Fame
Junior Leader
Distinguished Service
PGA Hall of Fame
Merchandisers of the Year

The PGA Tour
Sawgrass
Ponte Vedra Beach, FL 32082
(904) 285–3700

Other PGA Tour telephone numbers:

PGA Tour Productions—New York: (212) 838–8540
Family Golf Center: (813) 726–8481
The Players Championship: (904) 285–3301

KEY STAFF MEMBERS

Commissioner:
  Deane R. Beman

Deputy Commissioner & CEO:
  Timothy G. Smith

Director, Player Relations/Internal
  Operations:
    Mike Bodney

Special Assistant to the Commissioner:
  Gary Becka

Vice President, Tournament Affairs/Sponsor
  Relations:
    Steve Rankin

Tournament Director, Administration:
  David Eger

Tournament Director, Operations:
  Mike Shea

Director of Communications and
  Broadcasting/
  President PGA Tour Productions:
    Terry Hanson

Information Director:
  Tom Place

THE LADIES PROFESSIONAL GOLF ASSOCIATION

The first professional golf association for distaff players was born in 1944. Called The Women's Professional Golf Association, the group conducted a few tournaments, including the first U.S. Women's Open, but faded away by 1948.

That year, Wilson Sporting Goods helped finance a new tour with leadership from Patty Berg, Babe Zaharias, and Fred Corcoran, who was Mrs. Zaharias's personal manager. The Ladies Professional Golf Association, as it was named, was officially chartered in 1950. By 1952, the LPGA boasted a circuit of twenty-one events.

Top players of the era included Miss Berg, Mrs. Zaharias, Marilynn Smith, Peggy Kirk, Louise Suggs, Marlene Hagge, and Betsy Rawls.

Mickey Wright brought new attention to the LPGA in the early 1960s with a magnif-icent golf swing that most knowledgeable observers call the best swing ever, in women's or men's golf. Kathy Whitworth began her eight-year dominance of the women's game in 1965 and there were fine seasons by Judy Rankin, Sandra Haynie, and Carol Mann.

Early big-money input came from Sears and Roebuck, a prominent sponsor of televised events. The USGA also began telecasting the U.S. Women's Open in 1963, and television helped the women's tour just as it had aided the men's.

In the 1970s, the Colgate-Palmolive Company, under CEO David Foster, began a number of rich events, including the Colgate–Dinah Shore and Colgate-sponsored tournaments in Europe and the Far East. LPGA member Nancy Lopez became the darling of golf fans, boosting the LPGA much as Arnold Palmer had appealed to golf fans in the late 1950s and early 1960s.

The LPGA began its fortieth season in 1989 with a new commissioner, William A. Blue. Blue was former vice president and director of international marketing for The Kahula Group, a division of Allied-Lyons. Blue also held marketing positions with Brown-Forman International, Mead Johnson, Riviana Foods, and Iroquois Brands/ Archon.

As golf's popularity has grown, so has the LPGA. In the late 1980s, LPGA players vied for well over $12 million in purses, a giant step from 1959 when total purses were $200,000.

In one big leap, the LPGA jumped into man-sized prize money in 1989 when it was announced that the Centel corporation of Chicago, Illinois, would sponsor a 1990 LPGA event in Tallahassee, Florida, with a total purse of $750,000, the same amount of prize money that Centel had paid PGA Tour prosintheformermen'sevent.

The LPGA is the world's oldest professional sports organization for women.

"That year, Wilson Sporting Goods helped finance a new tour with leadership from Patty Berg, Babe Zaharias, and Fred Corcoran, who was Mrs. Zaharias's personal manager. The Ladies Professional Golf Association, as it was named, was officially chartered in 1950."

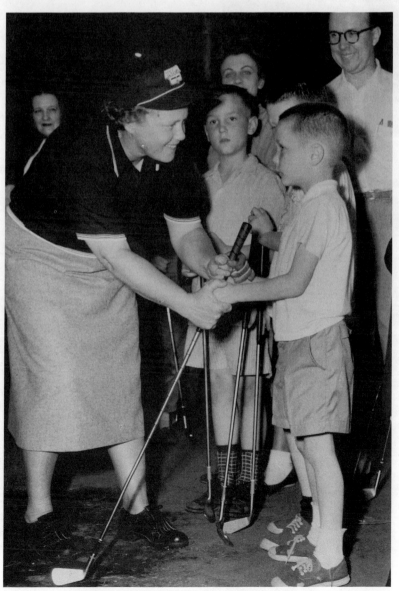

Patty Berg (left), *one of the founders of the Ladies Professional Golf Association* (Courtesy Wilson Sporting Goods)

Nancy Lopez, who burst upon the pro-golf scene in 1978, brought media attention to the LPGA Tour, much as Arnold Palmer did to the men's tour in the 1960s. (Dost & Evans)

Ladies Professional Golf Association
2570 Volusia Ave.
Suite B
Daytona Beach, FL 32114
(904) 254–8800

KEY STAFF MEMBERS

Commissioner:
 William A. Blue

Director of Communications:
 Gregg Shimanski

Media Services Coordinators:
 Beth McCombs
 Sandi Owen
 Elaine Scott

Director, Operations:
 Jim Webb

Tournament Director:
 Suzanne Jackson

Tournament Officials:
 Jim Haley
 Michael Milthorpe
 Jeff Morton
 Robert O. Smith
 Barbara Trammell

Sales and Promotions Manager:
 Carolyn Roskowski

Sponsor Support Manager:
 Mike Waldron

LPGA BOARD OF DIRECTORS

Robert M. Gardiner

N.P. Crockett

Kathy Whitworth

Dot Germain

William A. Blue

Alexander Calder, Jr.

Richard W. Kazmaier, Jr.

Judy Dickinson

Nancy Lopez

THE AMERICAN JUNIOR GOLF ASSOCIATION

While there are numerous junior golf associations in the United States, The American Junior Golf Association is indicative of the growing popularity of the game among young people.

The AJGA is an upstart, having gotten off the ground in 1977. That year the AJGA sponsored two tournaments. In 1989, that schedule boasted twenty-seven events between March and November, in eighteen states with more than 3,000 junior golfers participating.

The association conducts its tournaments at a high level, similar to pro tour events— big scoreboards, programs, tee time sheets, first tee announcers. The group scored a coup when it landed former Masters Champion Ben Crenshaw as National Chairman.

The group also reaps benefits from its AJGA Foundation and the foundation's One Percent Club. The club provides an opportunity for PGA Tour and LPGA Tour players to donate 1 percent of their yearly money-winnings to junior golf. In 1988, the club provided the foundation with $134,169—$55,898 came from touring professionals and $78,271 from matching sponsors.

The AJGA cosponsors several awards: Rolex, Golf magazine, and the AJGA combine to award the All-American and Player of the Year awards.

> *"The association conducts its tournaments at a high level, similar to pro-tour events—big scoreboards, programs, tee time sheets, first tee announcers."*

American Junior Golf Association
2415 Steeplechase Lane
Roswell, Georgia 30076
(404) 998–4653

KEY STAFF MEMBERS

Executive Director:
  Stephen Hamblin

AJGA Foundation Director:
  Chris Haack

Chairman of the Board:
  J.R. "Digger" Smith

Senior Rules Official:
  George Hannon

Communications Director:
  Scott Hodoval

AJGA SPONSORS

American Airlines	Ron Miller Golf	Taylor Made	United States Fidelity & Guarantee
AT&T	Merit Golf	Texace	
Buick Motor Division	Mizuno	Titleist	Wilson
Callaway Golf	Nabisco		
Coca-Cola U.S.A.	Ram Golf Corporation		
Coppertone	Rolex Watch, U.S.A.		
Ben Hogan Company	Smith Corona		
McDonald's	Square Two		

THE GOLF WRITERS ASSOCIATION OF AMERICA, INC.

The GWAA must be recognized for its role in developing the game in the United States. Its more than 600 members, golf writers for the nation's newspapers and magazines, have spread the word about golf since the GWAA was founded in 1947.

The GWAA has a continuing role in improving press coverage of the game. The association ensures professional working conditions, lobbying for improved media relations with tournament sponsors and players, and keeping members informed about new developments in golf.

The GWAA sponsors several of the key awards in golf: The Ben Hogan Award is given annually to an individual who has continued to be active in golf despite a physical phandicap. The Charlie Bartlett Award is presented to a playing professional for unselfish contributions to the betterment of society. The William H. Richardson Award is for one who has consistently made an outstanding contribution to golf. The GWAA also elects players to the PGA World Golf Hall of Fame.

> "Its more than 600 members, the golf writers for the nation's newspapers and magazines, have spread the word about the sport for decades."

Golf Writers Association of America
P.O. Box 37324
Cincinnati, OH 45222
(513) 631–4400

KEY STAFF AND OFFICERS

Secretary:
  Robert D. Rickey

President:
  Joseph Greenday
  Philadelphia Daily News

First Vice President:
  Bob Green
  Associated Press

Second Vice President:
  Furman Bisher
  Atlanta Journal

Treasurer:
  James Regan
  Springfield News

Other Key Organizations

American Golf Sponsors, Inc.
Box 41
Golf, IL 60029
(312) 724–4600

President: Ted May

Canadian Ladies' Golf Association
1600 James Naismith Drive
Gloucester, Ont Can K1B 5N4
(613) 748–5642

Executive Director: Leonard Murphy

Canadian Professional Golfers Association
430 Signet Drive, Unit D
Weston, Ontario Can M9L 2T6
(416) 744–2212

Executive Director: David J. Colling

Golf Coaches Association of America
583 D'Onofrio Drive, Ste 1
Madison, WI 53719–2004
(608) 833–6824

President: Doug Gordin

Golf Course Association
8030 Cedar Avenue, Suite 228
Minneapolis, MN 55420
(612) 854–8482

Executive Director: Curtis M. Walker

Group Fore–Women's Professional Golf Tour
1259 El Camino Real, Suite 153
Menlo Park, CA 94025
(415) 327–5207

President: Judy Horst

International Golf Association
3 East 54th Street
New York, NY 10022
(212) 223–4693

Executive Director: Birch Riber

National Association of Left-Handed Golfers
10105 Hammerly, No. 714
Houston, TX 77080
(713) 464–8683

President: Bob Linder

National Golf Car Manufacturers Association
4361 Northlake Blvd.
Palm Beach Gardens, FL 33410–7868
(407) 694–2977

Secretary/Treasurer: Don A. Rossi

Royal & Ancient Golf Club
St. Andrews, Fife KY16 9JD
Scotland

Royal Canadian Golf Association
Golf House
R.R. No. 2
Oakville Ontario Canada L6J 4Z3
(416) 844–1800

Executive Director: G.R. Hilton

World Amateur Golf Council
c/o United States Golf Association
Far Hills, NJ 07931
(201) 234–2300

Jt. Secretary: P.J. Boatwright, Jr.
Jt. Secretary: Michael F. Bonallack

2

ART AND COLLECTIBLES

A COMMON question, accompanied by a moan, can be heard today in locker rooms throughout America: "Why, oh why, did I ever give away that old set of Tommy Armour woods?"

It's the same predicament in which golfers found themselves after discovering that the cigar box full of baseball cards, tossed in with the goods of that 1960s garage sale, would be worth a small fortune today. Old golf clubs are in big demand, and they don't have to be all that old.

Many steel-shafted clubs made in the 1950s and 1960s are valued by collectors and command top prices. For example, the VIP by Nicklaus irons, made in 1966–1967, are considered collectibles. Wilson Staff irons made between 1958 and 1974 are also classic models. Bristol putters from the late 1950s and early 1960s can bring over $1,000. Many old Wilson wedges are considered classics.

If you're fortunate to sneak a look into a playing professional's bag, you may find that some of the best players in the game are carrying a Tommy Armour 3-wood, a Wilson R-90 sand iron, or an old George Low Wizard 600 putter. The fact that many fine professionals still use an older club increases the demand, and value, of that model.

Older clubs, from the wood shaft era (1890–1935) are also in great demand. Many are works of art, finely crafted by club makers like David Anderson and his five sons in St. Andrews. Knowledge of the true value of these clubs is a must—many are simply old golf clubs of little value.

Before paying a stiff price for a club at auction, learn more about what you're buying. Deal with a reputable dealer. Visit the best golf museums. Read as much as you can: An excellent reference book is *The Encyclopedia of Golf Collectibles: a Collector's Identification and Value Guide,* by John M. and Morton W. Olman.

The Olmans, by the way, own and operate the Old Golf Shop in Cincinnati, one of the best sources for golf art and artifacts.

Another means by which to determine the value of old clubs you are about to buy or sell is by joining The Golf Collectors Society. (See listings at end of chapter.)

Golf collectors welcome newcomers to their ranks and are generous in sharing information. Since 1970 the society's expert editor, Joe Murdoch, a noted authority on collectibles, has published periodic and fact-filled pamphlets for members. (See listings.)

Old golf publications have value in themselves. That stack of *Golf Digest* editions you've been saving since 1978 may be readable and informative, but has little cash value. However, a complete set of the *American Golfer,* published from 1908 to 1936, is

"Old golf clubs are in big demand, and they don't have to be all that old."

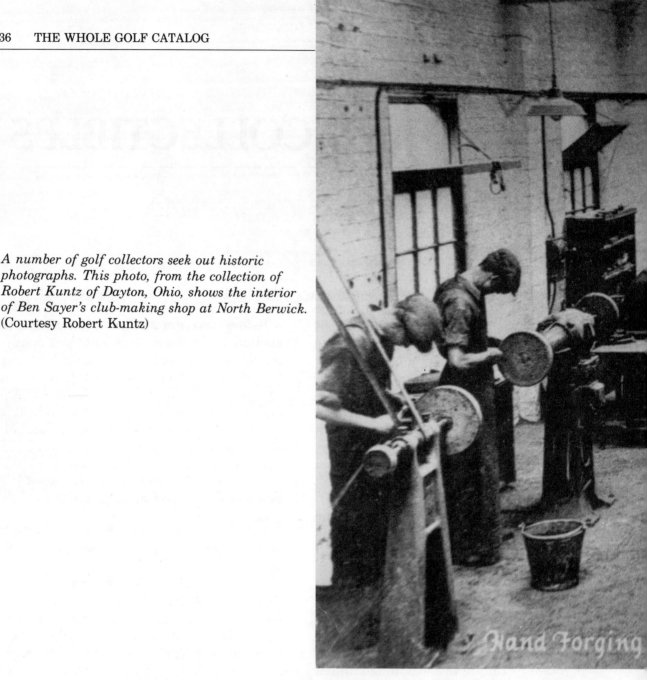

A number of golf collectors seek out historic photographs. This photo, from the collection of Robert Kuntz of Dayton, Ohio, shows the interior of Ben Sayer's club-making shop at North Berwick. (Courtesy Robert Kuntz)

a real collector's item. Even that relative upstart publication *Golf World,* published from 1947 to 1974 under the title *Golf World Newsweekly,* will bring a good price if you own a complete set in good condition.

John and Morton Olman point out in their excellent reference book that Great Britain's large auction houses—Sotheby's, Christie's, and Phillips—offer a number of interesting golf antiques. If you've scheduled a British golf vacation, and are a poten-

tial collector, it would be worthwhile to pick up a presale catalog from one of these auction houses and perhaps sit in on one of the auctions.

Clubs, books, and artwork command the largest prices. Old golf books can be bought at auction, in trades with other collectors, or even stumbled upon in old book sales. Richard E. Donovan (see listings) offers a periodic catalog of old golf books and will mail your purchase to your doorstep. Old golf

Heads in Ben Sayer's Workshops, The Links, North B...

books are a wonderful way in which to start collecting. Most are reasonably priced yet, if the booming market continues, will grow in value. Even if your golf book collection may not be the major item in your child's inheritance, you'll enjoy reading each of your classics.

Golf art makes a lovely and valuable addition to the decor of your home library or your corporate office. While the oldest and best paintings command higher prices,

there are many fine prints available at much less cost. Most of the golf museums (see listings) offer these prints at very reasonable prices.

Demand continues for framed magazine covers showing early golfers, and these are becoming popular decorating accessories in country clubs and locker rooms.

A good source of golf art is The Sporting Scene/Investors Gallery in Dallas. It's owned by Fred Oman, a member of the

USGA's Museum and Library Committee (as is Morton Olman). Mr. Oman is a most helpful source on buying golf art as an investment.

Ceramics and pottery with golf scenes are also collectible, and values sometimes soar over $500 for a fine item. Early trophies made of silver, old golf medals, and buttons and badges with club insignia are also considered treasures.

If you're interested in collecting, join the Golf Collectors' Society and visit the following dealers and museums. Other listings can be found in the chapter, Archives and Museums.

Golf Collectors' Society
638 Wagner Road
Lafayette Hill, PA 19444
(215) 828–4492

Read for Reference:

Golf Collectors' Society Bulletin
638 Wagner Road
Lafayette Hill, PA 19444
(215) 828–4492

The Encyclopedia of Golf Collectibles:
A Collector's Identification and Value Guide
Books Americana, Inc.
Florence, AL 35630

Museums (Some prints, artifacts available for sale):

United States Golf Association
Golf House
Far Hills, NJ 07931
(201) 234–2300

The PGA World Golf Hall of Fame
P.O. Box 1908
Pinehurst, NC 28374
(919) 295–6651

Golf collectors often look for offbeat golf equipment to include in their collections. In this picture, taken in about 1915, note the sandboxes on the tees. In golf's early days, golfers put a handful of sand on the teeing area and used it as a tee. (Courtesy Robert Kuntz)

Royal and Ancient Golf Club of St. Andrews, Scotland. Founded in 1754. (Courtesy USGA)

Dealers:

Richard E. Donovan Enterprises
305 Massachusetts Avenue
P.O. Box 7070
Endicott, NY 13760
(607) 785–5874

The Sporting Scene/Investor's Gallery
1203 Dragon
Dallas, TX 75207
(214) 748–7831

Old Golf Shop
325 West Fifth Street
Cincinnati, Ohio 45202
(513) 241–7789
(800) 227–8700

"Old golf books can be bought at auction, in trades with other collectors, or even stumbled upon in old book sales."

"Ceramics and pottery with golf scenes are also collectible, and values sometimes soar over $500 for a fine item."

3
ARCHIVES AND MUSEUMS

If GOLFERS are a family, and most of us who play seriously believe that indeed we are, then Golf House is golf's family album.

Golf House is the museum and library of the United States Golf Association in Far Hills, New Jersey. The building itself is an architectural treat, a stately old red brick mansion with a white-pillared portico, built in 1919 as a residence for the family of Thomas H. Frothingham. Today it serves as a sort of residence for the favorite sons and daughters of the family of golfers.

They're all here—Bob Jones, Ben Hogan, Glenna Collett Vare, Mickey Wright, Arnold Palmer, Patty Berg, Francis Ouimet, Babe Zaharias, and those others who reached heights of skill that most of us can only dream about. They don't actually live here, of course, but they are here—their presence can be felt as one strolls through the halls.

The Bob Jones Room is representative of the mood of Golf House. Wood paneled and lined with shelves of books, it's comfortable, the sort of room in which Jones and his cronies might have relaxed after a friendly round of golf. Jones's portrait hangs over the fireplace mantel. His championship medals in a glass case are a simple but awesome display. A book on the coffee table is opened to Herbert Warren Wind's wonderful story, "Robert Tyre Jones, Jr."

Don't expect to find a bunch of trophies here. There are a few, but Golf House was never designed as a trophy case. Neither does it really seem like a museum, although it has acquired an excellent reputation among museums, largely through the work of the tireless Janet Seagle, the USGA's museum curator and librarian, and the equally energetic USGA Museum and Library Committee.

One favorite part of the collection is the treasure trove of champions' clubs. Miss Seagle acquired a club from each USGA Champion. One can look at these clubs and imagine Hogan or Zaharias, with the curiously innate "feel" that they brought to the game, carefully gripping and regripping the old wrapped-leather grips.

Golf House has the most complete library of golf books ever assembled, and the room in which these volumes are shelved is a cozy retreat for writers and historians.

The USGA, which seeks to preserve the game's history as well as its integrity, has in recent years upgraded its exhibits on women's golf. The exhibit, "Women in Golf: Play Well, Have Fun!" is intriguing. A virtual review of the women's side of the game—amateur and professional—is displayed in wonderful old photographs and memorabilia. It's worth noting that among the most recently acquired portraits at Golf House are commissioned paintings of Babe

> "If golfers are a family . . . then Golf House is golf's family album." ◁

> "The Bob Jones Room is representative of the mood of Golf House. Wood paneled and lined with shelves of books, it's comfortable, the sort of room in which Jones and his cronies might have relaxed after a friendly round of golf."

Map to USGA

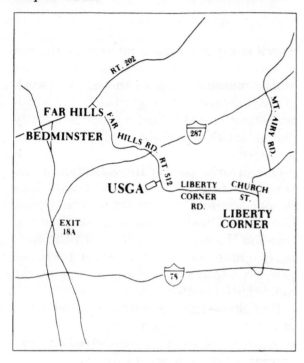

Zaharias and Patty Berg. Work on a portrait of Mickey Wright, the four-time U.S. Women's Open Champion, was completed in 1989.

Golf House includes hands-on exhibits, like the video-taped films of famous golfers swinging the club, computerized golf games, and a practice putting lane.

Collectors, players, and friends of golf will enjoy touring this wonderful old building, which was renovated a couple of years ago. Even the drive to the museum is lovely. A meandering lane twists and turns through the USGA's rolling property and deer peep out from their haunts in the spruce, pine, maples, magnolias, and oaks.

Museum memorabilia and prints are available for purchase.

Golf House
United States Golf Association
Far Hills, NJ 07931
(201) 234–2300

Museum Hours: Monday–Friday, 9 a.m.–5 p.m.
Saturday, Sunday, 10 a.m.–4 p.m.
Closed: New Year's Day, Easter Sunday,
Thanksgiving, and Christmas.

THE PGA WORLD GOLF HALL OF FAME

The PGA World Golf Hall of Fame is an entirely different type of museum, an awe-inspiring edifice to golf's great champions.

The museum buildings sprawl over a hillside overlooking the fourth hole of famed Pinehurst #2, the masterpiece of golf-course architect Donald Ross.

Historic black-and-white photographs of the early days of the Pinehurst golf resort are included in the museum's collection.

The main shrine awes even the players who are honored here. This building at the

back of the complex and overlooking the golf course is a sort of temple of golf. Upon entering, visitors first see a heroic-sized bronze sculpture of Bob Jones towering above a reflecting pool. That, in itself, would be enough to inspire the highest handicapper,

> "Upon entering, visitors first see a heroic-sized bronze sculpture of Bob Jones towering above a reflecting pool."

The PGA/World Golf Hall of Fame at Pinehurst, North Carolina (Courtesy PGA/World Golf Hall of Fame)

but there is more: Hallways on each side of the Jones sculpture house oil paintings and busts of the Hall of Fame's honorees. In the high-ceilinged shrine, where footsteps resound and echo, the silence reminds one a little of a cathedral and, indeed, players whose portraits hang here have often seemed a bit overcome by the grandeur.

Members of the Golf Writers Association of America select the inductees. The annual ceremonies are held in conjunction with a Hall of Fame Pro-Am tournament.

I've attended two induction ceremonies: In 1978 a banquet honored Billy Casper, Bing Crosby, Dorothy Campbell Hurd Howe, Harold Hilton, and Clifford Roberts. In 1982, in more informal ceremonies (outdoors, on the hillside behind the shrine), Julius Boros and Kathy Whitworth were inducted. The 1982 ceremony was the better of the two:

On a beautiful afternoon, about a hundred Pinehurst residents in casual dress sat on the shrine's back steps.

"We're all friends here," said Dick Taylor, the master of ceremonies and erudite editor of *Golf World,* who made a nice, casual affair of the induction. Boros and Miss Whitworth humbly recounted a bit of their early life in golf and paid tribute to those who had helped them get to this place of high honor.

While it was all very low-key, those attending were quite moved—Julius Boros was just recovering from heart surgery and, although it was late in her career, Miss Whitworth had begun to win again after a long dry spell.

The shrine alone is worth the trip to Pinehurst, but the PGA/World Golf Hall of Fame has two buildings. The Grand Hall offers a good collection of golf photographs, the old club-makers' shop, a major tournament showcase, and the Ryder Cup Room. The Auchterlonie collection of old clubs is housed here, and there are various good rotating exhibits.

The Hall of Fame opened in 1974 with the induction of Patty Berg, Walter Hagen, Ben Hogan, Robert T. Jones, Jr., Byron Nelson, Jack Nicklaus, Babe Zaharias, Francis Ouimet, Arnold Palmer, Gary Player, Gene Sarazen, Sam Snead, and Harry Vardon.

It is operated today by the PGA of America, under the expert guidance of Peter Ross Stilwell, the director, and Ray Davis, the curator.

Golf prints, books, and artifacts are available in the Hall of Fame's gift shop.

The PGA/World Golf Hall of Fame
PGA Boulevard
Post Office Box 1908
Pinehurst, North Carolina 28374
(919) 295–6651

March 1–November 30:   Open seven days a week,
9 a.m.–5 p.m.

> *"Boros and Miss Whitworth humbly recounted a bit of their early life in golf and paid tribute to those who had helped them get to this place of high honor."*

THE LPGA HALL OF FAME

Of all archives, the LPGA Hall of Fame gets the most press. It seems that each time a member of the Ladies Professional Golf Association closes in on qualifying for the Hall of Fame, the press begin to question the LPGA's high standards for induction.

Well, it makes good copy. The LPGA Hall of Fame is the only such archive where an athlete can actually qualify for entrance, even if no one likes her! The pioneers of the LPGA had good reason to establish this policy—many archives in other sports become

LPGA Hall of Fame member Kathy Whitworth. The swing that won eighty-eight tournaments. (Dost & Evans)

popularity contests. Golfers must play their way into the LPGA Hall of Fame.

There's an interesting history behind this esteemed collection of inductees, which stood at eleven members at the end of 1989. There was a previous Hall of Fame for women golfers at Augusta Country Club, the site of the old Titleholders' Championship (a sort of Masters' championship for women) in Augusta, Georgia. That Hall of Fame included several LPGA members— Babe Zaharias, Patty Berg, Betsy Rawls, Louise Suggs, Mickey Wright, and Betty Jameson—but also a few amateur players, Glenna Collett Vare, Pam Barton, Cecil Leitch and Joyce Wethered.

In 1967, a committee of LPGA players was appointed to decide how players would gain entry into the new LPGA Hall of Fame. The committee decided that, since this was to be named LPGA, it would be appropriate to honor only LPGA players. And so, the original LPGA players in the existing Hall of Fame members were automatically included. In order to keep induction from becoming a political issue, the committee also established the following criteria for admission:

A player must have been an LPGA member, in good standing, for ten consecutive years. She must have won at least thirty official events, including two different major championships, or have won thirty-five official events with one major championship, or have won forty official events exclusive of a major championship.

The LPGA Hall of Fame archives were housed in the PGA/World Golf Hall of Fame for many years. In 1982, the archives were moved to the new LPGA headquarters in Sugar Land, Texas, new displays were created, and dedication was held in 1985.

The LPGA Hall of Fame has an impressive and well-displayed collection of rare photographs of these great women golfers. A stirring videotape recalls the highlights of each player's career.

Several important trophies are housed in the LPGA Hall of Fame: The Glenna Collett Vare Trophy, which is awarded each year to the player with the lowest scoring average; the Rolex Player-of-the-Year Trophy, founded in 1966; the Rookie-of-the-Year Trophy; the Patty Berg Award; the Mazda-LPGA Series Trophy; and the William and Mousie Powell Award.

The LPGA Hall of Fame currently remains in Sugar Land, Texas. In August, 1989, the LPGA announced that its headquarters are moving to a new corporate site in Daytona Beach, Florida. When new facilities are built, the Hall of Fame will move to the Florida headquarters.

LPGA Hall of Fame
4675 Sweetwater Boulevard.
Sugar Land, Texas 77479
(713) 980–5742

Open year round: Monday through Friday, 9 a.m.–5 p.m.

> *"Of all archives, the LPGA Hall of Fame gets the most press."*

THE RALPH W. MILLER GOLF MUSEUM AND LIBRARY

One of the best private collections is housed in the Ralph W. Miller Golf Museum and Library, at Industry Hills Country Club in City of Industry, California.

Before he died in 1974, Ralph W. Miller, a well-known golfer and historian in southern California, collected one of the finest private assortments of golf artifacts and literature. The collection, housed in viewing rooms of the spacious clubhouse at Industry

"Before he died in 1974, Ralph W. Miller, a well-known golfer and historian in Southern California, collected one of the finest private assortments of golf artifacts and literature."

Hills Country Club, includes more than 7,000 golf journals and books (some are very rare, such as The Goff, published in 1743), many volumes of newspaper clippings about the game, antique golf clubs and golf balls, works of art, photographs, and other memorabilia.

Maintenance of the collection and its display rooms is provided by the City of Industry.

The display is open to the public and also may be used by researchers.

Ralph W. Miller Museum and Library
Industry Hills Golf Club
#1 Industry Hills Parkway
City of Industry, CA 91744
(818) 854–2354

Open to the public: 8:30 a.m.–5 p.m., seven days a week. Researchers are requested to visit from Monday through Friday.

Two private golf clubs house vast collections of historic clubs and artifacts.

JAMES RIVER COUNTRY CLUB

The museum at James River Country Club is in Newport News, Virginia, on the peninsula in the lovely Tidewater area of Virginia. The museum has on exhibit hundreds of early golf clubs, some of which date to the early 1600s. The golf-ball collection is extensive, going through each of the eras of the game.

The collection, which is housed in a room in the clubhouse, includes golf art and more than 1,000 books. It was assembled in the 1930s with private funds donated by Archer Huntington, who arranged shipment of many of the artifacts from Europe and funded construction of the room in which they are displayed.

James River Country Club
1500 Country Club Road
Newport News, VA 23606
(804) 595–3327

AMERICAN GOLF HALL OF FAME, FOXBURG COUNTRY CLUB

Another very fine collection of valuable golf artifacts is housed in the American Golf Hall of Fame at Foxburg Country Club in rural Pennsylvania. Among the treasures displayed at Foxburg are golf clubs once used by the early champions like J.H. Taylor and Old Tom Morris.

There's a complete assembly of featherie golf balls, gutta-perchas, and clubs used during the feather-ball era. Also in the collection are many valuable early clubs, including McEwan golf clubs dating from 1770.

If you're driving through rural Pennsylvania, a visit to Foxburg Country Club will make a delightful side trip. The collection is open to the public. Foxburg Country Club is fifty-five miles northeast of Pittsburgh and four miles off I-80 at Exit 6.

American Golf Hall of Fame
Foxburg Country Club
Box 1, Route 58
Foxburg, PA 16036

Open to the public: April to November only, 9 a.m.–8 p.m.

"If you're driving through rural Pennsylvania, a visit to Foxburg Country Club will make a delightful side trip."

BRITISH COLLECTIONS

Several golf clubs in Great Britain have fine private collections, most notably, England's North Manchester Golf Club in Lancashire, and, in Scotland, the Royal and Ancient Golf Club of St. Andrews.

The private North Manchester Golf Club is the home of the Harry B. Wood collection of golf memorabilia, which includes one of the finest assortments of clubs from the early twentieth century.

The wonderful collection of trophies, books, and golf clubs at the Royal and An-cient Golf Club is known worldwide, but may be viewed only by members or by special arrangements.

North Manchester Golf Club
Rhodes House
Middleton
Manchester, England M24 4FB

The Royal and Ancient Golf Club
St. Andrews, Fife KY16 9JD
Scotland

CLUB COLLECTIONS

A number of American country clubs house historic golf collections. These are private clubs, not open to the public. But, if you're fortunate enough to enjoy a day of golf at these clubs as a guest, be sure to ask if you may view the golf memorabilia.

The best of these collections is at the Colonial Country Club in Fort Worth, Texas. Colonial has longtime ties with Ben Hogan. The golf course is, in fact, known as "Hogan's Alley."

Hogan has stored many of his trophies in the Ben Hogan Trophy Room at Colonial, including the Hickock Belt, which was given to him when he was named Athlete of the Year in 1953, and replicas of his four U.S. Open medals. An interesting artifact is a fifth USGA medal, awarded to Hogan when he won a USGA-sponsored event which was staged to replace the U.S. Open when that championship was discontinued during World War II. The medal is identical to the four U.S. Open medals, and some historians call this medal Hogan's "Fifth Open" trophy.

The Broadmoor Golf Club in Colorado Springs, Colorado, has a collection of fine old golf books in a glass case near the stairway in the main clubhouse.

In Texas, Las Colinas Sports Club, in Irving, and Fossil Creek Golf Club, in rural Fort Worth, have chosen to decorate their clubhouses with golf collectibles. The Fossil Creek clubhouse has a number of me-

mentoes from Arnold Palmer, who designed the golf course with Ed Seay.

Many private clubs include golf collectors among their membership, and these collectors are often kind enough to display their artifacts in their home clubhouse. If you're interested in golf art and artifacts, it's worth checking out the nooks and crannies of any clubhouse in which you are a guest—you may be lucky enough to view some real treasures from the game's rich history.

4

AGENTS

THE MERE fact that touring professional golfers now sport a number of logos, insignia, and even, in Payne Stewart's case, team colors, reveals that golf agents are doing a bang-up job.

Never have touring professionals managed to make so much money away from the golf course.

One of the first player agents was the inimitable Fred Corcoran. Corcoran was the PGA tour's tournament manager in the late 1930s, and he went on to become what was called a "manager and sports promoter" of a number of colorful golf personalities. Sam Snead was a client of Corcoran's. So were Babe Zaharias, Tony Lema, and Ken Venturi.

Corcoran, a sharp businessman and a comfortable man with whom great people felt at ease, had a long and brilliant career in the golf industry. He was the PGA tour's tournament manager from 1936 to 1947, then was promotional director for a couple of years. He became the LPGA Tour's founding commissioner in 1948, when that organization was first getting off the ground.

Another pioneer golf agent was Mark McCormick, whose entry in the field happily coincided with the rise of his star player, Arnold Palmer. Today McCormick is chairman of International Management Group, the sports and entertainment empire he founded. McCormick's list of contemporary players includes a number of familiar names like Curtis Strange and Nancy Lopez.

The golf agent occupies an intriguing niche in modern golf. He or she is not only a player's deal maker, but often coach and father (or mother) confessor. Today, when professional golfers are nearly overwhelmed by their own growing celebrity, the agent is a friendly face among a crowd of strangers.

Most agents spend a great deal of time at

Mark McCormack, president of International Management Group, one of golf's premier player agents (Courtesy IMG)

professional tournaments, for that is where their clients spend their lives. Deals may be nailed down in a flashy office, but they are often "massaged" on tour, since that is where equipment reps and the giants of industry can also be found. Never underestimate the power of a pro-am partner!

Golfers today receive handsome checks for representing country clubs, golf clubs, and golf-clothing companies, just as in the old days. But, they also represent candy companies, chewing gum, beer, hamburger stands, ice-cream makers, soft drinks, banks, soap, medical supplies, and telephone books! Behind all this is the agent.

Outings and pro-ams have become a lucrative sideline for a number of touring professionals. Agents with large stables of players, like IMG, or agents who choose to represent a few very good players, like Pros Incorporated, can assure the success of a corporate golf outing simply by providing their own clients. Pros Incorporated, a Richmond-based firm representing Tom Kite, Lanny Wadkins, Kathy Whitworth, and Beth Daniel, among others, is headed by Vernon Spratley and Vinny Giles. Giles is a lawyer and stockbroker who made his own name in golf as an amateur and two-time Walker Cup player.

A good example of a player who generates a huge off-course income is Dave Stockton, a client of the Washington-based Advantage International. Stockton makes an estimated $250,000 a year for his corporate outings, where he dispenses camaraderie and expert golf advice.

Several women have become golf agents, most notably Clare Sheils of Santa Cruz, California, and Linda Giaolli, of Santa Monica, California. Ms. Giaolli represents Amy Alcott.

> "The golf agent occupies an intriguing niche in modern golf . . . deal maker . . . coach . . . father [or mother] confessor."

Golf agent Clare Sheils

Ms. Sheils represents only four players; Patty Sheehan, Sherri Turner, Shirley Furlong, and Mary Beth Zimmerman. She's content representing a small, select group for which she can do her best work. Ms. Sheils has managed to secure some unique and rewarding contracts for each of her players: Patty Sheehan, whose charity work includes helping troubled youngsters, has a tie-in with M & M Candy. Sherri Turner, a diabetic, has a contract with an insulin company. A career as an agent demands ingenuity as well as hard work.

Golf agents provide an umbrella of services for touring golf professionals. Top firms like IMG and Pros Incorporated include accounting services. The firm will pay the pro's bills and provide investment advice, if those services are requested.

Golf agents are beneficial to corporate executives as well as players. The agent is the contact to call if you want to hire a golf professional to represent your company or make an appearance at a company event. The agent signs the player to the contract, makes a place on the schedule, makes travel arrangements, and provides publicity photos and biographies.

Good agents save the golfer and the client a lot of legwork. Good agents also assure that today's top stars will enjoy a comfortable life-style well into their later years.

Below is a listing of men touring professionals and their agents, followed by a list of women touring professionals and their agents.

Agents and Managers

Advantage International
1025 Thomas Jefferson, NW
Washington, DC 20007
(202) 333-3838

Principle: Greg Hood

Representing:

Fulton Allem	Jim Nelford
Ronnie Black	Tom Pernice
Keith Clearwater	Dan Pohl
Fred Couples	Tom Purtzer
Danny Edwards	Jim Simons
Ian Baker-Finch	Joey Sindelar
Wayne Grady	Dave Stockton
Al Geiberger	Howard Twitty
Jay Haas	

Advantage International Pty. Ltd.
8-12 Sandilands Street
Suite 4
South Melbourne
Victoria, Australia 3205

Principle: Stephen Frazer

Representing: Bob Shearer

Anthony A. Asher
Sullivan, Ward, Bone Tyler, Fiotte & Asher
25800 Northwestern Highway
P.O. Box 222
Southfield, MI 48037
(313) 746-2701

Principle: Anthony A. Asher

Representing: Agim Bardha

Paul Azinger Enterprises, Inc.
4520 Bent Tree Boulevard
Sarasota, FL 34241
(813) 371-2113

Principles: Ralph Azinger, Joe Guadino

Representing: Paul Azinger

Doug Baldwin
316 Occidental Avenue South
Suite 500
Seattle, WA 98104

Principle: Doug Baldwin

Representing: Jodie Mudd, Mac O'Grady

William C. Boone, Jr.
3300 First National Tower Bldg.
Louisville, KY 40202
(502) 589-4200

Principle: William C. Boone, Jr.

Representing: Frank Beard

Choate Management
312 Belle Plaine
Gurnee, IL 60032
(312) 336-4778

Principle: Mike Choate

Representing: David Ogrin

R. Lorne Collins
Box 1043
Brandon, Manitoba
CANADA R7A 6A3
(204) 725-4503

Principle: R. Lorne Collins

Representing: Dan Halldorson

Continental Management
P.O. Box 255
Mobile, FL 36601
(205) 626-1900

Principle: David Strickland

Representing: Mike Blackburn, Woody Blackburn

Charles Coody
1555 Oldham Lane
Abilene, TX 79602

Principle: Charles Coody

Representing: Charles Coody

Jack Cook, Jr.
1600 West 38th Street
Suite 405
Austin, TX 78731
(512) 451–7541

Principle: Jack Cook, Jr.

Representing: Peter Thomson

John Cook Enterprises, Inc.
1111 Tahquitz East, Suite 121
Palm Springs, CA 92262
(619) 322–0610

Principle: Jim Cook

Representing: John Cook

Cornerstone Sports, Inc.
Chateau Plaza, Suite 940
2515 McKinney Avenue
Lock Box 10
Dallas, TX 75201
(214) 855–5150

*Principles: Rocky Hambric, Mike Dirks, David
Winkle, C.J. McDaniel*

Representing:

Tommy Armour, III	Larry Mize
Mark Brooks	Larry Nelson
Brandel Chamblee	Kenny Perry
Andy Dillard	Don Pooley
David Edwards	Scott Simpson
David Frost	Brian Tennyson
Bob Gilder	Doug Tewell
Lon Hinkle	Bob Tway
Steve Jones	Mark Wiebe
Bob Lohr	

CorpSport International
#204 Lemarchand Mansion
11523 100th Avenue
Edmonton, Alberta
CANADA T5K OJ8
(403) 488–4848

Representing: Richard Zokol

Pauline Crane
191 Lake Avenue
Kirkland, WA 98033
(206) 822–3136

Principle: Pauline Crane

Representing: Quinton Gray

James DeLeone, Esq.
88 East Broad Street
Suite 900
Columbus, OH 43215
(614) 223–9342

Principle: James DeLeone

Representing: Ed Sneed, Tom Weiskopf

Edwards, Belk, Hunter & Kerr
6070 Gateway East, Suite 211
El Paso, TX 79905
(915) 779–6464

Principle: J. Crawford Kerr

Representing: Tim Norris

Rose Elder & Associates, Inc.
1725 K Street, NW
Washington, D.C. 20006

Principle: Rose Elder

Representing: Lee Elder

Eddie Elias Enterprises
1720 Merriman Road
P.O. Box 5118
Akron, OH 44313
(216) 867–4388
NYC: (212) 245–1710

*Principles: Eddie Elias, Barry Terjesen, Kevin
Donahue, Eric McClenaghan.*

Representing:

Tommy Bolt	Gary McCord
Dale Douglass	Chi Chi Rodriguez
Ken Green	Ken Venturi
Bill Kratzert	Fuzzy Zoeller

Gator Golf Enterprises
135 Lamorak Lane
Maitland, FL 32751

Representing: Wally Armstrong

Golden Bear
11760 U.S. Highway One
N. Palm Beach, FL 33408
(407) 626–3900

*Principles: Larry O'Brien, Jim Wisler, Marilyn
Keough*

Representing: Jack Nicklaus

Clayton Hoskins, Esq.
Bricker & Eckler
100 East Broad Street
Columbus, OH 43215
(614) 227-2332

Principle: Clayton Hoskins

Representing: John Cook

Hale Irwin Golf Services, Inc.
745 Old Frontenac Square
Suite 200
St. Louis, MO 63131
(314) 997-4333

Representing: Hale Irwin

Hazel Hurt
15212 Pond Woods Drive East
Building 34
Tampa, FL 33618

Principle: Hazel Hurt

Representing: Jim Dent

Hewitt Properties
1411 Edgewater Drive
Suite 101
Orlando, FL 32804
(407) 894-6731

Representing: David Peoples

International Management Group
One Erieview Plaza, Suite 1300
Cleveland, OH 44114
(216) 522-1200

Principles: Andy Pierce, Kathy Repeta, Kathy Houlahan, David Yates, Alastair Johnston, Bill Colvin, Hans Kramer, Peter Malik, Mark McCormick, Dave Lightner, Hughes Norton, Jill Fanos, Mike Reilly, Jay Burton, John Laupheimer

Representing:

Tommy Aaron	George Burns
Billy Andrade	Bob Charles
Isao Aoki	T.C. Chen
Miller Barber	Bobby Clampett
Andy Bean	Bobby Cole
Chip Beck	Charles Coody
Jim Benepe	Steve Elkington
John Brodie	Nick Faldo
Billy Ray Brown	Brad Faxon
Bob Brue	Ray Floyd

David Graham	Jerry Pate
Lou Graham	Corey Pavin
Vance Heafner	Chris Perry
Hale Irwin	Gary Player
Peter Jacobsen	Nick Price
Bernhard Langer	Sam Randolph
Bruce Lietzke	Jack Renner
Sandy Lyle	Bill Rogers
Dave Marr	Bob Rosburg
Don Massengale	Doug Sanders
Orville Moody	Curtis Strange
Tommy Nakajima	Bob Toski
Greg Norman	Denis Watson
Mark O'Meara	D.A. Weibring
Arnold Palmer	Willie Wood

Leader Enterprises, Inc.
20 North Orange Avenue
Suite 1100
Orlando, FL 32801
(407) 425-4900

Principle: Robert Fraley

Representing: Payne Stewart

Richard Lloyd
4141 N. Scottsdale Road
Suite 333
Scottsdale, AZ 85251
(602) 990-1275

Principle: Richard Lloyd

Representing: Dan Halldorson

Paul Lufkin
Five Star Marketing
22599 Shelburne Road
Shaker Heights, OH 44122
(216) 831-2081

Principle: Paul Lufkin

Representing: Bill Glasson, Kenny Knox, Larry Mowry

Richard E. Madigan & Assoc.
311 Claremont Avenue
Montclair, NJ 07042
(201) 746-8381

Representing: Gary Hallberg, Scott Hoch, Wayne Levi

Richard Madigan, Rich Neumann Management Associates, Inc.
11 Edinburgh Drive
Palm Beach Gardens, FL 33418
(407) 622–0809

Principles: Skip Raine, Lou Palmer

Representing:

Butch Baird	Lyn Lott
Rex Caldwell	Bobby Nichols
Mike Holland	Mark Pfeil
Wayne Levi	Jim Thorpe

Richard Marshall
3100 Richmond Avenue #500
Houston, TX 77098
(713) 440–4065

Representing: John Mahaffey

Dr. W.R. Massey
P.O. Box 1408
Statesboro, GA 30458
(912) 764–5435

Representing: Gene Sauers

James McCumber
P.O. Box 490
Middleburg, FL 32068
(904) 282–5511

Representing: Mark McCumber

Mentor Management Company
4724 Center Lane Road NE
Olympia, WA 98506
(206) 456–1160

Principle: Norman Ratner

Representing: Lennie Clements

Johnny Miller Enterprises
1220 Soda Canyon Road
P.O. Box 2260
Napa, CA 94558
(707) 224–6444

Representing: Johnny Miller

Mo-Cat, Inc.
City Center East, 3rd Floor
150 South Palmetto Avenue
Daytona Beach, FL 32014
(904) 252–1561

Principle: Doyle Tumbleson

Representing: Morris Batalsky

North Enterprises
22 Oxwood Circle
Madison, WI 53717
(608) 833–4653

Representing: Andy North

Oxford Sports Management, Inc.
6305 Waterford Blvd., Suite 335
Oklahoma City, OK 73118
(405) 848–5600

Principle: David Hardin

Representing:

Ronnie Black	Andrew Magee
Andy Dillard	Scott Verplank
Mark Hayes	Willie Wood

Arnold Palmer Enterprises
P.O. Box 52
Youngstown, PA 15696
(412) 537–7751

Principle: Doc Giffin

Representing: Arnold Palmer

Jerry Pate Enterprises
1255 Country Club Road
Gulf Breeze, FL 32561
(904) 932–3500

Representing: Jerry Pate

> *"Golfers . . . also represent candy companies, chewing gum, beer, hamburger stands, ice-cream makers, soft drinks, banks, soap, medical supplies, and telephone books! Behind all of this is the agent."*

Pros, Inc.
100 Shockoe Slip
P.O. Box 673
Richmond, VA 23206
(804) 643-7600

Principles: Vinny Giles, Dave Maraghy, Allyson Hibbitts, Vernon Spratley

Representing:

Bruce Devlin	Davis Love, III
Hubert Green	Rocco Mediate
Mike Hulbert	Steve Pate
Joe Inman	Larry Rinker
John Inman	Bobby Wadkins
Tom Kite	Danny Wadkins
Gary Koch	Robert Wrenn

ProLink
3305 Golden Trails, #205
Kingwood, TX 77345
(713) 360-6168

Principles: Drew Gross

Representing: Frank Conner

ProServ, Inc.
888 Seventeenth Street, N.W.
Washington, D.C. 20006
(202) 457-8800   (800) 424-9821

Principles: Robert Morris, Steve Frei, John Mascatello

Representing:

Mark Calcavecchia	Steve Melnyk
Rex Caldwell	Calvin Peete
Billy Casper	Scott Verplank
Jim Ferree	Fred Wadsworth
Donnie Hammond	

Jeffrey Rhodes & Company
1370 Stewart Street
Seattle WA 98109
(206) 682-0504

Representing: Bill Sander

Charles Rubin, Esq.
1313 Commerce Tower
911 Main Street
Kansas City, MO 64105
(816) 421-4770

Principle: Charles Rubin

Representing: Tom Watson

John Sandquist
1756 114th S.E.
Suite 234
Bellevue, WA 98004
(206) 455-1157

Principle: John Sandquist

Representing: Rick Fehr

Scott P. Sayers, Jr.
2905 San Gabriel, Suite 213
Austin, TX 78705
(512) 482-8900

Principle: Scott Sayers

Representing: Ben Crenshaw

Tim Simpson, Inc.
c/o Springbrook Country Club
585 Camp Perrin Road
Lawrenceville, GA 30245
(405) 963-0966

Representing: Tim Simpson

J.C. Snead Enterprises
P.O. Box 1152
Ponte Vedra Beach, FL 32082
(904) 285-4418

Principle: Susan Snead

Representing: J.C. Snead

J. Kenneth Sowles, Esq.
2 Waterfront Place
86 Lake Street
Burlington, VT 05401
(802) 864-8181

Representing: Charlie Bolling

Craig Stadler Enterprises
Law Offices of Brentnall Turley, Esq.
2049 Century Park E., Suite 1200
Los Angeles, CA 90067
(213) 277–3097

Representing: Craig Stadler

Brent Turley, Margaret Fields, Betty Fukuzaki, Michael J. Sterbick
15 Oregon Avenue
Suite 301
Tacoma, WA 98409
(206) 475–0440

Representing: Ken Still

Sutton Enterprises
Suite 117—Energy Square
212 Texas Street
Shreveport, LA 71101
(318) 221–3121

Representing: Hal Sutton

Larry Thibeault
P.O. Box 677426
Orlando, FL 32867
(407) 273–5052

Principle: Larry Thibeault

Representing: Brett Upper

Tresal Enterprises, Inc.
14901 Quorum Drive, Suite 170
Dallas, TX 75240
(214) 392–0002

Principles: Albert Salinas, Arnold Salinas, Joseph Salinas

Representing: Lee Trevino

Brentnall P. Turley, Esq.
2049 Century Park East
Suite 1200
Los Angeles, CA 90067
(213) 277–3097

Principles: Brent Turley, Margaret Fields, Betty Fukuzaki

Representing: Aki Ohmachi, Mike Reid, Craig Stadler

UMI—Uni-Managers International
10990 Wilshire Blvd., Suite 1800
Los Angeles, CA 90024
(213) 470–6000

Principles: Edward Barner, Joan McCalation, Lynn Paulson

Representing: Victor Regalado, John Schroeder, Sam Snead

Venture Management
536 South High Street
Columbus, OH 43215
(614) 228–4653

Principle: J. Michael McGinley

Representing: Blaine McCallister

Moose Wammock
1335 Mount Pleasant Road
Jacksonville, FL 32225
(904) 221–0005

Principle: Moose Wammock

Representing: Ed Fiori

LPGA Players' Agents

Advantage International
1025 Thomas Jefferson St., N.W.
Washington, DC 20007
(202) 333–3838

Principle: Greg Hood

Representing:

Nancy Brown	Michelle McGann
Donna Caponi	Anne-Marie Palli
Heather Farr	Kathleen McCarthy
Nicole Lowien	Scribner
	Colleen Walker

Don Carner
3030 S. Ocean Blvd.
Palm Beach, FL 33480
(407) 582–0834

Representing: JoAnne Carner

Cornerstone Sports, Inc.
2515 McKinney Ave., Lock Box 10
Dallas, TX 75201
(214) 855–5150

Principle: Roscoe O. Hambric, Jr.

Representing:
  Tami Jo Henningsen
  Adele Lukken
  Martha Nause

Giaciolli & Company
Crocker Bank Bldg.
225 Santa Monica Blvd.
3rd Floor
Santa Monica, CA 90401
(213) 451–5862

Principle: Linda Giaciolli

Representing: Amy Alcott

Don Hegeman
702 Home Federal Tower
Tucson, AZ 85701
(602) 575–9156

Representing: Chris Johnson

International Management Group
One Erieview Plaza, Suite 1300
Cleveland, Ohio 44114
(216) 522–1200

Principles: Jay Burton, Dave Lightner, Peter Johnson (Nancy Lopez only)

Representing:

Kathy Baker	Betsy King
Laura Baugh	Nancy Lopez
Kay Cockerill	Liselotte Neumann
Mei-Chi Cheng	Ayako Okamoto
Laura Davies	Laurie Rinker
Lori Garbacz	Patti Rizzo
Jane Geddes	Jody Rosenthal
Cathy Gerring	Jan Stephenson
Juli Inkster	Barb Thomas
Caroline Keggi	Donna White
Tracy Kerdyk	

Keller & Heckman
1150 17th St., Suite 1000 NW
Washington, DC 20036

Principle: Carole Harris

Representing: Marta Figueras-Dotti

Lee Trevino has enlivened the American golf scene for two decades with his sterling play and colorful personality. (Dost & Evans)

Don Mason
Two Capitol Plaza
Suite 3–1
Concord, NH 03301
(603) 224–2000

Principle: Don Mason

Representing: Jane Blalock

Pros, Inc.
P.O. Box 673
Richmond, VA 23206
(804) 643–7600

Principles: Vinny Giles, Vernon Spratley

Representing: Beth Daniel, Kathy Whitworth

LPGA Tour star Jan Stephenson (Dost & Evans)

Clare Sheils
520 Mission Street
Santa Cruz, CA 95060
(408) 426–4481

Principle: Clare Sheils

Representing:
  Patty Sheehan   Sherri Turner
  Shirley Furlong Mary Beth Zimmerman

Tresal Enterprises, Inc.
14901 Quorum Dr., Suite 170
Dallas, TX 75240
(214) 392–0002

Principles: Albert Salinas, Arnold Salinas, Joseph Salinas

Representing:
Amy Benz   Vicki Fergon

5

THE BEST GOLF BOOKS

GOLFERS SHARE the game with all other golfers. We may learn golf in splendid isolation, but it is the same game for everyone. We play by the same rules. We use various models of the same clubs. Even our golf courses are alike—eighteen separate patterns of teeing area, fairway, and green. This shared challenge may be why golfers love to read. Books not only pare the game down to its lyrical grace, beauty, and test of individual character, but in books, we learn about one another. We read of Hogan or Nicklaus missing a short putt, and we share in their despair. We read about Tom Kite holing a key pitch shot, and we understand his moment of glory. We, too, are golfers. We have been there.

Over the years, thousands of books have described great courses and great players. We may never have played the Old Course at St. Andrews, but we have read about the Road Hole. Most of us never saw Bobby Jones play, but we have read of The Grand Slam. Through books, golfers can even learn how to play, or at least, how to play better, and our desperate search for greater knowledge is why golf instruction books remain the best-sellers in sports. Golf is a shared obsession.

Fortunately, the game has attracted a number of very fine writers. They have produced a body of work that we will call golf literature, because the best of it is that. It is a tribute to the game, and to its writers, so that one player can report to another, "I've been reading some Darwin and a bit of Wind," and the companion is likely to know what they're talking about.

Herbert Warren Wind, an American writer, and the late Bernard Darwin, an Englishman, are the best of golf's serious writers. Wind and Darwin are essayists, and their insightful reporting from both sides of the Atlantic has enriched our appreciation of golf's unique drama and personalities.

Who could not be moved by Wind's eloquent essay, "Robert Tyre Jones, Jr.," written in 1972, shortly after the death of Bobby Jones? In it, Wind recalls Jones's 1958 return to St. Andrews. In a ceremony in Younger Hall, that great American golfer, crippled by a rare and painful form of muscle disease, was made an Honorary Burgess of the Borough.

"Seventeen hundred fervent St. Andreans crammed it to the rafters, literally," Wind wrote. "Jones spoke without notes that evening, and the occasion and the warmth of the audience fired him to a high pitch of eloquence. (I remember that he said of the Old Course, The more you study it the more you love it, and the more you love it the more you study it, and also, I could take out of my life everything except my experiences at St. Andrews and I would still have a rich, full life.) At the end of his talk, he was helped from the stage to his electric golf cart, and as he directed it down the center aisle toward the door the whole hall suddenly burst into the old Scottish song 'Will Ye No' Come Back Again?' and it came pour-

Following Through—*Herbert Warren Wind on Golf*

ing out with all the wild, overwhelming emotion of a pibroch wailed in some lonesome glen."

The man who wrote that, Herbert Warren Wind, was born in 1916 in Brockton, Massachusetts. He graduated from Yale University in 1937 and earned his M.A. at Cambridge University in 1939. One of the original editors of *Sports Illustrated,* he has since worked for *The New Yorker* magazine as a Profile writer and a contributor to the Sporting Scene department. Wind himself has said that he was once "an acceptable golfer." He competed enough to gain an understanding of golf as it is played at the highest level. H.W.W. has produced more than a dozen books, and his devotees anxiously await his yearly assessments of the Masters and the U.S. Open, which appear in *The New Yorker.*

Bernard Darwin died in 1961 at the age of eighty-five. Darwin worked mostly on the other side of the pond and over a forty-five-year period produced vivid essays for *The Times* of London and the weekly *Country Life.* While he wrote on a number of subjects, Darwin found his niche covering golf, a game he played very well. He was a semifinalist in the British Amateur in 1921 and captained the British side in the first Walker Cup match in 1922.

Darwin attended Eton and Cambridge University, where he studied classics and law. He eventually passed the examinations to become a solicitor and, in 1903, a barrister, a profession which bored him. In 1908 he began writing golf pieces for various English newspapers and, in favor of his new career, bid farewell to the law at the age of thirty-two.

It was golf's gain. Bernard Darwin had a keen understanding of the human side of golf. His final paragraph in the story "Duncan and Mitchell," from his book *Golf Between Two Wars,* underlines Darwin's insight.

"I have written at some length about that championship because I cannot help feeling that it had a profound effect on Mitchell's career," Darwin observed. "He remained for years a grand golfer and was, I think, the best match player in the country, but he never again really looked like winning the Championship. Yet—and this is the biggest and most speculative 'if' of all—I can never get it out of my head that had he won at Deal he might have won several more times. As it was, the shadow of that Deal disaster lay heavy upon him. It strikes me—I may be wrong but I will say it nevertheless—that Abe is very fond of golf but not fond of big golf. By nature a gentle and peaceful creature, he never really enjoyed, as some more fortunate people do, the trampling and the hum of the crowd and the clash of battle. He has fought hard and well because it was his business to do so, but he did not like the fight for its own sake. In that respect he reminds me of another great player who was always happier in playing with his friends and disliked the 'fuss' of championships, Mr. Robert Maxwell. He never took the field again after the war and so does not come into my period, but I cannot refrain from saying what a tremendous golfer he was. Tremendous—that is the epithet for Abe Mitchell.

To see him at his best, serene and unworried, was to find it impossible to believe that anyone could beat him and I still find it surprising that anyone ever did."

To their credit, both Darwin and Wind knew a fine golfer when they saw one, even if she was a woman. Darwin gracefully chronicled the career of the great English amateur Joyce Wethered, along with other fine women golfers of the day. Wind's 1965 piece on American professional Mickey Wright in *The New Yorker* remains the definitive story about Miss Wright.

Both Bernard Darwin and Herbert Warren Wind wrote a number of books and if you have one, keep it.

There are other golf writers with unique style: Who hasn't chuckled at the observations of Charles Price, or Peter Dobereiner? Or laughed out loud at Dan Jenkins's stuff? And there are the fine English golf scribes: Peter Ryde, Pat Ward-Thomas, and Michael McDonnell. I'm particularly fond of McDonnell's stories about Ben Hogan from "Great Moments In Sport: Golf."

The following excerpt is from "Ben Hogan, Carnoustie, 1953."

". . . It took him into a lonely world where only he and the golf course existed—he and the task that he had to accomplish. Nobody else lived in that world.

"It was not arrogance nor gross presumption of his destiny, because Hogan's vision never stretched that far, never beyond exerting complete mastery over the stroke that confronted him. The only judgment

"Books not only pare the game down to its lyrical grace, beauty, and test of individual character, but, in books, we learn about each other. We read of Hogan or Nicklaus missing a short putt, and we share in their despair. We read about Tom Kite holing a key pitch shot, and we understand his moment of glory. We, too, are golfers. We have been there."

that mattered was his own, and there was none harsher.

"He could never share himself with others since he, Hogan, existed only with a club in his hands. He had nothing else to offer, and if others pitied his loneliness then it was a mistake, because within him there was a fullness of life which excited him so much that each day he could not wait for the hours of sleep to pass so that he might return to his beloved clubs and his foe, the golf course."

McDonnell's writing seeps into the subconscious. He is so good, and so subtle, that his perceptions become *our* perceptions.

Among newer writers, Thomas Boswell, whose stories from the *Washington Post* and *Golf* magazine were published in *Strokes of Genius,* in 1987, conveys a fine understanding of professional golfers and their exploits. Al Barkow, the editor of *Golf Illustrated,* made a contribution to golf literature in 1987 with *Gettin' to the Dance Floor,* an oral history of the American side of the game. This book was largely an editing task, and I believe Barkow's best writing came in *Golf's Golden Grind,* which was published in 1974.

Until now, women golfers have been relatively shortchanged in golf's literature.

Strokes of Genius—*Thomas Boswell*

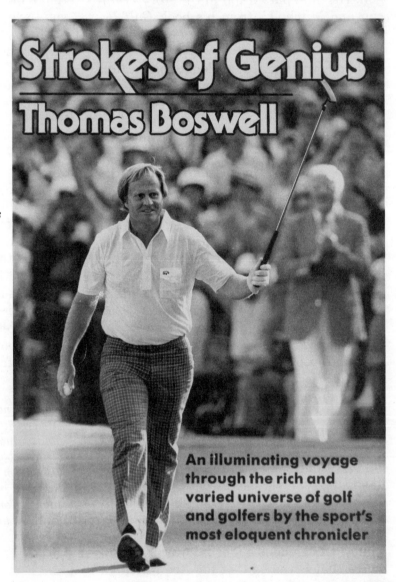

That sad fact will probably change in the near future: The National Golf Foundation has determined that, while women make up only 23 percent of all golfers, women make up 41 percent of all beginning golfers and are coming to the game in increasing numbers.

This shift should create a lively demand for more books about women players and, one hopes, will prompt writers to at least be more accurate and thorough in their stories about the women's side of the game. With a few notable exceptions, such as Darwin and Wind, and a couple of good magazine writers (Dick Taylor of *Golf World* and George Eberl of *Golf Journal* come to mind), writers are sometimes sloppy and inaccurate when writing about women golfers.

Women authors have written some very good golf books, but copies are rare and you'll have to search them out through dealers. In 1929, Glenna Collett came out with *Ladies in the Rough,* for Alfred A. Knopf. In 1934, Joyce Wethered penned *Golfing Memories and Methods,* well worth having for her unique view of competition and her graceful writing style.

More recently, Rosalynde Cossey wrote a fine history of British and Irish golf in *Golfing Ladies, Five Centuries of Golf in Great Britain and Ireland,* published by Orbis, London, in 1984.

My own favorite on the women's game is an old book, *After The Ball: Merry Memoirs of a Golfer,* a charming recollection of women's tournaments in the early twentieth century by the English golfer and golf writer Eleanor E. Helme. It was published by Hurst & Blackett, Ltd., in the early 1930s.

"So off we went," wrote Miss Helme, "and certainly found Ireland just the same as she always was and always will be, the most delightful of hostesses, who positively kills you with kindness. There might not be lobsters at Newcastle, but what about those iced cakes, and all the members, men and ladies, handing them round to you just as if you were at a private tea-party every day in the clubhouse, and when you could eat no more 'Now then, Captain, what are we going to do to entertain the ladies for the rest of the day?' And there would be a putting competition, or a driving competition, or a concert, whilst on the Sunday, every motor-car in the neighbourhood seemed to assemble outside the Slieve Donard, to whirl us off through the mountains of Mourne, where the gorse smelt sweeter than anything you could imagine, and the mountains looked bluer, and the sea more emerald."

The older golf books like *After the Ball* not only are of lasting value as a good read, but many have actually increased in value through the years: Miss Helme's book was priced at $40 in 1985. That's chicken feed, however, compared with the whopping $12,500 for a first edition of *Rules of the Thistle Golf Club: With Some Historical Notices Relative to the Progress to the Game of Golf in Scotland.* This volume, by James Cundell, privately printed in 1824, was the first attempt at a written history of the game.

Literature students are often surprised to learn that golf has lured fine novelists and short story writers to its ranks for a quick shot or two. John Updike, Alistair Cooke, and George Plimpton have all given golf writing a whirl. P.G. Wodehouse wrote numerous golf stories, while Ian Fleming's chapter on a golf match enhanced the drama and conflict in his book *Goldfinger,* in the James Bond series. Even F. Scott Fitzgerald used country club settings for some of his highly polished short stories. In fact, Jordan Baker, one of Fitzgerald's lead characters in his novel *The Great Gatsby,* was cast

> *"Through books, golfers can . . . learn how to play, or at least, how to play better, and our desperate search for greater knowledge is why golf instruction books remain the best-sellers in sports. Golf is a shared obsession."*

as a famous tournament golfer and was based on an actual American golfer, a great beauty named Edith Cummings.

Golf offers a very fine library. There are books on golf travel, course architecture, golf history, instruction, biography, autobiography, and fiction. Many of the best books are relatively inexpensive and some are available in reprints. In short, with a bit of research and money you can build your own fine collection, one that will give you many hours of pleasure. To that end, I've listed books about golf (alphabetically, by author) that are well worth reading and owning, with short reviews.

THE BEST GOLF BOOKS

Al Barkow. Gettin' to the Dance Floor. *New York: Atheneum, 1986.*

This book is, most of all, a great idea. Barkow's role was as interviewer and editor. He interviewed twenty-four veteran players, from William "Wild Bill" Mehlhorn and Henry Picard, to Patty Berg and Betsy Rawls. A history of American golf evolves, often in the golfer's own words. I say this because one chapter especially, with Rawls, doesn't seem to sound like Betsy and must have been heavily edited. The chapters with Byron Nelson and Berg are standard fare—we've read all this before—but the closing chapter with Jack Burke, Jr., is wonderful. Burke offers a fascinating perspective on the life of an up-from-the-ranks American golf professional.

Al Barkow. Golf's Golden Grind. *New York, London: Harcourt Brace Jovanovich, 1974.*

Barkow at his best. A lyrical, revealing book about the realities of the grind that is the PGA Tour. Includes a top-notch, colorful history of the PGA and its political evolution from the early road show of Walter Hagen and Gene Sarazen. Fine observations about the early years of Hogan, Snead, and Nelson.

The opening chapter, "Following the Sun," is beautifully written:

"They live by the sun and pay its dues," Barkow begins. "They are burnt red around chins and cheekbones; backs of necks are Oklahoma in drought—deep, dry crevices in baked hide; backs of hands are crumpled onionskin; permanent squint lines are deeply etched; lips are camphored. Few use oils. They are not on vacation. They are at work under King Hot, and oils can get on hands and make them slippery. Slippery is bad, dry is good . . . on the outside. On the inside, all the nerve ends, tendons, muscles, ligaments want to be, should be, as slick and free flowing as a fire pole."

Michael Bartlett. The Golf Book. *New York: Arbor House, 1980.*

Bartlett, who edited this collection, has combined profiles, glory, humor, instruction, and even the spirit of the rules in an homage to golf writers. The essays by Herbert Warren Wind, Bernard Darwin, Pat Ward-Thomas, and Michael McDonnell are lovely. The humor of Henry Longhurst, Frank Hannigan, Jim Murray, and Charles Price guarantee a merry afternoon. From various classic instruction books, Bartlett has culled the "secrets" of some of the game's best minds, including Robert Tyre Jones, Jr., Jack Nicklaus, Percy Boomer, Tommy Armour, and Ernest Jones. Even Harry Vardon makes a contribution, through the keen insights in Ken Bowden's "Harry Vardon, The Master Mold."

Bartlett offers wonderful surprises, too. He found Peter Ryde's stirring account of Jones's Grand Slam in, of all things, *The 1980 Bay Hill Classic Annual.* Bartlett also thoughtfully included "The Principles of Golf," from *The Principles Behind the Rules of Golf,* by Richard S. Tufts. Tufts, who developed Pinehurst, was a member of the USGA Rules Committee and believed so strongly in these principles that he published the book himself. Tufts manages to humanize a dry subject.

John Updike's story, "Thirteen Ways of Looking at the Masters," written in 1980 for *Golf*

Gettin' to the Dance Floor—*Al Barkow*

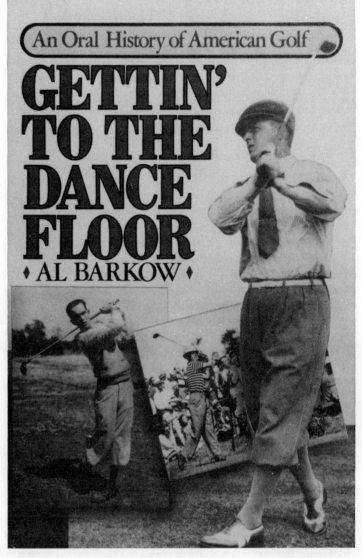

An Oral History of American Golf

GETTIN' TO THE DANCE FLOOR

◆ AL BARKOW ◆

Magazine, is, of course, wonderfully crafted, but may be slightly offensive to Southerners and to women.

Jolee Edmondson's story "The Whitwams Go to the Masters" won first prize in the annual awards for the Golf Writers Association of America in 1977, the first such prize won by a woman.

Thomas Boswell. Strokes of Genius. *New York: Doubleday & Co., 1987.*

An eloquent collection of Boswell's columns and stories from the *Washington Post* and *Golf* magazine. The moguls of modern journalism demand "people stories," and Boswell writes them beautifully. His reflections on Nicklaus as "The

Olden Bear" are masterful. "I Am the Walruz" is a nicely sympathetic piece on Craig Stadler, whose insistence on being "his own man" makes him a fascinating player in a sometimes stodgy game. Boswell writes with a psychoanalytical slant, which gives new insight into a quietly intense golfer like Tom Watson.

While Boswell clearly respects the game, he isn't awed by it. He may be the best of the newer golf reporters, however, he doesn't offer the sense of "place" always apparent in the work of Darwin and Wind. These two old masters could put a reader in the middle of a fairway at Augusta National, Pine Valley, or Troon. Reading Wind, you stand *with* Watson over a pitch shot at the Old Course. Boswell tries mightily in

"I Am the Walruz," a nicely sympathetic essay on Craig Stadler, is in Thomas Boswell's book, Strokes of Genius (Dost & Evans)

"Cathedral in the Pines," but it doesn't quite come off. You get the feeling that, while he surely plays the game, he never played at a high-enough level of competition to understand the subtleties of a course or the drama of champion-ship combat. He doesn't *explain* golf, yet he's a sort of psychologist who is at his best when he writes about players. His refreshing and peppery style will keep you reading.

Glenna Collett Vare. Ladies in the Rough. *New York: Alfred A. Knopf, 1927.*

America's greatest woman amateur, who died in 1989, was the Bobby Jones of distaff golf. Yet, she was an outspoken woman, and that quality is

captured here in her autobiography—especially in a chapter where she frankly rails against the financial boundaries of amateur competition. Mrs. Vare's code of fine sportsmanship crops up throughout, and she is generous in her remarks about players of the day like Edith Cummings, Virginia Wilson, Mrs. Caleb Fox, Dorothy Camp-bell Hurd, and Ada Mackenzie.

Mrs. Vare never pretended to be a great writer. In 1985 she told me that she had drafted friends to help her write this book. Still, this is a valuable look at Glenna's career and the golf-ers she played against. The black-and-white photographs are wonderful. A collector's edition, you'll have to track it down through a dealer or get lucky at someone's garage sale.

Geoffrey S. Cornish and Ron E. Whitten. The Golf Course. *New York: The Rutledge Press, 1981.*

This beautiful volume is a must for students of the game—a study of golf-course architecture with wonderful illustrations and photography.

Geoffrey Cornish and Ron Whitten charted new territory when they researched golf architects and the courses they designed. They describe the evolution of golf architecture, from the earliest innovations, like small greens and cross bunkers, to the modern fixation with railroad ties and stadium courses. Modern designers like Robert Trent Jones and Pete Dye get a lot of ink, but Cornish and Whitten also pay tribute to early artists like C.H. Alison and H.S. Colt, Donald Ross, A.W. Tillinghast, C.B. Macdonald, and Alister Mackenzie. The "Profiles" section is a series of short biographies of architects, famous and obscure.

Rosalynde Cossey. Golfing Ladies. *London: Orbis, 1984.*

This book is the closest we have to a history of women's golf. Miss Cossey thoroughly covers five centuries of players in Great Britain and Ireland. Her research is painstaking, and the writing is excellent. American readers who may not be accustomed to her charming British way with words might remember that it's *their* language.

The Golf Course—*Geoffrey S. Cornish and Ronald E. Whitten*

Golfing Ladies—*Rosalynde Cossey*

This volume offers rich anecdotes about players from Mary, Queen of Scots, to Vivien Saunders and complete records of women's competition on the other side of the Atlantic.

Beautifully designed, the book includes stylish photographs of early players and capsule biographies in a special section.

Bernard Darwin. Darwin on the Green. *London: Souvenir Press Ltd., 1986.*

This essay collection spans Darwin's fifty-three years with *Country Life.* "A Question of Style" was his first piece, written in 1908. "Stormy Weather," his last, was written in 1961. These are reflections related to golf of all levels, from club play to championships, and of interest to all Darwin fans.

"Confessions of a Practiser" (1919) will seem familiar and funny to any golf addict, as Darwin recounts his indoor exploits with clubs, carpets, and bedposts. "The Golfer's Cigarette" (1947) is a whimsical report of the smoking habits of various champions.

If these essays are read chronologically, it becomes obvious that Darwin was the rare writer who got better as he got older. Writers often peak at middle age and then, their energy spent, sink into self-parody. Darwin's enthusiasm for golf reporting remained keen. His clean, pointed style is at its best in "Stormy Weather," which he wrote in 1961, the year of his death, at the age of eighty-five. Darwin uses his memories in this one, but he enlightens us with them, rather than leaning on the past out of sheer laziness. The freshness of "Stormy Weather," written twenty-nine years ago, reminds us today that Darwin is the master.

Bernard Darwin. Golf Between Two Wars. *London: Chatto & Windus, 1944.*

While nearly all of Bernard Darwin's essays are enlightening, I think he was at his best as a reporter. Covering the Walker Cup, the Ryder Cup, or an Open Championship, Darwin had a unique ability to involve the reader in a golf course and a championship match. There's a lot of this kind of pure reporting in *Golf Between Two Wars,* a chronicle of the years between World War I and World War II. In the foreword he freely admits that this is no history book, but a series of his own recollections of golf in peacetime. They are vivid. The era from 1919 to 1939 included a number of the game's most dramatic innovations. International play picked up. The modern golf ball came into use, as did steel shafts. Great personalities emerged, like Walter Hagen, Gene Sarazen, and Henry Cotton. But, as Darwin stresses, this particular era will likely be remembered as that of Robert T. Jones, Jr., and Joyce Wethered, the fine English player who was the greatest woman amateur. He pays equal tribute to them.

This brings to mind a quality shared by Darwin and Herbert Warren Wind, his American counterpart. Darwin had, and Wind continues to have, a marvelous lack of prejudice toward women golfers. Both wrote about women golfers gracefully, assessing the women's game with seriousness and no apologies. In fact, to my knowledge, neither Darwin nor Wind ever attempted to compare women's golf with the men's side of the game. Accepting the obvious differences, neither indulged in frivolous comparisons.

Peter Dobereiner. The World of Golf. *New York: Atheneum, 1981.*

Dobereiner is among the most prolific of good golf writers, and this collection of short stories and columns—many from the *Observer* and the *Guardian*—is an extensive one. Dobereiner is thoughtful, amusing, and perhaps packs more wallop into three pages than any other golf writer.

He knows how to kick off a story and is a master of the great lead, for example, the first paragraph of "Obsession with Length," a *Golf Digest* piece on the USGA's equipment standards written in 1980:

"They are not worried about vampires at Golf House. As for ghosties and ghoulies and things that go bump in the night, the members of the United States Golf Association are terribly brave and do not even sleep with the light on, or so I believe. Nevertheless, they are gripped by a neurotic, superstitious fear of the supernatural, in the form of a golf ball that will need only a gentle tap to make it soar off a quarter of a mile down the fairway."

Dobereiner is excellent in almost every way, but he must have been stalled in an elevator for three decades of women's golf. In "The Sound of Nancy," Dobereiner makes two errors. The first is that he claims that French amateur Catherine Lacoste was treated badly by American women golfers on her way to winning the 1967 U.S. Women's Open, and that she cried herself to sleep at night as the result of "bitchy hostility" from the Americans. It never happened. Not only were the Americans cordial, Mlle Lacoste seemed quite cheerful that night before Sunday's final round when I saw her dancing at the old Homestead, whirling to the music until she fell laughing to the floor.

In Dobereiner's second misstep, he claims that Lacoste, Nancy Lopez, and Babe Zaharias were the only women to have hit their shots with a decided, "Crack!" It only means that he never saw, or rather, heard, JoAnne Carner, Patty Berg, or Mickey Wright, who hit the noisiest tee shots this side of men's golf. Having watched them all play, I must say that, compared to Miss Wright, Mlle Lacoste was a powder puff.

William Hallberg. Perfect Lies. *New York: Doubleday, 1989.*

Thanks to William Hallberg, who edited this wonderful book, not to mention a few fair writers like F. Scott Fitzgerald, Ring Lardner, John Updike, and Holworthy Hall, we now have a collection of great golf fiction in one volume. Hallberg did an admirable job of collecting the best and credits Herbert Warren Wind and Robert Mac-Donald with helping him in his detective work.

A few years ago, Ben Crenshaw was passing around a photocopy of a story called "Dormie One" at Austin Country Club. It remains the most dramatic piece of golf fiction I've ever read, and the best, and I was delighted to find it in Mr. Hallberg's collection. "Dormie One" was written in 1917 by Holworthy Hall, a pen name for Harold E. Porter.

Hallberg also includes the poignant and lovely "Winter Dreams," an F. Scott Fitzgerald story from *All The Sad Young Men.* Ring Lardner is here ("A Caddy's Diary") and P.G. Wodehouse ("The Heart of a Goof").

But Hallberg has unearthed at least three short stories, written in today's lean style, that you will soon count among the best you've read. "An Afternoon with the Old Man," by Andre Dubus, is from his collection *Adultery and Other Choices* and first appeared in *The New Yorker.* "The Year of Getting to Know Us," by Ethan Canin, is from *Emperor of the Air* and originally ran in *Atlantic Monthly.* Both stories are about young men and their relationships with their fathers. Because the fathers are golfers, we know them better. You will love these stories. They may even break your heart.

"The Mower," by James Kaplan, is offbeat and terrific. It originally ran in *The New Yorker.*

Eleanor E. Helme. After the Ball. *London: Hurst & Blackett, Ltd., approximately 1930.*

Another collector's edition which will be difficult to find. Miss Helme was a secretary at the Ladies Golf Union during the early twentieth century. She was also a fine player, in a semifinalist sort of way, and a charming writer. It's not fluff. Helme veils her pithy observations with wit. She knew and watched some of the best early golfers—Gladys Ravenscroft, Joyce Wethered, Alexa Stirling, and Glenna Collett—and she keenly assesses their play. That's only part of it. I've run into no other writer who so vividly and truthfully describes women's competition; the rivalries, frivolities, and the sweet joy of combat as women became serious about their golf and traveled to tournaments in England, Scotland, and Ireland. This lovely little book includes some very funny line drawings. It is well worth the search.

Dan Jenkins. The Dogged Victims of Inexorable Fate. *New York and Canada: Sports Illustrated Books as published by Little, Brown and Company, 1970.*

Just when you think you've nailed Jenkins as a "Texas" writer, you pick up something like his story "The Game of Golfe," a lot of which is written in a brogue. Frankly, the story is not his best, and one wonders why he included it in this otherwise wonderful collection of stories from *Sports Illustrated* in the 1960s. But "The Game of Golfe" reminds us that Jenkins cannot be typed. He's a lot more than the man who wrote *Semi-Tough,* the title of his football novel, or *Dead Solid Perfect,* his account of the life of a professional golfer. Jenkins isn't really a Good Old Boy. He's a sensitive writer, when he drops the dialect. He'll also probably be remembered as one of the great humorists of our time.

Jenkins is just plain funny. He can make you laugh out loud when he writes about any sport, tossing verbs and adjectives at you in frenzied delight. Jenkins is also an insider. He manages to get close to athletes, puts his own unique twists on their stories, and leaves us entertained and feeling privileged to be this close to a sport. He loves golf, was a good player, and therefore understands it. In this collection, "Sam Snead With Hair" gets close to the early professional tour. "America's Guest" is an irreverent profile of George Low.

But, in "The Glory Game," he brings us public links golf on a platter, the game at its most fundamental. And, in "The Dogged Victim," he has written one of the best profiles of Arnold Palmer that you'll ever read. Jenkins not only gives you the meat and potatoes of golf, he also serves dessert.

Robert Tyre Jones, Jr., and O.B. Keeler. Down the Fairway. *New York: Minton, Balch & Company, 1927.*

Jones was already a legendary golfer when he teamed with O.B. Keeler, the fine Atlanta golf writer, to write this autobiography. At twenty-five, he had won two U.S. Opens, the British Open, and two U.S. Amateur Championships. In five years, he had never finished lower than second in the U.S. Open. The Grand Slam would not come until 1930, but this book is interesting because Jones writes of his early life and career, and expresses his great love for the game and the people in it.

He was a fine writer, as everyone knows, and his inherent modesty shines through in his accounts of 1926, the year in which he captured both the U.S. and British Opens. Great golfer that he was, Jones was also intensely human, and his very brief account of his welcome in New York after capturing the British Open will cause the throat to tighten.

Curiously, Jones often refers to "fate" and the role that it played in his career. "Fate" is a factor that Glenna Collett also credited during her best years, which paralleled Bob Jones's era. What a steely-eyed glare we would receive from Jack Nicklaus if we credited his success to "fate," or any factor beyond his control.

You will love this book. Herbert Warren Wind has written that it is his favorite. Part Two is devoted to Jones's golf theories.

Charles Price. Golfer-at-Large. *New York: Atheneum, 1982.*

If you haven't read Charles Price, you haven't read about golf. Often funny, always irascible, Price remains one of the best writers the game has known. He can make you laugh, as in "How Bobby Jones and I Blew the British Open at St. Andrews," a sly, and true, account of how Price briefly led the oldest championship, or "Pinehurst Revisited," his blithe memories of life at the old golf resort and a look at Pinehurst's more recent changes. But Price can be poignant, as in

Golfer-at-Large—*Charles Price*

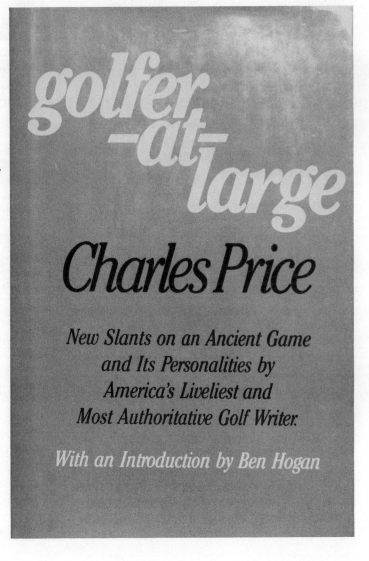

"The Haig and I," perhaps the best profile of the late Walter Hagen.

Charles Price was, and probably still is, a very fine golfer who played on the PGA tour as an amateur. He befriended Jones, Hagen, Hogan, Demaret, and a host of other pals, and those connections have enhanced his writing. He understands the game and appreciates its great tracks, which he explains so well in stories like "Baltusrol."

Price doesn't use any fifty-cent words. He's truly an American writer, complete with the effortlessly witty turn of phrase.

Charles Price was a founder of *Golf Magazine* and its original editor-in-chief. This is a collection of his stories and columns from that publication. I've always had the feeling that Price, more than most writers, gets under golf's skin and tells the truth about the game. This book is superb.

Art Spander and Mark Mulvoy. Golf, The Passion and the Challenge. *New York: Rutledge Books, Inc., 1977.*

A number of almost-poets have tried to pin a number of near-poetic words on this game. Spander and Mulvoy, a couple of fine sportswriters, have pulled it off, well describing golf's beauty and terror.

The authors delve into golf's universality. They've connected us. To Spander and Mulvoy, we are all one—you, Tommy Bolt, Jack Nicklaus, Lefty Stackhouse, and me. The game, they contend, is the thing. This book was written thirteen years ago, but the wonderful writing and glorious photographs are timeless. Spander and Mulvoy help you understand golf's ancient lure.

Pat Ward-Thomas, Herbert Warren Wind, Charles Price, and Peter Thomson, with Foreword by Alistair Cooke. The World Atlas of Golf. *London: Mitchell Beazley Publishers, Ltd., 1976.*

Do not dismiss *The World Atlas of Golf* as merely a coffee-table volume of beautiful design. The book was produced by some of the game's premier writers: Ward-Thomas, Wind, Price, and Thomson, and their essays never fail to convey a sense of place as they describe the best courses in the world.

Additionally, they review course design from the old links to the modern creations, peruse the evolution of clubs and balls, and present a readable and thorough look at the basics of course architecture and construction.

Ward-Thomas's "Elements of Greatness—A Classic Course" is a beautiful piece. He floats from one favorite hole to another, combining eighteen classic golf holes from around the world into his "classic course."

We then tour the great courses of Europe and Africa (Ward-Thomas), North and South America (Price), and Asia and Australia (Thomson).

This is a thoughtful, lyrical book and the color art and photographs are breathtaking.

Joyce Wethered. Golfing Memories and Methods. *London: Hutchinson and Co., Ltd., 1934.*

Joyce Wethered was the finest woman amateur in the history of the game. Even Glenna Collett, the best American amateur, could not beat her, although Miss Collett tried mightily, most notably in the British Women's Amateur at St. Andrews where their encounter was called the "Match of the Century."

In this lovely old book, Joyce Wethered also shows that she is a very fine writer.

She recalled her entry in the Open Amateur at St. Andrews after a long layoff from tournament golf:

"... this was the championship that I certainly

"John Updike, Alistair Cooke, and George Plimpton have all given golf writing a whirl. P.G. Wodehouse wrote numerous golf stories, while Ian Fleming's chapter on a golf match enhanced the drama and conflict in his book Goldfinger, *in the James Bond series. Even F. Scott Fitzgerald used country club settings for some of his highly polished short stories. In fact, Jordan Baker, one of Fitzgerald's lead characters in his novel* The Great Gatsby, *was cast as a famous tournament golfer and was based on an actual American golfer—a great beauty named Edith Cummings."*

enjoyed the most. Perhaps one of the reasons was that I was able to enter after an interval with much less expected of me than usual. There could be no justification for such remarks as, 'Of course you will do well,' which in a game like golf spell ruin if they are believed for one moment. I was prepared for anything or everything to happen, however disastrous or extraordinary. It created an enchanting sense of freedom to feel that the well-meaning friends who come up after a bad shot and say, 'That really wasn't like you!' would not this time allow themselves to be so easily shocked."

The narrative is intriguing and the long section on her swing theories, illustrated with photographs, is of historical note.

Herbert Warren Wind. Following Through.
New York: Ticknor & Fields, 1985.

A collection of Wind's essays from *The New Yorker* from 1962 to 1985. The book would be a must for collectors, if only for the stirring profile of Bobby Jones, "Robert Tyre Jones, Jr.," written in 1972, shortly after Jones's death. All great athletes deserve as fine a chronicler as Wind.

Reading Wind's prose, you feel the turf beneath your feet, the sock of the club against the ball, the gale at your back, and the sun falling warm upon your shoulders. Wind can make you feel the tension and glory of playing championship golf, even if you sport a double-digit handicap.

Lee Trevino is the subject of a thoughtful profile in Herbert Warren Wind's Following Through. *(Dost & Evans)*

He set the standard in golf reporting.

His stunning essay "Nicklaus and Watson at Turnberry" includes this: Watson, on the final hole, drove into the fairway. Nicklaus, trailing Watson by a stroke, drove into the rough and . . . "He was faced with an almost unplayable lie: the ball had ended up two inches from the base of a gorse bush; and, to complicate matters, a branch of the bush, some two feet above the ground, was directly in the line of his backswing. He would be hard put to it to manufacture any kind of useful shot. Watson to play first, going with a 7-iron. He couldn't have hit it much better: the ball sat down two feet from the pin. Nicklaus now, playing an 8-iron. Still not giving up. With his great strength, he drove his club through the impeding gorse branch, managed to catch the ball squarely, and boosted it over the bunker on the right and onto the green thirty-five feet from the cup. He worked on the putt, studying the subtleties carefully, as if the championship depended on it. Then he rammed it in for his 3. Tremendous cheers. Watson chose not to give himself too much time to think about the two-footer he now had to hole to win. After checking the line, he stepped up to the ball and knocked it in. Another salvo of cheers—for Watson, and also for both Watson and Nicklaus and the inspired golf they had played over the last thirty-six holes of the Open."

All the pieces in *Following Through* are memorable. Special favorites, after the Jones and Turnberry stories, are "Trevino," "Hogan: Something to Remember Him By," and "The Women: Mickey Wright, Babe Zaharias, and Joyce Wethered."

Herbert Warren Wind. The Story of American Golf. *New York: Alfred A. Knopf, Inc., 1948, 1956, 1975.*

If you own only one golf book, it should be this one. It was published in 1948 but Wind has conscientiously updated it twice since. In *The Story of American Golf,* he traces the roots of the game in this country in lyrical and precise words.

As a reference book alone, the work is wonderful and while golf history can be a pretty dry subject—all that old stuff about the Apple Tree Gang and Francis Ouimet—Wind's ear for detail and colorful little tidbits keep the eyes racing. He lingers over the great players, Hogan, Snead, Nelson, and the modern-day giants, and pays fair tribute to the women—there's an especially fine chapter on Glenna Collett Vare—but there are pleasant surprises, too, like an assessment of the great American golf instructors.

When Wind analyzes a golf swing, or a golf course, he is so apt a student that you know it's best to believe him. His career as a writer has spanned some of the most exciting eras of golf. The game is lucky to have had him.

CLASSIC GOLF INSTRUCTION BOOKS

The following instruction books are not reviewed—only the individual golfer knows if he or she can glean something useful from their pages—but the books listed here are considered the classics of the genre. They are worth reading for their historical merit. Several include the only written record of the swing theories of golf's greatest players and instructors.

Frank Kenyon Allen, Tom LoPresti, Dale Mead, and Barbara Romack. *Golfer's Bible.* New York: Doubleday, 1968.

Tommy Armour. *How to Play Your Best Golf All the Time.* New York: Simon and Schuster, 1953.

Patty Berg and Otis Dypwick. *Golf.* New York: A.S. Barnes, 1941.

Percy Boomer. *On Learning Golf.* New York: Alfred A. Knopf, 1946.

Leo Diegle and Jim Dante, with Len Elliott. *The Nine Bad Shots of Golf.* New York: Whittlesey House, 1947.

Ben Hogan, with Herbert Warren Wind. *Ben Hogan's Five Lessons—The Modern Fundamentals of Golf.* New York: A.S. Barnes, 1957.

Ben Hogan—Five Lessons—The Modern Fundamentals of Golf

Ernest Jones, and Innis Brown. *Swinging into Golf.* New York: Whittlesey House, 1937.

Ernest Jones and David Eisenberg. *Swing the Clubhead.* New York: Dodd, Mead, 1952.

Robert Tyre Jones, Jr. *Bobby Jones on Golf.* New York: Doubleday, 1966.

Bob MacDonald. *Golf.* USA: Wallace Press, 1927.

Alex J. Morrison. *A New Way to Better Golf.* New York: Simon and Schuster, 1932.

Jack Nicklaus, with Ken Bowden. *Jack Nicklaus's Lesson Tee.* Norwalk, CT: Golf Digest, 1977.

Gary Player, with Desmond Tolhurst. *Golf Be-gins at 50.* New York: Simon and Schuster, 1988.

Sam Snead. *How to Hit a Golf Ball.* New York: Doubleday, 1950.

Louise Suggs. *Par Golf for Women.* New York: Prentice-Hall, 1953.

Harry Vardon. *The Complete Golfer.* New York: McLure, Phillips, 1905.

Tom Watson. *Getting Up and Down.* New York: Random House, 1983.

Kathy Whitworth: *Golf For Women.* NY: St. Martin's Press, 1990.

Mickey Wright. *Play Golf the Wright Way.* New York: Doubleday & Company, 1962.

6

THE BEST GOLF VIDEOS AND FILMS

I N THE last decade the advent and popularity of home videocassette recorders has brought yet another innovation to the game of golf. Through videos, golfers can work on their swings, improve their mental approach, review great championships, learn The Rules Of Golf, and even speed up their play.

The popularity of golf videos reached new heights in 1987 when an American company released a video that aroused more interest than many recent developments in the game. The video wasn't even original but a copy of a film first produced fifty-six years before. And it was expensive.

However, SyberVision's landmark video of Bobby Jones in the instruction films that had first been produced by Warner Brothers

The great Bobby Jones (Courtesy USGA)

in 1931 proved that there is a sophisticated market for golf videos.

The production begins with historical footage of Jones as he won golf's Grand Slam and became a national hero. Jones then narrates eighteen classic instruction shorts, complete with a cast of the era's movie stars, including James Cagney, W.C. Fields, Loretta Young, Walter Huston, and Joan Blondell.

The package, two videocassettes and a book about Jones by Charles Price, cost the consumer about $250, yet the release of the video was greeted with the kind of hoopla that might have attended the discovery of the Holy Grail, or at least the longest ball. Since their release, touring professionals as well as country club members have enjoyed the videos and used them to analyze Jones's genius. Not only have they studied that famous swing, many have also sought to incorporate the Atlantan's theories into their own games.

Golfers love to try to mimic great swings, thus instruction videos have been produced by the hundreds. Golfers also love the lore of the game, and production companies have fulfilled that interest by producing films of the great moments in golf. In the following listings, you'll find many videos that appeal to you as a golfer and as a golf historian.

Many of these videos are sold through the National Golf Foundation and the United States Golf Association. When ordering an NGF or USGA tape, inquire about special prices for NGF members and members of the USGA Associates program.

Videos are available in VHS and Beta, which you'll need to specify in your order.

INSTRUCTION

An Inside Look—

Instruction from famed teachers Bob Toski, Jim Flick, and Peter Kostis. 56 minutes. $49.95.

GolfSmart
P.O. Box 639
Chicago Park, CA 95712–0639

Telephone toll free 1–800–637–3557
Collect in California 916–272–1422

Arnold Palmer's Play Great Golf—

Instruction video in two volumes, 60 minutes each, with Arnold Palmer. Volume I, "Mastering the Fundamentals," helps develop and sharpen the proper fundamentals. Volume II, "Course Strategy," helps the golfer evaluate any shot in real golf-course situations. 60 minutes. $41.95 each. Available through the National Golf Foundation.

Telephone toll free 1–800–733–6006

The Art of Putting—

Instruction video with Ben Crenshaw, who teaches you how to be a better putter. 44 minutes. $36.95. Available through the National Golf Foundation.

Telephone toll free 1–800–733–6006

The Azinger Way—

Instruction tape with Paul Azinger using driver, pitching wedge, and putter. $29.95

International Sports Video
302 S. Massachusetts Ave.
Lakeland, FL 33801
(813) 683–3177

Better Golf Now—

Ken Venturi teaches the fundamentals of golf on a 40-minute cassette. $41.95. Available through the National Golf Foundation.

Telephone toll free 1–800–733–6006

Ben Crenshaw, arguably modern golf's best putter, explains his methods in The Art of Putting *video. (Dost & Evans)*

Billy Casper Golf Basics I and Billy Casper Golf Basics II—

Tips from the Hall-of-Famer and former U.S. Open Champion. 30 minutes each. $14.95 each.

GolfSmart
P.O. Box 639
Chicago Park, CA 95712–0639

Telephone toll free 1–800–637–3557
Collect in California 916–272–1422

Bob Toski Teaches You Golf—

Toski's complete teaching program for success in golf. 56 minutes. $52.95. Available through the National Golf Foundation.

Telephone toll free 1–800–733–6006

Bobby Jones Instructional Series—

Instruction excerpts from Jones's famous series *How I Play Golf*, with commentary by Jack Nicklaus. 45 minutes. $72.95. Available through the National Golf Foundation.

Telephone toll free 1–800–733–6006

Challenge Golf: Home Edition; Individuals and Personal Teachers—

Peter Longo teaches the handicapped how to play golf. 53 minutes. $52.95. Available through the National Golf Foundation.

Telephone toll free 1–800–733–6006

Challenge Golf: Teaching Edition; Hospitals, Park Districts, Schools—

Instruction video adapted for therapists, park directors, school coaches, and other professionals. 60 minutes. $52.95. Available through the National Golf Foundation.

Telephone toll free 1–800–733–6006

Chi Chi's Bag of Tricks—

Chi Chi Rodriguez, one of the masters of invention, teaches golfers how to get out of trouble. 60 minutes. $49.98. Available through the National Golf Foundation.

Telephone toll free 1–800–733–6006

Difficult Shots—

Hale Irwin helps the golfer master the game's ten most difficult shots. 60 minutes. $52.95. Available through the National Golf Foundation.

Telephone toll free 1–800–733–6006

18 Tips from 18 Legends of Golf—

18 lessons from senior players; Mike Souchak, Peter Thomson, Butch Baird, Doug Ford, Miller Barber, Sam Snead, Art Wall, Tommy Bolt, Gene Littler, Don January, Gardner Dickinson, Doug Sanders, Jerry Barber, Bob Goalby, Billy Casper, Gay Brewer, Charlie Sifford, and Julius Boros. Sections include: "Before You Hit," "The Full Swing," "The Fairway Shots," "Around the Green," "Strategy and Equipment. 120 minutes. $59.95. Includes postage and handling.

Telephone toll free 1–800–321–5700
or write:

18 Tips
P.O. Box 2459
Secaucus, NJ 07094.

Exercise for Better Golf—

Designed to improve your game and lessen your chance of golf-related injuries. 73 minutes. $52.-95. Available through the National Golf Foundation.

Telephone toll free 1–800–733–6006

Nick Faldo's Golf Course—

The 1989 Masters Champion's keys to consistency. 60 min. $29.98.

GolfSmart
P.O. Box 639
Chicago Park, CA 95712–0639

Telephone toll free 1–800–637–3557
Collect in California 916–272–1422

Faults and Cures—

Famed instructor John Jacobs answers questions about the game's most troubling swing faults. 58 minutes. $72.95. Available through the National Golf Foundation.

Telephone toll free 1–800–733–6006

Feel Your Way to Better Golf—

PGA touring pro Wally Armstrong teaches what good golf feels like. 52 minutes. $15.95. Available through the National Golf Foundation.

Telephone toll free 1–800–733–6006

Finding Fundamentals—

Bob Toski and Jim Flick teach the basics of golf. 26 minutes. $32.00. Available through the National Golf Foundation.

Telephone toll free 1–800–733–6006

Gary Player on Golf—

Veteran star Gary Player gives lessons on all aspects of the game. 90 minutes. $32.95. Available through the National Golf Foundation.

Telephone toll free 1–800–733–6006

Gene Littler's: The Ten Basics—

A 30-day program designed to shave 5–10 strokes off your game. 45 minutes. $21.00. Available through the National Golf Foundation.

Telephone toll free 1–800–733–6006

Get Rid of Your Back Problems and Play Better Golf—

Dr. K.J. Keggi, Sam Snead, and Pamela Kazeme-kas provide a conditioning program to give you a healthier back. 60 minutes. $41.95. Available through the National Golf Foundation.

Telephone toll free 1–800–733–6006

The Golden Tee—

Excellent instruction tips from vintage champions, including Byron Nelson and Mickey Wright, Bob Rosburg, Billy Casper. From a filmed presentation of 25 years ago. 72 min. $29.-95.

GolfSmart
P.O. Box 639
Chicago Park, CA 95712–0639

Telephone toll free 1–800–637–3557
Collect in California 916–272–1422

Golf—

Instruction from Al Geiberger. 60 minutes. Videocassette only. $69.95. Audio and videocassette. $89.95.

GolfSmart
P.O. Box 639
Chicago Park, CA 95712–0639

Telephone toll free 1–800–637–3557
Collect in California 916–272–1422

Golf for Kids of All Ages—

Instruction for juniors with PGA tour veteran Wally Armstrong, son Scott, and Gabby Gator, an animated character. $19.95. Postage and handling, add $2.50.

Brentwood Home Video
P.O. Box 1347
Alpharetta, GA 30239–1347
1–800–762–3851, ext. 420

The Golf Digest Schools Learning Library—

Your choice of ten cassettes based on the instruction principles of the Golf Digest golf schools, featuring Bob Toski and various staff professionals.

Vol. 1: "A Swing for a Lifetime"
Vol. 2: "Find Your Own Fundamentals"
Vol. 3: "Driving for Distance"
Vol. 4: "Sharpen Your Short Irons"
Vol. 5: "Saving Par from the Sand"
Vol. 6: "Putting for Profit"
Vol. 7: "When the Chips Are Down"
Vol. 8: "Winning Pitch Shots"
Vol. 9: "Hitting the Long Shots"
Vol. 10: "Trouble Shots"

Priced at $29.95 each. Five for $129.75. Ten for $239.50.

Telephone toll free 1–800–451–7020, Operator 106

Golf for Winners—

Mark O'Meara and Hank Haney teach the importance of the "swing plane." 42 minutes. $63.95. Available through the National Golf Foundation.

Telephone toll free 1–800–733–6006

Golf Is Mental Imagery—

Mike Austin uses the principles of kinesiology to teach the golf swing. 56 minutes. $41.95. Available through the National Golf Foundation.

Telephone toll free 1–800–733–6006

Golf the Miller Way—

Former U.S. Open Champion Johnny Miller with swing tips. 30 min. $29.95.

GolfSmart
P.O. Box 639
Chicago Park, CA 95712–0639

Telephone toll free 1–800–637–3557
Collect in California 916–272–1422

Golf My Way—

A classic video from modern golf's premier player, Jack Nicklaus, in two hours of golf instruction. 128 minutes. $89.95. Available through the National Golf Foundation.

Telephone toll free 1–800–733–6006

In Chi Chi's Bag of Tricks, *veteran star Chi Chi Rodriguez offers advice on trouble shots.* (Dost & Evans)

Golf's One in a Million Shots—

Steve Melnyk is the narrator. 60 minutes. $29.95.

GolfSmart
P.O. Box 639
Chicago Park, CA 95712–0639

Telephone toll free 1–800–637–3557
Collect in California 916–272–1422

The Golf Swing—

With Tom Weiskopf, who had one of the best. 45 minutes. $19.95.

GolfSmart
P.O. Box 639
Chicago Park, CA 95712–0639

Telephone toll free 1–800–637–3557
Collect in California 916–272–1422

Golf Your Way—

Phil Ritson's instruction tape, which received *Golf Magazine*'s five-star rating. 78 minutes. $23.99. Available through the National Golf Foundation.

Telephone toll free 1–800–733–6006

The Greater Golfer in You—

In Volume I, Dr. Gary Wiren teaches the golf swing. 84 minutes. $59.95. In Volume II, Dr. Gary Wiren teaches the short game. 87 minutes. $59.95. Available through the National Golf Foundation.

Telephone toll free 1–800–733–6006

Greg Norman: The Long Game—

Exciting instruction from one of modern golf's premier big hitters. 63 minutes. $79.95. Available through the National Golf Foundation.

Telephone toll free 1–800–733–6006

How I Play Golf—

The 1987 release of the Bob Jones classic 1931 instruction series, first-generation copies of the black-and-white Warner Brothers films, 18 lessons, and a highlight film of the American hero's career. 3 hours. 2 cassettes. $250.00. Available through the National Golf Foundation.

Telephone toll free 1–800–733–6006

How to Break 90 in 30 Days—

Golf instruction geared for the average player to help avoid the most common mistakes of high-handicap golfers. 50 minutes. $32.00. Available through the National Golf Foundation.

Telephone toll free 1–800–733–6006

The Jimmy Ballard Golf Connection—

Famed instructor Jimmy Ballard outlines the seven common denominators of all great ball strikers. 90 minutes. $52.95. Available through the National Golf Foundation.

Telephone toll free 1–800–733–6006

Keys to Consistency—

Nicklaus's teacher, Jack Grout, divulges his methods for playing solidly all the time. 59 minutes. $39.95. Available through the National Golf Foundation.

Telephone toll free 1–800–733–6006

Keys to the Effortless Swing—

Swing tips from Michael McTeigue. 80 minutes. $39.95.

GolfSmart
P.O. Box 639
Chicago Park, CA 95712–0639

Telephone toll free 1–800–637–3557
Collect in California 916–272–1422

King of Clubs—

Peter Longo offers great trick shot entertainment and instruction. 40 minutes. $24.95. Available through the National Golf Foundation.

Telephone toll free 1–800–733–6006

Tom Kite & Friends; Reach Your Potential—

Instruction with Tom Kite as he helps Julius Erving, Claude Akins, and Ron Masak learn to play better by playing their own style of game. Practice tee sessions and on-the-course playing tips for shaving strokes. Two-hour video on two cassettes: $59.95. Add $2.50 for postage and handling.

Telephone toll free 1–800–762–3851

Brentwood Home Video
P.O. Box 1347
Alpharetta, GA 30239–1347

"Through videos, golfers can work on their swings, improve their mental approach, review great championships, learn the Rules of Golf, and even speed up their play."

Tom Kite and friends team up in Kite's golf video, Reaching Your Golf Potential. (Dost & Evans)

The Last 100 Yards—

Jack Grout details the "how and why" of the short game. 45 minutes. $39.95. Available through the National Golf Foundation.

Telephone toll free 1–800–733–6006

Learning Golf—

Mike Calbot makes the swing simple to understand and accomplish. 90 minutes. $49.95. Available through the National Golf Foundation.

Telephone toll free 1–800–733–6006

Lee Trevino's Golf Tips for Youngsters—

The ace shot maker, Lee Trevino, helps juniors with valuable advice. 40 minutes. $24.95. Available through the National Golf Foundation.

Telephone toll free 1–800–733–6006

Lee Trevino's Priceless Golf Tips—

In Volume I, Trevino helps the golfer learn how to improve chipping and putting. 25 minutes. In Volume II, Lee handles troublesome shots and difficult lies. 25 minutes. Volume III is about swing fundamentals, gaining distance and control. 25 minutes. $21.00 each. Available through the National Golf Foundation.

Telephone toll free 1–800–733–6006

Make Every Shot a Nice Shot!—

Video on mental approach to golf comes with two audio tapes and cartoon booklet. Designed by Sports Enhancement Associates to move golfers away from mechanics and into thinking and sensory perception. $89.95. Add $3.05 for postage, insurance, and delivery.

Telephone toll free 1–800–633–2252, ext. 4245

Sports Enhancement Associates
5816 Shakespeare Road
Box 5826
Columbia, SC 29250

The Master System to Better Golf: Vol. I—

A series featuring Craig Stadler, Davis Love III, Tom Purtzer and Gary Koch on the short game, driving, iron accuracy, and putting. 60 minutes. $39.95.

Craig Stadler on the Short Game—Stadler discusses the basics of wedge play and course strategy. 20 minutes. $14.95.

Davis Love III on Driving—Davis Love III gives a comprehensive lesson on driving. 20 minutes. $14.95.

Tom Purtzer on Iron Accuracy—Purtzer on the basics of long and short iron play. 20 minutes. $14.95.

Gary Koch on Putting—Koch covers putting fundamentals and how to read greens. 20 minutes. $14.95.

All available through the National Golf Foundation.

Telephone toll free 1–800–733–6006

Lee Trevino's Priceless Golf Tips *offers advice on putting and chipping, along with trouble shots, the swing, distance, and control.* (Dost & Evans)

The Master System to Better Golf, Vol. II—

Paul Azinger, Fred Couples, and Bobby Wadkins cover sand play, tempo, and trouble shots. 60 minutes. $39.95.

> **Paul Azinger on Fairway and Green Sand Traps**—Azinger on bunker play. 20 minutes $14.95.
>
> **Fred Couples on Tempo**—Couples discusses the timing of the swing. 20 minutes. $14.95.
>
> **Bobby Wadkins on Trouble Shots**—Wadkins tells you how to get out of awkward lies and positions. 20 minutes. $14.95.

All available through the National Golf Foundation.

Telephone toll free 1–800–733–6006

The Master System to Better Golf, The Seniors—

Different aspects of the game covered by Miller Barber, Dale Douglas, and Orville Moody. 115 minutes. $41.95. Available through the National Golf Foundation.

Telephone toll free 1–800–733–6006

Mastering the Long Putter—

John Schlee demonstrates the proper techniques in maximizing the advantages of the long putter. 50 minutes. $39.95. Available through the National Golf Foundation.

Telephone toll free 1–800–733–6006

PGA Tour star Hal Sutton is featured with four others in the PGA Tour Golf *video.* (Dost & Evans)

Veteran Ray Floyd offers useful advice on the short game in his video, Sixty Yards In. *(Dost & Evans)*

Men's Golf—

Al Geiberger demonstrates the picture-perfect golf swing. 60 minutes. Video only, $72.95. Video and audio cassettes, $95.00. Available through the National Golf Foundation.

Telephone toll free 1–800–733–6006

PGA Tour Golf—

Three volumes. In Vol. I, Tom Kite, Craig Stadler, Payne Stewart, and Hal Sutton on the fundamentals of the swing. 60 minutes. $63.95. Vol. II, putting, bunker play, pitching and chipping with PGA tour stars. 60 minutes. $63.95. Vol. III, course strategy lessons as the pros play nine holes together. 60 minutes. $63.95. Available through the National Golf Foundation.

Telephone toll free 1–800–733–6006

Play Your Best Golf—

Bob Toski, Jim Flick, Conrad Rehling, Gary Wiren, Peggy Kirk Bell, Rod Meyers, and Carol Johnson give instructions on two videos. Vol. I, "The Clubs," is 69 minutes and costs $29.95. Vol. II, "The Strategies," is 109 minutes and costs $29.95. Both volumes for $59.95. Available through the National Golf Foundation.

Telephone toll free 1–800–733–6006

"Golfers love to try to mimic great swings, thus instruction videos have been produced by the hundreds. Golfers also love the lore of the game, and production companies have fulfilled that interest by producing films of the great moments in golf."

Power Driving—

Mike Dunaway teaches the secrets of hitting for distance. 30 minutes. $52.95. Available through the National Golf Foundation.

Telephone toll free 1–800–733–6006

Precision Putting—

PGA tour player Dave Stockton on the secrets of putting. 30 minutes. $49.95.

GolfSmart
P.O. Box 639
Chicago Park, CA 95712–0639

Telephone toll free 1–800–637–3557
Collect in California 916–272–1422

Saving Par from the Sand—

Bob Toski and John Elliot explain the elements of successful bunker play. 26 minutes. $32.00. Available through the National Golf Foundation.

Telephone toll free 1–800–733–6006

Secrets for Seniors—

Sam Snead's secrets of shot making, and his approach to physical and mental fitness. 60 minutes. $39.95. Available through the National Golf Foundation.

Telephone toll free 1–800–733–6006

Al Geiberger, a star of the PGA Senior Tour, offers golf tips in the video Winning Golf. *(Dost & Evans)*

Sharpen Your Short Irons—

Jim Flick demonstrates the four fundamentals of short-iron play. 26 minutes. $32.00. Available through the National Golf Foundation.

Telephone toll free 1–800–733–6006

The Short Way to Lower Scoring—

Paul Runyan shows you how to save strokes around the green. Vol. I is about putting and chipping. 35 minutes. $32.00. Vol. II is on pitching and sand play. 26 minutes. $32.00. Available through the National Golf Foundation.

Telephone toll free 1–800–733–6006

Sixty Yards In—

Ray Floyd, master of the short game, on the finesse shots. 60 minutes. $59.95. Available through the National Golf Foundation.

Telephone toll free 1–800–733–6006

So You Stand on the Wrong Side of the Ball Too—

Instructional information for left-handed golfers. $63.95. Available through the National Golf Foundation.

Telephone toll free 1–800–733–6006

Super Power Golf—

Dr. Gary Wiren presents a specific program on how to hit the ball farther. $52.95. Available through the National Golf Foundation.

Telephone toll free 1–800–733–6006

A Swing for a Lifetime—

Bob Toski and Jim Flick demonstrate how to build a golf swing. 26 minutes. $32.00. Available through the National Golf Foundation.

Telephone toll free 1–800–733–6006

Ten Fundamentals of the Modern Golf Swing—

The basics of the swing, with David Glenz and Jim McLean. 60 minutes. $34.95. Available through the National Golf Foundation.

Telephone toll free 1–800–733–6006

Winning Golf—

Al Geiberger's easy step-by-step program for golfing improvement. 60 minutes. $29.95. Available through the National Golf Foundation.

Telephone toll free 1–800–733–6006

FOR WOMEN GOLFERS

The 1988 U.S. Women's Open: A Star Is Born—

Liselotte Neumann holds off Patty Sheehan and Colleen Walker to win her first Women's Open at Five Farms in Baltimore. Includes historic film of past Women's Open champions. The first video of a women's championship. A collector's item. 53 minutes. $29.95. Available from the United States Golf Association.

Telephone toll free 1–800–336–4446
Or write:

Golf House
United States Golf Association
P.O. Box 2000
Far Hills, NJ 07931–2000

Basic Instructional Films—

A six-cassette series of golf instruction filmed in 1965 under the guidance of PGA, LPGA, and National Golf Foundation educators. $29.95 each. $150.00 for the entire series.

"A Special Kind of Joy"—16 minutes.
"How to Build a Golf Swing"—30 minutes.
"The Short Approach Shots"—9 minutes.
"The Special Challenge Shots"—14 minutes.
"Putting—Golf's End Game"—12 minutes.
"Courtesy on the Course"—18 minutes.

Available through the National Golf Foundation.

Telephone toll free 1–800–733–6006

LPGA Tour star Donna White reviews the fundamentals in her video, Beginning Golf for Women. (Dost & Evans)

The glamorous Jan Stephenson, who has ventured into exercise and fitness videos, also stars in an instructional tape, How to Golf. (Dost & Evans)

Beginning Golf for Women—

LPGA touring professional Donna White teaches basic fundamentals for beginners. 40 minutes. $15.95. Available through the National Golf Foundation.

Telephone toll free 1–800–733–6006

Jan Stephenson's How to Golf—

Jan covers every aspect of the game, for men and women. 50 minutes. $32.00. Available through the National Golf Foundation.

Telephone toll free 1–800–733–6006

Keys to Great Golf—

JoAnne Carner helps you learn the basics, and how to hit the ball with more power. 90 minutes. $41.95. Available through the National Golf Foundation.

Telephone toll free 1–800–733–6006

Mastering the Basics: A Guide for the Woman Golfer—

Introduction by Patty Berg. Features Michele Bell and Annette Thompson. 40 minutes. $19.95. Available through the National Golf Foundation.

Telephone toll free 1–800–733–6006

Two-time Women's Open Champion JoAnne Carner is her effervescent self in The Keys to Great Golf! *(Dost & Evans)*

Nancy Lopez's Golf Made Easy—

Nancy gives step-by-step demonstrations on golf's fundamentals. 48 minutes. $41.95. Available through the National Golf Foundation.

Telephone toll free 1–800–733–6006

Women's Golf—

In two volumes. Vol. I, "The Full Swing," teaches greater accuracy and distance. Vol. II, "The Approach Game," emphasizes the short game. Each cassette, 40 minutes. Priced at $32.00 each. Available through the National Golf Foundation.

Telephone toll free 1–800–733–6006

Women's Golf—

A Sybervision production in which Patty Sheehan presents her golf-training program for women. 60 minutes. $72.95. Available through the National Golf Foundation.

Telephone toll free 1–800–733–6006

CHAMPIONSHIPS AND SPECIAL EVENTS

The British Open Golf Championships—

Ask about specific years. The Open Championships from 1970 through 1986 are available. 52 min. each. $79.95 each.

GolfSmart
P.O. Box 639
Chicago Park, CA 95712–0639

Telephone toll free 1–800–637–3557
Collect in California 916–272–1422

Fast Play Makes Fast Friends—

The USGA video on how to make golf more fun. 28 minutes. $19.95. Available through the National Golf Foundation.

Telephone toll free 1–800–733–6006

Golden Greats of Golf—

Historical highlights of golf's great players. 60 minutes. $52.95. Available through the National Golf Foundation.

Telephone toll free 1–800–733–6006

Golf's Greatest Moments—

Celebrating 100 years of golf with its greatest players. 77 min. $29.98.

GolfSmart
P.O. Box 639
Chicago Park, CA 95712–0639

Telephone toll free 1–800–637–3557
Collect in California 916–272–1422

Golf Memories—

Vintage golf with Bobby Jones, W.C. Fields, Bob Hope,Gene Sarazen, and many others. 60 minutes. $41.95. Available through the National Golf Foundation.

Telephone toll free 1–800–733–6006

Golf's One in a Million Shots—

Steve Melnyk narrates as we relive the "great shots" of golf. 60 minutes. $29.95. Available through the National Golf Foundation.

Telephone toll free 1–800–733–6006

Golf Shots—

Golf's first video magazine in a quarterly edition. Brings the game to life four times a year. Each video is 90 minutes long. Subscription price for four issues, $99.95. Add $12.00 for shipping and handling. Available through the National Golf Foundation.

Telephone toll free 1–800–733–6006

Great Moments of the Masters: The Video—

The legends of golf and their shot-making triumphs at Augusta National Golf Club. Official video of the Masters. $49.95. Handling and postage of $3.50. In Texas, add $4.00 sales tax.

Telephone toll free United States: 1–800–888–1188
Telephone toll free Canada: 1–800–268–1121
Or write:

Golf Videos
P.O. Box 13121
Austin, TX 78711

Jack Nicklaus Shows You the Greatest 18 Holes of Major Championship Golf—

Jack hosts an exciting review of golf's great holes and championships. 65 minutes. $49.95. Available through the National Golf Foundation.

Telephone toll free 1–800–733–6006

Jack Nicklaus is the host of several golf videos including Jack Nicklaus Shows You the Greatest 18 Holes of Major Championship Golf. *(Dost & Evans)*

Juli Inkster, three-time U.S. Women's Amateur Champion, joins Tom Watson and Peter Allis in The Rules of Golf Explained. *(Dost & Evans)*

Legacy of the Links—

Lee Trevino hosts an homage to the game from St. Andrews, Scotland. 90 minutes. $32.00. Available through the National Golf Foundation.

Telephone toll free 1–800–733–6006

The 1986 Masters Tournament—

Jack Nicklaus charges from behind in the final nine in one of his most thrilling victories. 60 min. $19.95.

GolfSmart
P.O. Box 639
Chicago Park, CA 95712–0639

Telephone toll free 1–800–637–3557
Collect in California 916–272–1422

The 1987 Masters Tournament—

Features the play-off between Larry Mize, Greg Norman, and Seve Ballesteros, and Mize's famous pitch shot. 60 minutes. $19.95.

GolfSmart
P.O. Box 639
Chicago Park, CA 95712–0639

Telephone toll free 1–800–637–3557
Collect in California 916–272–1422

The 1988 Masters Tournament—

More thrills from the Masters, including Sandy Lyle's shot from the fairway bunker on 18 to win. 60 minutes. $19.95.

> **GolfSmart**
> P.O. Box 639
> Chicago Park, CA 95712–0639
>
> *Telephone toll free 1–800–637–3557*
> *Collect in California 916–272–1422*

The Rules of Golf Explained—

Tom Watson, Juli Inkster, Peter Allis. A rundown on the rules. Includes a USGA Rules of Golf book. 23 minutes. $29.95.

> **GolfSmart**
> P.O. Box 639
> Chicago Park, CA 95712–0639
>
> *Telephone toll free 1–800–637–3557*
> *Collect in California 916–272–1422*

U.S. OPEN CHAMPIONSHIPS:

All U.S. Open videos are available through the United States Golf Association. Films of the videos can be rented for $20.00 each. Order by telephone or mail.

Telephone toll free 1–800–336–4446
In New Jersey: 201–234–2300.
Or write:

Golf House
P.O. Box 2000
Far Hills, NJ 07931–2000

The U.S. Open: Golf's Greatest Championship—

How the U.S. Open has evolved since 1895. 55 minutes. $29.95.

The 1988 U.S. Open: Strange Days at the Country Club—

Curtis Strange secured his position as one of the game's top players at the historic Country Club, where Frances Ouimet (1913) and Julius Boros (1963) preceded him as U.S. Open champions. 50 minutes. $29.95.

An Olympic Duel—

Scott Simpson's 1987 U.S. Open victory at San Francisco's Olympic Club. 59 minutes. $20.00.

A Vintage Year—

Ray Floyd, at 43 in 1986, becomes the oldest U.S. Open Champion in history. At Shinnecock Hills Golf Club. 28 minutes. $29.95.

North Survives at Oakland Hills—

In 1985, Andy North overcame Oakland Hills' famed monster to win his second Open. 30 minutes. $29.95.

Fuzzy Flew at Winged Foot—

Fuzzy Zoeller shoots 67 in a play-off with Greg Norman to win the 1984 U.S. Open. 37 minutes. $29.95.

The Nelson Touch at Oakmont—

In 1983, Larry Nelson shot 132 for the final 36 holes to pass Watson and Ballesteros at Oakmont Country Club. 36 minutes. $29.95.

Tom Watson at Pebble Beach—

In 1982, Watson's miraculous pitch shot at the 17th at Pebble Beach dashed Nicklaus's hopes for a record fifth Open victory. 36 minutes. $29.-95.

When Down Under Finished on Top—

Australia's David Graham wins the 1981 U.S. Open at the legendary Merion Golf Club. 36 minutes. $29.95.

The Day Jack Came Back—

Nicklaus won his fourth U.S. Open in 1980 in a classic duel with Isao Aoki at Baltusrol Golf Club, breaking his own Open scoring record in the process. 40 minutes. $29.95.

Irwin: Two-Time Man at Toledo—

In 1979, Hale Irwin withstood the charge of Gary Player and Jerry Pate to win his second Open title. 30 minutes. $29.95.

The Mile High Drama—

Andy North hung on to clinch his first Open title in 1978 at Cherry Hills Country Club. 26 minutes. $29.95.

The Heat Was On—

In 1977, Hubert Green outlasted the stifling heat and a challenge from the field to win the Open at Southern Hills Country Club in Tulsa. 36 minutes. $29.95.

Pate's Shot to Remember—

Jerry Pate hit his 5-iron to within two feet of the final hole at Atlanta Athletic Club and won the 1976 Open. 27½ minutes. $29.95.

Two-time U.S. Open Champion Curtis Strange is the star of the USGA's video on the 1989 U.S. Open, Strange Reigns at Oak Hill. *(Dost & Evans)*

Lou Graham Survives Medinah—

Lou Graham won the 1975 U.S. Open at Medinah Country Club when he beat John Mahaffey in a playoff. 30 minutes. $29.95.

Hale and Travail at Winged Foot—

Hale Irwin survived the difficult Winged Foot and won the 1974 U.S. Open by two strokes. 32 minutes. $29.95.

Miller's Miracle at Oakmont—

Johnny Miller's final round 63 vaulted him from six strokes behind to the 1973 U.S. Open title. 31 minutes. $29.95.

Pebble Beach—The 1972 Open—

Jack Nicklaus never faltered as he won his third U.S. Open title at the historic Beach. 30 minutes. $29.95.

Trevino at Merion—

Lee Trevino beat Jack Nicklaus by 3 in an 18-hole playoff in 1971 to claim his second Open championship. 34 minutes. $29.95.

Tony Jacklin Conquers Hazeltine—

In 1970, Tony Jacklin became the first Englishman in fifty years to win the Open at Hazeltine National Golf Club. 33 minutes. $29.95.

Orville Moody at Champions—

Orville Moody was a surprise winner when he captured the 1969 Open in Houston. 37 minutes. $29.95.

Trevino's Four Rounds in the 60s—

In 1968, Lee Trevino burst open the championship scene when he won his first U.S. Open. At Oak Hill Country Club. 39½ minutes. $29.95. USGA Associate Members: $19.95.

Nicklaus and the Record at Baltusrol—

Nicklaus foiled the efforts of amateur Marty Fleckman when he set an Open record of 275 at famed Baltusrol. 39 minutes. $29.95.

Triumph and Tragedy: Casper and Palmer at Olympic—

With nine to play, Billy Casper trailed Arnold Palmer by seven strokes but beat Palmer in a play-off to win the 1966 Open. 40 minutes. $29.95.

Gary Player at Bellerive—

Player, the first foreign winner since 1920, conquered Bellerive in St. Louis in 1965. 36 minutes. $29.95.

The Comeback of Ken Venturi—

Venturi's classic battle with the heat and Congressional Country Club as he won the 1964 Open. 32 minutes. $29.95.

Ouimet and Boros at Brookline—

On the course where Francis Ouimet outdueled Vardon and Ray in 1913, Julius Boros won the 1963 U.S. Open. 39 minutes. $29.95.

Oakmont and the Open—

Rookie professional Jack Nicklaus captures his first Open title by defeating Palmer in an 18-hole play-off in 1962. 33 minutes. $29.95.

Golf's Longest Hour—

In 1956, Cary Middlecoff posted 281 at Oak Hill Country Club and waited as Ben Hogan, Julius Boros, and Ted Kroll failed to equal his score. 17½ minutes. $24.95. Special price for USGA Associate Members: $16.95.

GOLF COMEDY

Caddyshack—

The movie, with Rodney Dangerfield and Chevy Chase. 90 min. $29.95.

GolfSmart
P.O. Box 639
Chicago Park, CA 95712–0639

Telephone toll free 1–800–637–3557
Collect in California 916–272–1422

Dorf on Golf—

Tim Conway and his hilarious friends. 30 min. $29.95.

GolfSmart
P.O. Box 639
Chicago Park, CA 95712–0639

Telephone toll free 1–800–637–3557
Collect in California 916–272–1422

I Hate This Game—

With Thom Sharp. More funny bits on golf. 40 min. $24.95.

GolfSmart
P.O. Box 639
Chicago Park, CA 95712–0639

Telephone toll free 1–800–637–3557
Collect in California 916–272–1422

Just Missed . . . Dammit!

A collection of golf's immortals acting like the rest of us. 40 min. $19.95.

GolfSmart
P.O. Box 639
Chicago Park, CA 95712–0639

Telephone toll free 1–800–637–3557
Collect in California 916–272–1422

7
BROADCASTING

IT'S LITTLE wonder that Jack Nicklaus has become an icon of sorts. We not only admire his record, we know him. He has been a guest in our living rooms for nearly thirty years.

The golfing public was a bit slow in warming up to the man. He toppled that other pal, Arnold Palmer, and, thanks to television, we'd been on a first-name basis with Arnie since his Masters victories in 1958 and 1960.

1960. That's when Palmer virtually jumped out of the small screen with his brave birdies on the last two holes to edge Venturi by a stroke. Shirttail flying, visor perched at a cocky angle, his muscles fairly rippling under that cotton knit shirt, he swaggered toward us in black-and-white. What a combo—Arnold Palmer and televised golf.

Along came the chunky kid from Ohio, an intruder, slugging his way into our homes. Television, however, is an intimate medium, and on that little screen we shared the most glorious golfing moments of Jack's life. And a few tragic losses. This is what we saw.

1962. Jack was only twenty-two. He beat Arnie in that play-off for the U.S. Open title.

1970. St. Andrews. He outlasted Doug Sanders in a play-off for the British Open. On the final hole, Jack removed his sweater and crashed a 380-yard drive over the back of the green of this par-4 hole. He pitched close, sank the 7-foot birdie putt, then tossed his putter into the air in a rare burst of emotion.

Jack Nicklaus has been a guest in our living rooms for nearly thirty years. (Dost & Evans)

"Shirttail flying, visor perched at a cocky angle, his muscles fairly rippling under that cotton knit shirt, he swaggered toward us in black-and-white. What a combo—Arnold Palmer and televised golf."

1975. Once again, the bear roared at Augusta, rolling in an "impossible" 40-footer at the par-3 sixteenth to trample the hopes of Tom Weiskopf and Johnny Miller.

1977. The British Open at Turnberry. Tom Watson versus Jack in one of golf's greatest duels. In the third round, both fired 65's. On the final day, Watson edged Nicklaus by a stroke, shooting 65 to Jack's 66.

Arnold Palmer virtually jumped out of the small screen during his colorful career. (Dost & Evans)

1978. St. Andrews. The British Open again. Jack said his triumphal walk up the seventy-second fairway was one of the most emotional moments of his life.

1980. Baltusrol. The U.S. Open. He's slimmer now and has a better haircut. Barbara and the kids are there. Jack, the aging bear and family man, is our guy. He won, after a long slump, and cries of "Jack is back!" crash through the final holes of this historic New Jersey course.

1982. The U.S. Open. Pebble Beach. Watson, his modern-day nemesis, holes that historic chip shot and Nicklaus loses another heartbreaker.

1986. The Masters. Jack begins his rally on the final nine of the course that forever owns the award for set design. We watch one birdie, then another, and another. It has been a long time since he managed to pull off such heroics. He is older now. So are we. On the par-3 sixteenth, a hole we know and love so well, he fires it at the flag. The gallery's roar thunders through the pines. The ball nearly goes in and stops a foot from the hole. His sight has dimmed. He cannot see the ball. Through the sudden mist that comes to our eyes, neither can we.

Can broadcasting get any better than this? To paraphrase an old line—golfers have great character, and it is television that reveals it.

Through the years, the game has become almost better on television than in person, a tribute to the modern era's technological advances.

In the 1940s, golf tournaments were filmed for showing in movie theaters. In 1953, the first nationally televised tournament was George S. May's World Championship in Chicago. That first broadcast was a lulu. Lew Worsham holed a wedge shot on the final hole to win the tournament and the staggering sum of $50,000.

In 1956, the Masters was telecast for the first time and by 1966 was beamed into our living rooms in living color.

In 1957, ABC began to broadcast the popular *All-Star Golf,* followed in 1959 by NBC's *World Championship Golf.*

Perhaps the best-known and most beloved televised golf series was Shell's *Wonderful World of Golf,* created by Fred Raphael in 1962. For nearly a decade, WWOG escorted American television audiences around the world to the great courses in Britain, the Philippines, and even Monaco, where the best players of the day teed it up in combat for cash.

The World Series of Golf was originated in 1962 by Walter Schwimmer, who pitted the champions of the U.S. Open, the British Open, the Masters, and the PGA Championship against each other at the end of the golf season.

Since those earlier days, when television cameras were perched atop station wagons camouflaged by foliage, golf broadcasting has become a near-perfect operation. Each of the three major commercial networks—ABC, CBS, and NBC—spend millions on televising golf. It shows.

In the course of long hours of golf (ABC now televises the entire eighteen holes of the final round of the U.S. Open and the PGA Championship, and CBS covers all eighteen on Sunday at the Masters), we begin to know our heroes and heroines on an intimate basis. In close-ups, we note their ravaged faces and grins of joy. Today the players are at home with the camera. They share their thoughts and goals with us. Profiles of their families and teachers tell us more about them. We are with them as they trudge around their dramatically beautiful battlefields.

Golf is highly visual. On TV, golf is greenness, the silver flash of a club shaft, and the soaring white dot against the sky. On the U.S. Open and Masters telecasts, we can even comprehend the futility of the golfer's

". . . golfers have great character, and it is television that reveals it."

Tom Watson edged Jack Nicklaus by a stroke in one of golf's greatest duels. At the 1977 British Open, Watson fired a final round 65 to Nicklaus's 66. (Dost & Evans)

ABC sports commentators: (left to right) Jack Whitaker, Roger Twibell, Dave Marr, and Frank Hannigan (Courtesy ABC Sports)

war against the waiting course—we see the great, silent fairways and greens from crane shots.

Each network differs in its golf production techniques. The talented young producer Terry Jastrow has brought a new philosophy to ABC's telecasts. Jastrow, once a crack college golfer at the University of Houston, is a former movie producer and has a keen eye for both drama and scene set.

"On TV, golf is greenness, the silver flash of a club shaft, and the soaring white dot against the sky."

His sweeping camera vistas are never better than at the USGA championships. Veteran sports producer Bob Goodrich lends a hand on some telecasts of major championships.

ABC's team lit up the screen covering the dramatics of Curtis Strange's 1988 U.S. Open victory—a telecast that is considered to be one of the best in golf broadcast history.

ABC puts an anchor team in a studio adjacent to the 18th green and a second anchor team at another on-course location. ABC's chief advantage is that the network uses roving on-course reporters, usually former champions, who walk with the golfers and report the lie and course conditions as well as describing the characteristics of the upcoming shot. Because ABC reporters normally stay with a pairing from the first tee to the last green, they can offer keen insights of the golfer's overall round.

CBS golf producer Frank Chirkinian has a different philosophy, stationing reporters in on-course towers at various holes where they astutely preside over the action. CBS offers some of the liveliest golf telecasts. The game is admittedly slow, and Chirkinian encourages his announcers to enhance the action by bouncing conversation back and forth. With frequent camera switches and this beautifully done "golf banter," Chirkinian is able to keep golf broadcasts from becoming dull.

The network was at its best in the telecast of the 1986 Masters. When Jack Nicklaus made one of the most stunning comebacks in the history of the game to capture the green jacket, the CBS team clicked and the drama of that program will be remembered by everyone who saw it.

The network includes televised golf tips from former U.S. Open Champion Ken Venturi. CBS, which telecasts the Masters, is also able to offer viewers golf's most picturesque broadcast when the production team works Augusta National in the Spring.

NBC offers mobility. The network gets out

> "Jastrow, once a crack college golfer at the University of Houston, is a former movie producer and has a keen eye for both drama and scene set."

Mark Rolfing (with microphone), one of NBC's "foot soldiers" in a post-tournament interview. (Dost & Evans)

Donna Caponi won two U.S. Women's Open Champions and many other LPGA Tour titles before her new career as a golf announcer for ESPN. (Dost & Evans)

"With frequent camera switches and this beautifully done 'golf banter,' Chirkinian is able to keep golf broadcasts from becoming dull."

with the leaders early on through the use of hand-held radio-frequency cameras which need no cables. NBC producer Larry Cirillo likes to liven up his telecasts by weaving a number of players into the fabric of the show, without losing the thread of the day's main story.

Like ABC, NBC uses on-course foot soldiers as well as stationary anchor teams in towers.

In 1990, NBC introduced a new anchor team, former U.S. Open champion Johnny Miller and veteran newsman Bryant Gumble. Gumble, new to the golf scene, will share anchor duties with longtime golf announcer Charlie Jones.

Cable networks are relatively new entries in the golf broadcasting market. Two cable networks, ESPN and USA, telecast a number of professional tournaments during the year. ESPN and USA have a unique role at the major championships. ESPN carries the first two rounds of the U.S. Open, the PGA Championship, the British Open, and the U.S. Women's Open, using the core of the ABC announcing team. USA carries the first two rounds of the Masters, the TPC at Sawgrass, and the Ryder Cup, with other events.

The most innovative development in modern golf broadcasting came not in television, but in radio.

In 1986, the SportsBand network went on the air at the J.C. Penney Classic in Largo, Florida. SportsBand is a new concept originated by Dallas oil executives Frank Mitchell and Theis Rice.

With a twenty-one-person production staff, as many as six on-course roving reporters, two anchors, and various personalities who do features and interviews, the Sports-Band signal is broadcast to galleries through a foam earpiece about the size of a nickel. Listeners also wear a tiny receiver, the size of a pager or beeper. The signal can be heard only through the SportsBand receivers, yet can't be heard by the golfers.

Mitchell and Rice invented the concept as a way to keep galleries entertained as well as informed about what's happening elsewhere on the course. Since most tournament patrons choose a favorite spot and stay there, the network offers spectators a chance to keep up with the leaders.

Called "The Big Picture on the Little Radio," SportsBand offers a state-of-the-art signal and a very big sound emanates from the tiny earpiece. SportsBand has been used at a number of recent PGA Tour events, including the TPC at Sawgrass, and it's popular among PGA players. Many "off-duty" PGA pros can be seen wearing the Sports-Band receiver and headset, tuning in to the action still on the course, and wives of players are among SportsBand's most ardent fans.

All facets of golf broadcasting are so good

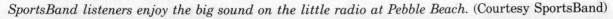

> *"NBC producer Larry Cirillo likes to liven up his telecasts by weaving a number of players into the fabric of the show . . ."*

SportsBand listeners enjoy the big sound on the little radio at Pebble Beach. (Courtesy SportsBand)

> *"Called 'The Big Picture on the Little Radio,' SportsBand offers a state-of-the-art signal—and a very big sound emanates from the tiny earpiece."*

now that it's difficult to see how they'll get any better, but innovations in technology and production concepts promise to further improve this key new arena of the game.

Golf Broadcasting Companies

RADIO:

SportsBand Network
Premier Place—Suite 675
5910 North Central Expressway
Dallas, TX 75206
(214) 891-6226

Sports Head: Frank Mitchell, President; Theis Rice, Vice President

Producer: Steve Rathe

Directors: Doug Johnson, Phil Garfinkel

Announcers: Nanci Donnellan, Lou Palmer, Greg Powers, Carol Mann, David Sullivan, Mary Bryan, Al Barkow, Rhonda Glenn. Feature anchor—Bob Drum.

TELEVISION:

American Broadcasting Co. (ABC)
47 W. 66th Street
New York, NY 10023
(212) 887-2186

Executive Producer: Geoffrey Mason

Producers: Terry Jastrow, Bob Goodrich

Director: Jim Jennett

Announcers: Jack Whitaker, Dave Marr, Peter Alliss, Roger Twibell, Frank Hannigan, Bob Rosburg, Judy Rankin, Jerry Pate, Ed Sneed, Rhonda Glenn. Special Commentator—Jack Nicklaus.

Mark Wiebe is interviewed "live" by SportsBand's mobile field reporter Greg Powers just after completion of his Saturday round in San Diego. The popular Powers, a current and active PGA Tour professional, is a veteran announcer on SportsBand's PGA Tour on-course broadcast. For more information contact: A.G. Longoria, Information Director, SportsBand Network, (214) 891-6226.
(Courtesy SportsBand)

Ed Sneed, a former PGA Tour standout, is one of the on-course reporters in ABC's golf broadcasts. (Dost & Evans)

Judy Rankin was an LPGA Tour star before becoming an announcer for ABC. She was the first woman to win over $100,000 in a single season. (Dost & Evans)

Pat Summerall ably anchors the CBS golf telecasts. (Courtesy CBS Sports)

Former U.S. Open Champion Ken Venturi is a golf analyst for CBS Sports. (Courtesy CBS Sports)

Steve Melnyk, former Walker Cup player and touring professional, now mans the microphone for the golf broadcasts of CBS Sports. (Courtesy CBS Sports)

Charlie Jones, a commentator for NBC, anchors some of that network's golf telecasts.

The NBC golf broadcasts have a totally new look for 1990 with commentators Johnny Miller and Bryant Gumble.

NBC's new golf reporting team for 1990 includes Bob Trumpy, longtime NFL analyst.

Jay Randolph, veteran golf broadcaster for NBC Sports (Courtesy NBC Sports)

Mark Rolfing is a new addition to the NBC golf broadcast team. (Courtesy NBC Sports)

Columbia Broadcasting System (CBS)
51 W. 52nd Street
New York, NY 10019
(212) 975–4321

Executive Producer/Director: Frank Chirkinian

Associate Producer: Chuck Will

Announcers: Pat Summerall, Jim Nantz, Ken Venturi, Ben Wright, Gary McCord, Steve Melnyk, Verne Lundquist. Masters only—Tom Weiskopf, Bob Murphy.

National Broadcasting Company (NBC)
30 Rockefeller Plaza
Room 1445
New York, NY 10112
(212) 664–4444

Executive Producer: Terry O'Neil

Co-ordinating Producer: Larry Cirillo

Director: Andy Rosenberg

Announcers: Bob Trumpy, Charlie Jones, Bryant Gumble, Johnny Miller, Mark Rolfing, Marlene Floyd, Jay Randolph.

CABLE TELEVISION:

ESPN
ESPN Plaza
Bristol, CT 06010
(203) 585–2000

Executive Producer: Don Ohlmeyer

Producer: Paul Spengler

Directors: Andy Young, Steve Beim

Announcers: Jim Kelly, Bob Murphy, Jim Colbert, Mary Bryan, Donna Caponi, Terry Diehl, Lori Garbacz.

USA Network
1230 Avenue of the Americas
New York, NY 10020
(212) 408–9100

Executive Producer: Gordon Beck

Producer: Garland Simon

Announcers: Ted Robinson, Joel Meyers, Jim Simpson

8

THE BUSINESS OF GOLF

Paul Hencke, editor-in-chief of the National Institute of Business Management newsletter, documented the golf boom in his February 1989 issue.

"Golf is on the verge of becoming a national mania, a sport reshaping life-styles, spending habits, real estate development, and investment patterns," he wrote.

Hencke charted golf's recent growth, saying that the game has become a $20-billion-a-year industry, and optimistically predicted that the industry will double its gross over the next twelve years.

Golf services have grown to meet this new demand and offer new job opportunities in an exciting field. We've covered two relatively new careers in the game, golf agents and broadcasters, in other chapters. Add golf administration, golf-course architecture, country-club management, and the roles of golf director, club professionals and assistant professionals, green superintendent, and rules officials to the virtual bonanza in new careers in and around the game.

1. Administration:

In administration, golf's power positions exist in three key organizations: the United States Golf Association, the PGA Tour, and the LPGA Tour.

Deane Beman, PGA Tour commissioner, a former Walker Cup player and touring professional, has boosted the PGA Tour to new prosperity. Not only are tournament purses higher than ever before, the PGA Tour is also enjoying greater broadcasting revenue from the sale of rights to PGA tournaments. Under Beman, the tour has embraced golf-course design with its TPC courses, stepped up the marketing of products bearing the PGA Tour logo, and kicked off the successful Senior PGA Tour.

One of Beman's plans is to obtain the video rights to all televised tour events, much as Major League Baseball owns the rights to its televised games. In this plan, the Tour would own exclusive rights to televised pictures of its players and would start a video file to be made available to the media and commercial enterprises.

David Fay is the newest addition to golf's power brokers. In July 1989, Fay was named senior executive director of the United States Golf Association, replacing the USGA's longtime leader, Frank Hannigan, who resigned to pursue writing and broadcasting projects.

Fay, at thirty-eight the youngest of golf's key executives, worked his way up through the ranks. A former member of the golf

Golf House, the USGA headquarters in Far Hills, New Jersey (Diane C. Becker)

team at Colgate University, from which he graduated after a semester at Stanford, he joined the USGA in 1978 after a stint as communications director of the (New York area) Metropolitan Golf Association. At the USGA, Fay was given responsibilities in almost every area, including rules and tournament administration.

Not only does the USGA conduct major championships, it also determines the rules of play (jointly with the Royal and Ancient Golf Club of St. Andrews), establishes equipment standards, sponsors international amateur team competition, has an active publishing and communication arm, and is at the forefront of turfgrass research. While Fay is the USGA's chief administrator and supervises the day-to-day activities of the staff at Golf House, the direction of the association is determined by the USGA's Executive Committee, with input from any number of other committees of USGA volunteers.

The third position is commissioner of the Ladies Professional Golf Association, a job newly occupied by Bill Blue. Blue took on the job in 1989 after former commissioner John Laupheimer resigned in 1988. Blue was hired, in large part, because of his strong marketing skills.

In his first year, Blue faced some stern tests: to decide upon a new site for LPGA headquarters and to boost the LPGA's purses and tournament schedules. In mid-summer, the LPGA announced that a new corporate headquarters site near Daytona Beach, Florida, had been selected. Blue was instrumental in adding the biggest purse in history to the LPGA's 1990 schedule—a $750,000 tournament in Tallahassee, Florida, sponsored by the Centel Corporation of Chicago, Illinois.

It's chancy to capsule the means by which an aspiring administrator trains for a job in golf. While strong business, marketing, and administration skills are obviously necessary, each of golf's three key administrators got the job through a different route. Deane Beman was a successful insurance executive before going to work for the PGA Tour, and Bill Blue was involved in sales and marketing with a number of large companies before taking on the LPGA commissioner's job. David Fay's path was more clearly directed toward a golf job—early on he worked in a number of positions at the Metropolitan Golf Association.

Fay's route to the helm of the USGA was by way of his work with a regional golf association (the Met Golf Association embraces the greater New York area), but there are other career possibilities with big golf organizations, such as the National Golf Foundation and the Western Golf Association.

USGA
Golf House
Far Hills, NJ 07931
(201) 234-2300

PGA Tour
Sawgrass
112 TPC Boulevard
Ponte Vedra Beach, FL 32082
(904) 285-3700

LPGA
2570 Volusia Avenue
Suite B
Daytona Beach, FL 32114
(904) 254-8800

National Golf Foundation
1150 U.S. Hwy. 1
Jupiter, FL 33477
(407) 744-6006

Western Golf Association
Golf, IL 60029
(312) 724-4600

2. ARCHITECTS

With the influx of new players, the design and building of golf courses is a burgeoning field. According to the National Golf Foundation, the United States will need some 4,500 new courses by the end of the century; that's about 375 new courses per year, or 1 a day for the next eleven years.

Current development is lagging—it's closer to 120 new courses a year—but the demand is there, and the need for golf-course designers promises to continue.

The job of the course architect was perhaps best defined by William S. Flynn, who, in the 1920s, designed some of this country's premier golf courses, including Cherry Hills Country Club in Denver, Shinnecock Hills Golf Club in Southampton, and The Homestead, in Hot Springs, Virginia.

Flynn said simply, "The principal consideration of the architect is to design his course in such a way as to hold the interest of the player from the first tee to the last

green and to present the problems of the various holes in such a way that they register in the player's mind as he stands on the tee or on the fairway for the shot to the green."

Over the decades, a number of distinguished architects have proven to be artists in carrying out those seemingly simple concepts; Donald Ross, A.W. Tillinghast, Perry Maxwell, Alister Mackenzie, and Flynn are among the most noted.

The appeal of golf-course design as a career has only recently begun to lure women into the field. Alice Dye, a fine amateur player and the wife of noted architect Pete Dye, is the only woman member of the American Society of Golf Course Architects. Mrs. Dye has become known as an advocate of a shorter set of tees for women golfers. Another woman involved in golf-course architecture is Betty Peter, who has long been drawing course construction plans for the

Robert Trent Jones (Courtesy American Society of Golf Course Architects)

noted Florida-based architect Joe Lee. Jan Beljan, who works as an architect for Tom Fazio, and Rachel Therrien, of Cornish & Silva, are the only other women in the field.

The directory of golf-course architects was compiled by the National Golf Foundation. These are not recommendations or endorsements but simply a reference source of firms experienced in golf-course planning, design and construction. Names that are starred (*) are members of the American Society of Golf Course Architects.

For further information, contact:

American Society of Golf Course Architects
221 North LaSalle Street
Chicago, IL 60601
(312) 372–7090

Golf Course Builders of America
4361 Northlake Blvd.
Palm Beach Gardens, FL 33410
(407) 694–2977

A new system of placing the forward tees was devised by Alice Dye, the lone woman member of the American Society of Golf Course Architects. (© 1989 Dye/Timberman Art and Image)

Position of New Forward Tees
A   Correct forward tee
B   Position for back tee for women
C   Incorrect position for forward tee

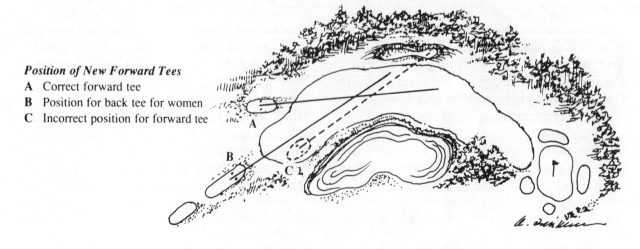

DIRECTORY OF GOLF COURSE ARCHITECTS

The individuals and firms listed below are experienced in the planning, design, and construction of golf courses. This list has been compiled as a reference source to expedite golf facility development planning.

Recommendations or endorsements cannot be made by the National Golf Foundation. It is suggested communication be made directly to arrange for consultation, contractual agreement and information on fee, terms and other details.

William W. Amick*

P.O. Box 1984
Daytona Bch., FL 32015

(904)767-1449

Charles F. Ankrom*

Charles F. Ankrom, Inc.
P.O. Box 170
Stuart, FL 33495

(407)283-1440

Architects Four Professional Association

David M. White, AIA
99 Middle Street
Manchester, NH 03101

(603)627-3844

Architectural Design Group, Inc.

W. Wade Setliff, AIA
President
P.O. Box 1070
Lakeland, FL 33802-1070

(813)682-8955

Branch Offices
1512 East Broward Blvd., Ste. 100
Fort Lauderdale, FL 33301

(305)522-1667

200 Lake Morton Drive, Ste. 400
Lakeland, FL 33801

(813)683-7501

905 West Main St., Ste. 25B
Box 53
Durham, NC 27701

(919)683-2548

Edmund B. Ault*

Ault, Clark & Assoc. Ltd.
2311 University Blvd., W
Wheaton, MD 20902

(301)942-0716

Gary Roger Baird*

Gary Roger Baird, Inc.
2505 Hillsboro Road
Suite 200
Nashville, TN 37212

(615)298-3537

Bob Baldock

Bob Baldock & Son
3001 Red Hill Ave.
Building #2, Suite 217
Costa Mesa, CA 92626

(714)557-2097

Gene Bates and Associates

Gene Bates
Principle
1150 South U.S. Hwy. 1
Jupiter, FL 33477

(407)744-0350

Belt, Collins & Associates

680 Ala Moana Blvd., #200
Honolulu, HI 96813

(808)521-5361

Benz & Poellot*

Bradford Benz & Michael Poellot
Old Town, Suite 36
50 University Avenue
Los Gatos, CA 95030

(408)354-7618

DIRECTORY OF GOLF COURSE ARCHITECTS *(Continued)*

Berson, Ackermann & Associates, Inc.
Nicholas T. Psiahas
279 New Brunswick Avenue
P.O. Box 478
Fords, NJ 08863
(201)738–4141

Richard A. Bigler
5807 So. Del Rey
P.O. Box 308
Del Rey, CA 93616
(209)888–2882

Warner Bowen & Sons
115 W. Washington St.
Sheridan, MI 48884
(517)291–3322

Brauer & Associates Ltd.
Paul S. Fjare, President
7901 Flying Cloud Dr.
Eden Prairie, MN 55344
(612)941–1660

Bruce Co. of Wisconsin, Inc.
Leland C. Bruce, Pres.
2830 W. Beltline Hwy.
P.O. Box 330
Middleton, WI 53562
(608)836–7041

Burns Golf Design
Stephen R. Burns, President
9 Marsh View Lane
Fernandina Beach, FL 32034
(904)277–4474

Lloyd Clifton & Associates, Inc.
1541 Islay Court
Apopka, FL 32712
(407)886–8272

Coore & Crenshaw, Inc.
1800 Nueces Street
Austin, TX 78701
(512)478–3483

Geoffrey S. Cornish*
Cornish & Silva
Fiddler's Green
Amherst, MA 01002
(413)253–3913

Cupp Design, Inc.
Robert E. Cupp
Two Piedmont Center, Suite 504
Atlanta, GA 30305
(404)237–0040

DBA-Country Club Designs, Knickers, Inc.
Jane Baxter
14 S. Swinton Avenue
Delray Beach, FL 33444
(407)243–1719

Deutsche Golf Consult
Rainer Preissmann
Agnesstrasse 2
U300 Essen
West-Deutschland Germany
0201/2 58 82

DVL DeVictor Langham, Inc.
D. J. DeVictor
77 Crossville Rd., Ste. 210
Roswell, GA 30075
(404)642–1255

Mark DeVries & Associates
2020 Monroe Ave., N.W.
Grand Rapids, MI 49505
(616)363–9801

Diedrich Architects
Richard Diedrich
3399 Peachtree Rd., Suite 820
Atlanta, GA 30326
(404)364–9633

Perry O. Dye
Dye Designs, Inc.
498 W. Oak Hills Drive
Castle Rock, CO 80104
(303)790–4224

DIRECTORY OF GOLF COURSE ARCHITECTS *(Continued)*

Pete Dye*	3247 Polo Drive Delray Beach, FL 33444	(407)276–9728
Eagle Golf Design, Inc.*	Gary Kern 15444 Clayton Road, Suite 216 St. Louis, MO 63011	(314)394–7789
Environetics, Inc.	Dana Hepler 7 Lakebridge Drive South Kings Park, NY 11754	(516)269–1031
Lindsay Ervin & Associates*	16 Village Green, Suite 202 Crofton, MD 21114	(301)793–0310 (301)261–0449
Fairway Design, Inc.*	Steve Smyers 4375 Creek Woods Lane Mulberry, FL 33860	(813)425–2849
George & Jim Fazio Golf Course Design	1225 U.S. Highway One Suite 203 Juno Beach, FL 33408	(407)627–3208
Tom Fazio*	Fazio Golf Course Designers, Inc. 17755 S.E. Federal Highway Jupiter, FL 33458	(407)746–4539
Finger-Dye-Spann Inc.*	1001 S. Dairy Ashford, Suite 213 Houston, TX 77077	(713)496–4300
Ronald Fream Des. Group Ltd.	3820 Sebastopol Road P.O. Box 1823 Santa Rosa, CA 95402	(707)526–7190
Gage Davis International	Ian Forrest, General Manager 1007 Pearl Street Boulder, CO 80302	(303)449–1166
Ferdinand Garbin*	R.D. 2, Box 186 Export, PA 15632	(412)327–4704
Ronald M. Garl	Golf Course Design, Inc. 704 So. Missouri Ave. Lakeland, FL 33801	(813)688–8383
David & Garrett Gill*	The David Gill Corp. 202 West Main Street St. Charles, IL 60174	(312)584–2883
Golf Design Associates	Andy Johnson P.O. Box 810 Avon, CO 81620	(303)926–3436
GolfScapes	Jeffrey D. Brauer 2225 E. Randol Mill Road Suite 218 Arlington, TX 76011	(817)640–7275
Robert Muir Graves*	Blackwood Farm P.O. Box 2156 Walnut Creek, CA 94595	(415)939–6300

DIRECTORY OF GOLF COURSE ARCHITECTS *(Continued)*

Greenwood, Frazee & Associates, Inc.
Neil Frazee
5120 Paddock Village Ct, Ste. B-11
Brentwood, TN 37027
(615)373–4910

Denis Griffiths & Assoc., Inc.*
P.O. Box 886
Norcross, GA 30071
(404)448–5616

Hale Irwin Golf Services, Inc.
Patrick J. Fister
Vice President—Development
745 Old Frontenac Square, Ste. 200
St. Louis, MO 63131
(314)997–4333

John C. Harvey
John C. Harvey, Partner
405 Lexington Avenue, 71st Floor
New York, NY 10174
(212)953–0007

X.G. Hassenplug Assoc.*
1300 Freeport Road
Pittsburgh, PA 15238
(412)781–6994

Arthur Hills & Assoc.*
7351 West Bancroft
Toledo, OH 43617
(419)841–8553

Horn Landscape Architects
David E. Horn
P.O. Box 6389
Lehigh Valley, PA 18001-6389
(215)264–2588

Howard Golf, Inc.
Leon Howard, President
P.O. Box 1501
Bryan, TX 77806
(409)775–2075

Howard Needles Tammen Bergendoff
F. Christopher Dimond, ASLA
Director of Urban Design
9200 Ward Parkway
PO Box 419299
Kansas City, MO 64141
(816)333–4800

Frank Hummel
1530 Ninth Street
Greeley, CO 80631
(303)353–3083

Ives/Ryan Group, Inc.
Gregory E. Martin
4932 Main Street
Downers Grove, IL 60515
(312)960–4055

Jensen Engineering
George Jensen
12 Broad Street
Asheville, NC 28801
(704)252–0537

Clyde B. Johnston*
One St. Augustine Place
P.O. Box 6242
Hilton Head Island, SC 29938
(803)842–3367

Rees Jones*
Rees Jones, Inc.
P.O. Box 285
Montclair, NJ 07042
(201)744–4031

Robert Trent Jones*
Robert Trent Jones, Inc.
31 Park Street
Montclair, NJ 07042
(201)744–3033

Robert Trent Jones II*
705 Forest Avenue
Palo Alto, CA 94301
(415)326–3833

DIRECTORY OF GOLF COURSE ARCHITECTS *(Continued)*

Stephen Kay

Main P.O. Box 81
Purchase, NY 10577

(914)738-3399

Dr. Michael J. Hurdzan* & Jack Kidwell*

Kidwell & Hurdzan
1668 McCoy Road
Columbus, OH 43220

(614)457-9666

Kenneth K. Killian*

Killian Design Group Inc.
639 First Bank Drive
Palatine, IL 60067

(312)358-8884

Klages, Carter Vail & Partners

David Klages, Controller
200 Baker St., Suite 201
Costa Mesa, CA 92626

(714)641-0191

Klages, Carter Vail & Partners

David Klages, Controller
200 Baker St., Suite 201
Costa Mesa, CA 92626

(714)641-0191

Joseph L. Lee

P.O. Drawer 1270
Boynton Bch., FL 33435

(407)732-2421

Lee Trevino/William Graves, Inc.

Albert Salinas
14901 Quorum Drive, Suite 170
Dallas, TX 75240

(214)392-0002

Gordon G. Lewis

2022 Constitution Cr.
Fort Myers, FL 33908

(813)267-3322
(813)267-0030

Karl Litten Inc.

5130 Linton Blvd., Suite B1
Delray Beach, FL 33484

(407)498-0209

Robert M. Lohmann*

Lohmann Golf Designs Inc.
800 McHenry Avenue, Suite H
Crystal Lake, IL 60014

(815)455-0445

R. F. Loving, Jr.

P.O. Box 100
Moon, VA 23119

(804)293-4249

Dan Maples Design, Inc.*

Dan Maples
P.O. Box 3014
Pinehurst, NC 28374

(919)944-2879

Matthews & Associates*

2724 E. Michigan Ave., Suite 200
Lansing, MI 48912

(517)485-0480

Thomas McBroom Assoc., Ltd.

Thomas McBroom, President
120 Carlton St., Suite 305
Toronto, Ontario
CANADA M5A 2K1

(416)967-9329

Mark McCumber & Associates

James L. McCumber
Chairman
P.O. Box 490
Middleburg, FL 32068

(904)282-5511

Meta 4 Design

Michael S. Johnstone
5927 Almaden Lane
Oakland, CA 94611

(415)339-2964

DIRECTORY OF GOLF COURSE ARCHITECTS *(Continued)*

Johnny Miller Design, Ltd.

Gene Bates
Golf Course Architect
1150 South U.S. Highway One, Suite 305
Jupiter, FL 33477

(407)744–9980

R.F. Moote*

38 Roberts Crescent
Brampton, Ontario
CANADA L6W 1G8

(416)451–3952

Jay Morrish & Assoc., Ltd.

10820 E. 45th St., Suite 205
Tulsa, OK 74146

(918)655–2937

Greg H. Nash*

Greg H. Nash, Inc.
8453 N. Black Canyon Hwy., Suite 104
Phoenix, AZ 85021

(602)864–0444

William H. Neff*

4951 Cottonwood Lane
Salt Lake City, UT 84117

(801)277–1791

Larry Nelson Design Assoc.

2500 Windy Ridge Pkwy.
Marietta, GA 30065

(404)565–3355

William Newcomb Associates

201 E. Liberty, Suite 16
Ann Arbor, MI 48104

(313)663–3064

Jack Nicklaus Golf Services

Mark Hesemann
President
11760 U.S. Hwy. #1
North Palm Bch., FL 33408

(407)626–3900

Richard P. Nugent*

Dick Nugent Associates
Orchard Hill Farm
20540 W. Hwy. 22
Long Grove, IL 60047

(312)438–5222

Olson Associates

Cal Olson, President
3070 Bristol St., Ste. 460
Costa Mesa, CA 92626

(714)756–1990

Roger B. Packard

Packard, Inc.
1113 West Armitage
Chicago, IL 60614

(312)348–5800

Arnold Palmer-Ed Seay*

Palmer Course Des. Co.
572 Ponte Vedra Blvd.
P.O. Box 1639
Ponte Vedra Beach, FL 32082

(904)285–3960

Gary Panks Associates

Gary Panks, President
7819 E. Greenway Rd., Suite #1
Scottsdale, AZ 85260

(602)483–9500

Richard M. Phelps*

P.O. Box 3295
Evergreen, CO 80439

(303)670–0478

Gary Player Design Group

4440 P.G.A. Boulevard, Suite 105
Palm Beach Gardens, FL 33410

(407)624–0300

David Rainville*

100 W. Main Street, Suite 9
Tustin, CA 92680

(714)838–7200

DIRECTORY OF GOLF COURSE ARCHITECTS *(Continued)*

Russell Roberts Co. Inc.
14431 Turkey Foot Road
Gaithersburg, MD 20878
(301)762-3270

Robinson* & Carrick* Associates, Ltd.
C.E. Robinson*
Douglas Carrick*
112 Merton St., Suite 400
Toronto, Ontario, Canada M4S 2Z9
(416)489-4442

William G. Robinson*
1450 Johnston Road
Box 237
White Rock, B.C.
CANADA V4B 5E9
(206)671-1410

Sanford & Ewseychik Golf Course Architects
John Sanford, Jr., President
1300 N. Florida Mango Rd. Ste. 14
West Palm Beach, FL 33409
(407)689-3521

Donald R. Sechrest, Inc.
712 Broadway, #218
Kansas City, MO 64105
(205)344-1921

William James Spear*
William J. Spear & Associates
16 North First Avenue
St. Charles, IL 60174
(312)584-8200

Earl Stone & Associates
P.O. Box 16225
Mobile, AL 36616
(205)344-1921

Sugar Tree Properties
Bill Bowerman
P.O. Box 68
Dennis, TX 76037
(817)594-5435

THK Associates, Inc.
Matthew A. Eccles
40 Inverness Drive East
Englewood, CO 80112
(303)790-2435

Kevin Tucker
Kevin Tucker & Assoc., Inc.
312 19th Ave. N.
Nashville, TN 37203
(615)320-0091

Urban Associates, Inc.
Marvin F. Armstrong, V.P.
360-2 Route 101 West, Pine Tree Place
Bedford, NH 03102
(603)472-5576

von Hagge Design Associates
16757 Squyres
Spring, TX 77379
(713)376-8282

A. James Wall Associates, Inc.
A. James Wall, President
1727 Coachman Place Drive
Clearwater, FL 34619
(813)253-3612

Wilson-Moreth Partnership, Ltd.
Ronald D. Wilson, President
Five East Cary Street
Richmond, VA 23219
(804)649-7697

Philip A. Wogan*
17 Walker Road
Topfield, MA 01983
(617)887-3672

Wyss Inc.
Patrick H. Wyss, Pres.
522 7th Street, Suite 214
Rapid City, SD 57701
(605)348-2268

DIRECTORY OF GOLF COURSE ARCHITECTS *(Continued)*

Yamao, Hisao   20-10 Hirao Kowata   0774–32–5553
                                    Uji Kyoto, Japan 611

Mike Young Golf Services, Inc. Mike Young   (404)769–7415
                                    P.O. Box 289
                                    Watkinsville, GA 30677

*Member of American Society of Golf Course Architects

3. COUNTRY-CLUB MANAGERS

With the boom in new country clubs, this is another growing field. The qualifications and responsibilities of the country-club general manager are diverse. While clubs seek individuals suited to their particular needs and memberships, the following job description for a Wisconsin country club of about 350 members typically outlines the demands of the job. For further information, contact:

Club Managers Association of America
7615 Winterberry Place
Bethesda, MD 20817
(301) 229–3600

JOB DESCRIPTION:
Country Club General Manager (sample)

POSITION: General Manager

FACILITY: An outstanding country club in southeastern Wisconsin between Kenosha and Racine, WI, with 18-hole golf course, four tennis courts, swimming pool, modern clubhouse, and membership of about 350.

REPORTS TO: The Board of Directors

RESPONSIBILITIES: 1) Provide care and services in accordance with modern club management techniques to ensure member satisfaction.
2) Manage, direct, and administer the activities of all of the various club departments in an effort to maximize member service in an efficient and economical way in accordance with the available business.
3) Implement new ideas and projects which encourage maximum membership participation in all club activities.
4) Direct, manage, and supervise assigned staff (golf pro, greens superintendent, tennis pro, swimming instructor, kitchen and dining room personnel) to insure cooperation and achieve maximum membership satisfaction.
5) Participate with the Board of Directors in the development of an annual operating and capital budget and manage the club's operations within the approved budget.
6) Recommend policies to strengthen the financial position of the club.
7) Perform other duties as assigned by the Board of Directors.

EDUCATION: Bachelor's degree (or equivalent) in hotel administration or related field plus 5–7 years of effective experience.

CHARACTERISTICS: The candidate must have the ability to plan and organize effectively. Must be: 1) self-motivated, and sensitive to the needs of the members. 2) able to recruit, screen, select, train, and motivate staff and employees, and 3) flexible and have a high level of energy.

COMPENSATION: $30,000 range, depending upon qualifications and experience.

4. GOLF DIRECTOR

The job Director of Golf is coming into use in the nation's larger clubs. This position is perhaps one step higher than the more widely used title Head Golf Professional and came into vogue because of the growing number of large golf resorts and large country club memberships.

The following job description for a director of golf was prepared by the Professional Golfers Association of America. For further information, contact:

Professional Golfers Association of America
P.O. Box 109601
Palm Beach Gardens, FL 33418
(407) 626–3600

JOB DESCRIPTION FOR A GOLF DIRECTOR
Function

Responsible to the Board of Directors for ensuring that overall objectives, policies, programs and fiscal practices of the facility are implemented, administered and maintained. The Di-

Golf Director (Courtesy PGA of America)

rector shall sit at board meetings as a non-voting member. Responsible for delegating to subordinates appropriate authority to fulfill portion of assigned responsibility, but may not delegate or relinquish overall responsibilities for results or any portion of final accountability.

ASSIGNED DUTIES AND RESPONSIBILITIES

1) Act as chief operating officer and be responsible for marketing total assigned facilities and services of the enterprise.
2) Interpret and enforce the policies, rules and regulations of the Board.
3) Prepare and have approved an annual budget and administer that budget in a fiscally responsible manner.
4) Prepare an employee manual and job descriptions and conduct semi-annual employee evaluations. One such session shall include the use of a performance rating sheet and setting of performance objectives.
5) Be responsible for daily cash receipts and account for safekeeping of same according to established written policy and procedures. Certify and categorize all invoices for payment.
6) Promote various functions that are within the bylaws and policies of the organization which will generate operating revenues and create member interest.
7) Maintain close cooperation with community officials and develop a strong community awareness with the people of the community.
8) Be current on developments in the world of golf and present the facility as being a leader in positive innovation.
9) Work closely with the other officials associated with the facility, allied associations of golf, and others that might contribute to the facility's function.
10) Be responsible for membership development and maintenance of related records and files.
11) On behalf of the facility, speak at various club, educational or civic functions as required.
12) Strive to operate the facility according to established fiscal parameters. Assist in budgetary development and related matters as required.
13) Oversee the publishing and distribution of informational and promotional literature.
14) Supervise and be responsible for the detailed operation of the golf courses, clubhouse, and pro shop, including supervision of the greens superintendent and head golf professional. Duties may also include supervision of all recreational personnel including tennis, pool, and health spa.
15) Be responsible for hiring, disciplining, and/or terminating employees according to facility policy and procedure. Establish wage rates for assigned employees.
16) Ensure that members and guests adhere to club policies and/or regulations.
17) Devise and control purchasing policies and procedures; establish inventory levels and ensure the distribution of merchandise and supplies to assigned departments. Prepare related reports and records.
18) Be responsible for the overall scheduling of the courses to insure that members, guests, tournament functions, etc., do not pose any conflicts. Revise schedules as required.
19) Should create an increased public interest in golf which includes all age groups.
20) Ensure that golf educational programs are conducted for members and guests as needed.
21) Participate and become involved in organizations whose purpose will be of benefit to the facility.
22) Coordinate and communicate with local news media, commercial firms, civic organizations, and other entities to promote the development of the golf facility's policies and programs.
23) Perform other duties as assigned.

CONTRACT

The contract shall be for three years, renewable 120 days prior to its expiration, and shall be self-renewed unless advised to the contrary.

BOND

The Director shall be capable of being bonded in the amount of $100,000. This bond will be paid for by the facility.

QUALIFICATIONS

1) Must be a PGA member.
2) Must possess a personality that will make

people feel welcome and that reflects favorably on the facility. This includes public speaking skills as well as personal human relations abilities.

3) Must be qualified administrator and have demonstrated that quality.

4) Shall possess a college degree from an accredited college or university or its equivalent from other training courses and/or an experience background which would equal such proficiency.

5) Must have the ability and skills to administer the entire golf and recreational complex.

6) Shall be a competent golfer with considerable experience in teaching and organizing instructional programs and in the management of tournaments.

7) Must have demonstrated merchandising and golf shop operational skills.

8) Must have promotional ability, physical and mental energy, and have demonstrated creative talents.

9) Should have the respect of his peers.

CHANGES

It must be recognized that all specific duties cannot be listed and that responsibilities will change accordingly as the need arises. The Director will be responsible for accomplishing unforeseen tasks that relate to assigned function. As conditions warrant, this job description shall be amended from time to time.

REVIEW

The contractual agreement, salary, and fringe benefits shall be subject to an annual review on the part of the supervising body of the Golf Director. This review to be completed no later than 120 days prior to the anniversary date of any contractual period.

5. GOLF PROFESSIONAL

The Professional Golfers' Association of America has established strict guidelines for its members—all of which help the memberships and management of the nation's golf clubs assure that they are getting a qualified new member of the staff.

The club professional is one of the game's greatest ambassadors. He or she is the person who introduces new golfers to the game and assures that every player enjoys golf. To help local clubs hire a golf professional, the PGA outlines ten steps:

- Contact the local PGA Section or PGA National.
- Appoint a selection committee.
- Evaluate your golf facility's needs.
- Write a job description and identify the type of individual sought.
- Complete the Job Information Worksheet.
- Meet with the PGA.
- Receive and screen applications.
- Interview selected applicants.

- Make selection and sign contract.
- Notify candidates, PGA, and media.

The following job description, provided by the PGA, is a detailed list of the golf professional's duties. I might comment that any individual who can responsibly handle this vast array of chores probably deserves a salary as high as the membership can afford to pay!

JOB DESCRIPTION
(Private Club Sample)

GENERAL DUTIES

1. Supervise, as directed by the Golf Committee, the starting of play by golfers.

2. Supervise proper charging of greens fees and season privilege fees.

3. Supervise the rental and use of golf cars and the maintenance of equipment for cleaning members' golf clubs.

Eagle Creek Country Club head professional, Tim Eaton (right), *discusses merchandise with a member.* (Courtesy PGA of America)

4. Supervise such rangers, if any, as may be employed by the Club.

5. Provide competent golf instruction for all groups and levels of players.

6. Supervise the operation of a handicap system at such times and to the extent directed by the Golf Committee.

7. Supervise competent personnel such as assistant professionals, starters, bag room attendants, shop manager, golf car maintenance man, etc., in the performance of their duties. The division of the employment of such personnel to be determined in the contractual arrangement.

8. Enforce all the Club's rules and regulations governing the use of the golf course, golf cars and other golf facilities.

9. Operate and maintain a reputable pro shop and practice range staffed with competent personnel and featuring quality merchandise and services.

10. Maintain close relationship and cooperation with the Club's Greens Superintendent.

11. Devote a reasonable number of hours to playing golf with members regardless of their golf excellence; such play not to be considered a playing lesson.

12. Plan golf evenings to promote golf and fellowship in the club/at the course. Prepare golf clinics, films, etc., for such evenings. Prepare rule clinics, golf educational programs, etc., for such evenings. Enthusiastically promote golf.

13. Represent the Club in the area professional golf activities including the Local Section of the PGA and in tournaments such as Pro-Ams with members, and state or national golf events as his time will permit, but only with the approval of the club's golf committee.

SPECIFIC DUTIES (WHERE APPLICABLE)

A. Men's & Women's Tournament Committee

1. Meet with the Tournament Committee Chairman and Event Chairman for the purpose of preparing and planning the details of golf events in writing.

2. Secure adequate caddies and golf cars for each event.

3. Handle starting times.

4. Assign golf cars.

5. Prepare score cards and scoring sheets.

6. Post all event information on first tee Bulletin Board including all rules under which each event shall be played.

7. Prepare and distribute event information sheets for participants.

8. Secure bag boys and fore-caddies.

9. Have bags and caddies ready at first tee.

10. Keep the tournament field on starting time schedule.

11. Keep players in field moving.

12. Record scores.

13. Determine winners.

14. Be available for rules decisions.

B. Junior Golf Committee

1. Determine which Juniors are qualified to play.

2. Instruct and test Juniors in the knowledge of golf rules and courtesies.

3. Advise parents and/or the Junior Golf Committee of problems and rule infractions.

4. Prepare and plan Junior golf clinics.

5. Prepare and plan with the Junior Golf Committee Junior tournaments for June, July and August.

C. Golf Car Operations

1. Take car reservations either by phone or by person from members.

2. Deliver golf cars to starting area.

3. Return cars to storage area.

4. Place golf cars on recharge.

5. Report mechanical deficiencies.

6. Account for all cars at the end of the day.

7. Return all disabled cars to golf car maintenance area.

8. Take responsibility for rental forms or cash tickets.

D. Golf Shop Operations

1. Maintain pro shop in clean and presentable condition.

2. Keep shop open from time agreed upon with management; keep help on duty until all bags and cars have been returned for storage.

3. Maintain merchandise at a reasonable level commensurate with members' needs.

E. Golf Range

1. Provide balls in respectable condition for rental by members.

2. Develop convenient system for dispensing balls.

3. Pick up balls daily and keep tee area neat.

F. Handicap Operation

1. Send master computer sheets to the data center for processing per schedule posted by the Handicap Committee.

2. Post Junior golf scores on master computer sheets.

3. Record changes requested by members on required forms. NOTE: All changes requested by members should be accumulated in the pro shop prior to recording changes.

G. Caddy Operation (Where Appropriate)

1. Secure and maintain a top flight group of Class "A" and "B" caddies.

2. Bring in enough "B" caddies each year to guarantee continuity of Class "A" caddies for future years.

3. Establish a caddy training program on an upgraded basis throughout the summer.

4. Keep open lines of communication between the caddies, the golf professional, and the golf committee.

5. Help organize and plan the annual Caddy Dinner in conjunction with the Caddy Committee and the Manager.

6. Insure proper maintenance and cleanliness of Caddy housing facilities.

Another key to running a successful golf operation is the role of the assistant golf professional. The head professional at a large club will hire several assistants to help take care of the membership. Assistants who train under the PGA Apprentice Program must fill the criteria outlined below.

The PGA Apprentice Program

Description: The purpose of the PGA Apprentice Program is to prepare prospective members for membership in the Professional Golfers' Association of America by providing the best possible foundation to produce qualified golf professionals. The program is designed to provide high standards for prospective members through involvement, education, motivation, and communication.

Requirements: A registrant must be (1) employed in the golf profession on a full-time basis (minimum 40 hours per week); (2) be employed in a Section of the PGA of America; (3) be at least 18 years of age; (4) working in eligible duties as defined in the PGA Constitution.

Assistant Golf Professionals:

1. Must be employed for 6 months by a Class A PGA Member or a Class A LPGA member who is the Head Golf Professional at a Recognized Club, Course, Recognized Par 3, Recognized Golf Range or Course under Construction.

   a. Only two (2) registered Apprentices for each nine (9) holes allowed at Recognized Clubs or Courses.

   b. Only one (1) registered Apprentice allowed for each 15 tees (no more than a total of four (4) regardless of the number of tees) at a Recognized Golf Range.

      (1) Assistants can only accumulate a MAXIMUM OF 18 CREDITS AT ANY TIME *DURING THE APPRENTICESHIP* AT RECOGNIZED AND APPROVED GOLF RANGES.

   c. Assistants can only accumulate a MAXIMUM OF 12 CREDITS *DURING THE APPRENTICESHIP* WORKING AT COURSES UNDER CONSTRUCTION.

2. Must provide substantiation of prior 6 months employment by a Class A Head Golf Professional on an EMPLOYMENT VERIFICATION FORM.

3. May be allowed up to 6 months retroactive credit for time actually worked in the *one year period immediately preceding the initial registration date.*

Courtesy PGA of America

For information, contact:

The PGA of America
100 Avenue of Champions
Palm Beach Gardens, FL 33410
(407) 626–3600

6. GREEN SUPERINTENDENT

If there is one thing a golfer appreciates more than anything else, it may well be consistency in a course and the way the ball behaves. If a golf course has been properly prepared, the ball is much more likely to do what it is supposed to do—and players are much more likely to enjoy the game.

The person who has more to do with making the golf course playable than anyone else is the golf course superintendent.

Not too many years ago, the golf course superintendent was known as the "greenkeeper." Horses pulled mowers down the fairways, and greens were mowed with push mowers. As golf grew in popularity, players began to demand better playing surfaces. The greenkeeper answered the challenge by bringing science and technology—as well as art—into the profession. Today's golf course superintendent is a highly trained professional who is ultimately responsible for every facet of the care and playing conditions of a course.

In carrying out his or her responsibilities, the golf course superintendent must train and supervise the maintenance staff, see that equipment is kept in good condition, and guard the course against the ravages of heat, cold, rain, drought, wind, disease, infestations and the wear and tear of the game. And all this has to be done within the constraints of time and budget.

The superintendent deals daily with everything from chemicals to insects, weeds, irrigation, and drainage. And, in dealing with all these, the superintendent must be sure that everything is done within local, state, and federal environmental and safety guidelines.

Many superintendents today have formal education in turfgrass science. Often, this consists of two- or four-year college degree in horticulture with an emphasis in turfgrass management.

The typical day of a golf course superintendent starts around dawn so the staff can finish before golfers arrive to play. Cups, for example, are moved to even out wear on greens. Greens are mowed, tees are made ready, and many other tasks are performed. Often the superintendent's day doesn't end until after dark. And sometimes he or she is awakened in the middle of the night to cope with emergencies on the course. Such things as long-range planning and budget preparation also have to be done. And all the while, the superintendent must find time to keep up with changes in the industry.

Indeed, the golf course superintendent is a busy and important person. He or she is responsible for property that often is worth millions of dollars. The goal is always to provide the best possible playing conditions under all circumstances.

Reprinted: Courtesy of the Golf Course Superintendents Association of America.

For further information, contact:

Golf Superintendents Assn. of America
1617 St. Andrews Drive
Lawrence, KS 66044
(913) 841-2240

> " 'Golf is on the verge of becoming a national mania, a sport reshaping life-styles, spending habits, real estate development, and investment patterns.' "

One of the game's biggest advances has been in golf course maintenance. In the early days, fairways were cut by horse-drawn mowers, such as in this photograph taken at a course in Elkhart, Indiana, in about 1915. (Courtesy Robert Kuntz)

7. RULES OFFICIAL

Through the joint efforts of the United States Golf Association and the Royal and Ancient Golf Club of St. Andrews, Scotland, the Rules of Golf have been simplified in recent years. Still, they make up a complex credo and total knowledge of the Rules and the related rules decisions is a rare achievement. A few individuals who have mastered the intricacies of the rules enjoy challenging careers in this complex side of the game. Most notable is P.J. Boatwright, Jr., the USGA's long-time Executive Director, Rules and Competitions, who is regarded as the premier rules official in golf.

Boatwright has become a sort of celebrity in his own right—the familiar tall, lanky man in his white porkpie hat, on call at the USGA's championships whenever a ruling is in doubt.

Boatwright's USGA colleagues are fond of paying him tribute by saying that, in his field, Boatwright is the best in the world.

Boatwright was preceded in this field by Joseph C. Dey, Jr., for many years the USGA's executive director and later commissioner of the PGA Tour. When Dey was the unofficial czar of the Rules of Golf, the officiating of golf tournaments was mostly handled by volunteers. Even today, rules officials at USGA events are largely drawn from the pool of USGA committee members, all of whom have attended Rules school and are virtual experts on these complicated standards.

But officiating is a growing career for professionals—the paid staffs of the USGA, the PGA Tour, and the LPGA Tour include people who monitor the Rules of Golf for a living.

This is a high-pressure job. After all, who wants to give bad news on a ruling to a player in contention for a top title? But the benefits are many. Rules officials have a front-row seat from which to watch key

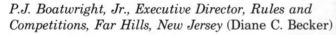

P.J. Boatwright, Jr., Executive Director, Rules and Competitions, Far Hills, New Jersey (Diane C. Becker)

The Newport Golf Club, Newport, Rhode Island. Site of the first U.S. Open in 1895. (Courtesy USGA)

shot-making by fine players in important tournaments. They spend much of their time outdoors, enjoying some of the finest scenery in sport. And officiating offers another great opportunity to simply spend one's time around the game.

Requirements are simple: One must have an unquestionable knowledge of The Rules of Golf and the ability to act reasonably and decisively in stressful situations. A diplomatic personality is a great asset.

Each year the United States Golf Association and the PGA jointly sponsor a series of "rules schools," around the United States. These regional gatherings offer intensive study of the rules and are well attended by officials from regional and national golf organizations, and by serious players who simply want to soak up knowledge about the game.

For information about attending a rules school in your area, contact the United States Golf Association or the Professional Golfers Association of America.

United States Golf Association
Golf House
Far Hills, NJ 07931
(201) 234–2300

Professional Golfers Association of America
P.O. Box 109601
Palm Beach Gardens, FL 33418
(407) 626–3600

"There's a virtual bonanza in new careers in and around the game."

9
CAMPS AND SCHOOLS

I N RECENT years, more than 100 golf schools and camps have sprung up in the United States. These schools offer a number of modern golfers a new social outlet as well as a great deal of satisfaction from working on their games.

Golf schools are designed for group instruction, although the student-teacher ratio is kept small, usually to a minimum of four or a maximum of eight students per teacher. Group lessons can be a lot of fun, for families or your favorite foursome, but golf schools also offer individual instruction.

"Semesters" also vary, most often from a three-day to seven-day course of instruction. Most modern schools offer the latest in golf technology, like swing aids and video instruction, to help you learn how to play the game better.

There are golf schools for children, schools for beginners, and schools for advanced players, but most schools cater to all ranges of handicaps just by varying the level of instruction.

With the growth of golf and sports marketing, a unique type of instruction, closely

related to golf schools, is often sponsored by companies and corporations for their executives, employees, and favored clients. These are corporate "outings" and clinics conducted by well-known professionals, often PGA and LPGA tour players, in one- or two-day sessions.

The corporate outing and golf school is a newly popular way in which to entertain important business guests. After all, nearly everyone in the business world plays golf, and there is a growing awareness among young executives that golf offers the perfect opportunity for establishing better relations with new clients. While no one would be so crass as to actually try to make a sale on the golf course, important business negotiations often begin in casual conversation at the nineteenth hole.

Here's how such outings work: A corporation spokesman contacts any one of a number of player agents. (Refer to "AGENTS" section for information on agents and their respective playing professionals.) The corporate spokesman and the agent discuss the player's appearance fee and work out a date. The agent may also offer useful tips on the program for the outing since the agent's players usually have made extensive appearances before business groups.

The corporate spokesman then arranges dates with a country club or golf resort. The program revolves around the celebrity golf professional. You may negotiate, for example, to have the pro conduct a morning golf clinic, eat lunch with the clients, then play a few holes with each foursome in an after-noon tournament and have drinks with the clients at an informal after-golf cocktail party.

Clients enjoy an opportunity to rub elbows with a top player. Touring professionals, both men and women, are also adept at helping the business clients improve their games. The golf clinic is a great way to give aspiring contacts some serious new golf information. If clients are able to knock two or three strokes off their average score, they'll be forever grateful, not only to the pro, but to the company that sponsored the occasion.

Golf schools are designed to help you improve all phases of your game: from hitting longer tee shots and more precise irons, to the scoring techniques of better bunker play, chipping, pitching, and putting. Not all of the students' efforts are confined to the practice tee, however. Many schools include playing lessons and most sponsor actual tournaments for students.

Instruction series are often staged in or near golf resort hotels, which means golfers can practically fall out of bed and onto the lesson tee. Attendance at a golf school can make an ideal getaway for a week of "golf only." A golf school scholarship also makes a unique gift for your favorite stressed-out golfer!

Prices vary, depending upon the length of the session and whether food and lodging are provided. Most schools include green fees at the host course.

The following listings include golf camps and schools of every variety:

North Central Region:

Ben Sutton Golf Schools
P.O. Box 9463
Canton, OH 44711
(216) 453–4350
(800) 225–6923

Cyclone Country Golf Camp
P.O. Box 1995
Ames, IA 50010
(515) 232–3999

Jayhawks Golf Camp (Boys)
2104 Inverness Dr.
Lawrence, KS 66046
(913) 842–1907

Jayhawks Golf Camp (Girls)
3809 Overland Dr.
Lawrence, KS 66044
(913) 842–1907
(913) 842–6724

Katke Golf Camp
Ferris State University
Big Rapids, MI 49307
(616) 592–3765

MI State University/Summer Sports School
222 Jenison Fieldhouse
East Lansing, MI 48824
(517) 355–5264

Minnesota PGA Jr. Golf Academy
701 Bunker Lake Boulevard
Ham Lake, MN 55304
(612) 754–0820

Murray St. University Summer School
222 Jenison Fieldhouse E.
Lansing, MI 48824
(517) 355–5264

Rob Hay Golf School
6300 Auto Club Road
Bloomington, MN 55438
(612) 884–1744

Sam Carmichael Golf School
Indiana Univ., Assembly Hall
Bloomington, IN 47405
(812) 335–7950
(317) 342–4336

Silver Sands Golf Academy
South Shore Drive
Delevan, WI 53115
(414) 728–6120

U.S. Golf Academy
5203 Plymouth LaPort Trail
Plymouth, IN 46563
(219) 935–5680

University of Michigan Camps
1000 S. State St.
Ann Arbor, MI 48109
(313) 763–6870

NORTHEAST REGION:

Berkshire School of Golf
55 Lee Road
Lenox, MA 01240
(413) 637–1364

Chase Golf Camp
Box 1446
Manchester, MA 01944
(508) 526–7514

Golf Digest Instructional Schools *
5520 Park Avenue, Box 395
Trumbull, CT 06611
(800) 243–6121
(203) 373–7130

Golf Digest Junior Instructional Schools
Box 395
Trumbull, CT 06611
(800)243–6121

Kiski Golf Camp
1888 Brett Lane
Saltsburg, PA 15681
(412) 639–3586

Penn State Golf Camp
Penn State University
409 Keller Blvd.
University Park, PA 16802
(814) 863–3550

* More than 250 regional schools nationwide

"Instruction series are often staged in or near golf resort hotels, which means golfers can practically fall out of bed and onto the lesson tee."

Pepsi Met PGA Golf School
P.O. Box 268
Wykagyl Station
New Rochelle, NY 10804
(914) 235–0312

Philadelphia PGA Golf Academy
Recreation Bldg., Penn State University
University Park, PA 16802
(814) 863–0425

Roland Stafford Golf School
Kass Inn, Route 30
Margaretville, NY 12455
(914) 586–4841

Swing's The Thing Golf Schools
P.O. Box 67
Shawnee-on-Delaware, PA 18356
(717) 421–6666
(800) 221–6661

The Golf School
Mount Snow Resort
Mount Snow, VT 05356
(802) 464–3333
(800) 451–4211

The Golf School at Stowe Acres Country Club
58 Randall Road
Stowe, MA 01775
(508) 568–9090

The Stratton Golf School
The Stratton Corporation
Stratton Mountain, VT 05155
(802) 297–2200
(800) 843–6867

The Woodlands Golf Academy
Route 40
Farmington, PA 15437
(412) 329–6900

SOUTHERN REGION:

Arnold Palmer Golf School
9000 Bay Hill Boulevard
Orlando, FL 32819
(407) 876–3944

Bertholy Method Golf Schools
Foxfire Village
Jackson Springs, NC 27281
(919) 281–3093

Bill Skelley's Schools of Golf
Main Street
Miami Lakes, FL 33014
(800) 231–4173
(305) 821–1150

Campbell University Golf School
P.O. Box 10
Buies Creek, NC 27506
(919) 893–8591

Charleston School of Golf
2110 Maybank Hwy.
Charleston, SC 29412
(800) 888–5347
(803) 795–5856

Conrad Rehling Golf Academy
Box 3355
Tuscaloosa, AL 35404
(205) 348–7041

Crimson Tide Golf Academy
Box 3355
Tuscaloosa, AL 35404
(205) 553–0997

Dave Pelz Short Game
1200 Lakeway Dr., Suite 21
Austin, TX 78734
(512) 261–6493

Duke Youth School
Route 751 at Science Dr.
Durham, NC 27706
(919) 684–2817

Elon College Golf School
Box 2197
Elon College, NC 27244
(919) 584–2248

FCA Golf Camps
P.O. Box 253
Winter Park, FL 27244
(407) 629-1073

Furman University Golf School
Furman Golf Course
Greenville, SC 29613
(803) 294-2983

GA Junior Golf Academy
4200 Northside Pkwy, Bld. 9 #100
Atlanta, GA 30327
(404) 233-4742
(800) 992-4742

Gator Camp
P.O. Box 2313
Gainesville, FL 32602
(904) 375-4683

Georgia Southern Golf Camp
Box 8082
Statesboro, GA 30460
(912) 681-5795
(913) 681-5736

Howie Barrow Golf School
Mission Inn Resort, Box 441
Howey-in-the-Hills, FL 32737
(800) 342-4495
(904) 324-3101

Innisbrook Golf Institute
P.O. Drawer 1088
Tarpon Springs, FL 34286
(813) 942-2000

Jack Nicklaus Grand Cypress Academy of Golf
One North Jacaranda
Orlando, FL 32819
(407) 239-1975
(800) 835-7377

Jeri Reid's Golf School
2035 S.W. 15th St., Suite 182
Deerfield Beach, FL 33442
(305) 429-0623

Jesse Haddock Golf, Inc.
Wake Forest Univ., Box 7567
Winston-Salem, NC 27109
(919) 761-6000

Jimmy Ballard Golf Workshop
4400 N.W. 87th Avenue
Miami, FL 33178
(305) 592-2000

Kinemation Studio of Golf
250 International Pkwy., #140
Heathrow, FL 32746
(800) 544-8727

Lakeway Academy of Golf
One World of Tennis Square
Austin, TX 78734
(800) 444-5606

Louisiana PGA Tiger Golf Camp
P.O. Box 16362
Baton Rouge, LA 70893
(504) 388-8808

Margo Walden Golf School
Seabrook Island Resort
Box 32099
Charleston, SC 29417
(803) 768-1000

Mike Holder's Cowboy Golf Camp
Oklahoma State University
Stillwater, OK 74078
(405) 377-4289

N.C. State Wolfpack Golf Camp
3000 Ballybunion Way
Raleigh, NC 27613
(919) 846-5380

National PGA Academy of Golf
Box 109601
Palm Beach Gardens, FL 33410
(407) 626-3600

North Texas Golf Academy
500 N. Central, Suite 213
Plano, TX 75074
(214) 881-4653

> *"Golf schools are designed to help you improve all phases of your game; from hitting longer tee shots and more precise irons, to the scoring techniques of better bunker play, chipping, pitching, and putting."*

Ole Miss Golf Camp
Univ. of Mississippi
P.O. Box 879
University, MS 38677
(916) 481–4506

PGA National "Killer" Golf School
1000 Avenue of the Champions
Palm Beach Gardens, FL 33418
(407) 627–7593

Paradise Golf Schools
281 U.S. 27 North
Sebring, FL 33870
(800) 624–3543
(813) 382–6200

Pine Needles Resort/Golf Camps
P.O. Box 88
Southern Pines, NC 28387
(919) 692–7111

Pinehurst Advantage Golf School
P.O. Box 4000
Pinehurst, NC 28374
(919) 295–6811
(800) 634–9297

Practice Tee Golf Academy
3742 Upper River Road
Louisville, KY 40207
(502) 895–4144

Roland Stafford Golf School
14800 Hollywood Boulevard
Hollywood, FL 33027
(305) 431–8800
(800) 327–9246

Ronnie Scales Golf Camp
University of Maryland Golf Course
College Park, MD 20740
(301) 454–2131

South Texas PGA Golf Academy
1 World of Tennis Square
Austin, TX 78738
(800) 444–5606

Tennessee Golf Academy
4711 Trousdale Dr.
Nashville, TN 37220
(615) 833–9689

Texas A&M Golf School
Texas A&M, Athletic Dept.
College Station, TX 77843
(409) 845–4533

The Academy of Golf/Lakeway
One World of Tennis Square
Austin, TX 78734
(512) 261–6000

The Florida Golf Academy
720 Goodlette Rd., Suite 303
Naples, FL 33940
(813) 649–6600

The Florida Golf School
2703 North A1A, Suite D
Fort Pierce, FL 34949
(407) 464–3706
(800) 365–6727

The Golf Academy of the South
P.O. Box 3609
Winter Springs, FL 32708
(407) 699–1990

The Golf School
Plantation Golf Resort, Box 1116
Crystal River, FL 32629
(904) 795–4211
(800) 632–6262

University of North Carolina Golf School
Box 2675
Chapel Hill, NC 27514
(919) 962–2041

Vintage Golf Schools
Port Royal Resort, Box 5045
Hilton Head, SC 29938
(803) 681–2406

WESTERN REGION:

Billy Casper Golf Camp
5764 Paradise Drive #7–531
Corte Madero, CA 94925
(415) 924–8725
(800) 542–6005

Craft-Zavichas Golf School
600 Dittmer Avenue
Pueblo, CO 81005
(303) 564–4449

Falcon Summer Golf Camp
U.S. Air Force Academy
Colorado Springs, CO 80840
(719) 472–1895

Gene Littler Golf Schools
2195 Faraday, Suite K
Carlsbad, CA 92008
(619) 931–9044

Golf University at San Diego
2001 Old Highway 395
Fallbrook, CA 92028
(619) 723–9077
(800) 426–0966

John Jacobs Practical Golf School
7350 East Evans, C-112
Scottsdale, AZ 85260
(800) 472–5007
(602) 991–8587

John Schlee's Maximum Golf School
4923 Avila Avenue
Carlsbad, CA 92008
(800) 444–0244
(619) 434–7497

Northern California PGA Resident School
3645 Fulton Ave.
Sacramento, CA 95821
(916) 481–4506

San Diego Golf Academy
P.O. Box 3050
Rancho Santa Fe, CA 92067
(619) 756–2486

Sports Enhancement
P.O. Box 2788
Sedona, AZ 86336
(602) 284–9000
(800) 345–4245

Sun Country Section PGA
111 Cardenas N.E.
Albuquerque, NM 87108
(505) 260–0167

SyberVision Golf Schools
111 Maiden Lane, Suite 400
San Francisco, CA 94108
(800) 432–2582

The Golf Clinic at Pebble Beach
P.O. Box M
Carmel, CA 93921
(800) 321–9401
(800) 821–1586

Tommy Jacobs Golf School
La Costa Hotel & Spa
Carlsbad, CA 92008
(619) 438–9111

For youngsters, one of the advantages of playing a good game is that one's ability on the golf course may be the source of a college education. College golf has become highly competitive, and a growing number of colleges and universities now offer golf scholarships to good young players.
It should be noted that these scholarships are given only to the nation's top junior players, but the growth in the sheer number of college golf teams means that more golf scholarships are available than ever before.
The following schools have intercollegiate golf teams. To inquire about the availability of golf scholarships, write to the athletic department at the individual schools.

NCAA SCHOOLS SPONSORING MEN'S GOLF TEAMS
1988–89

Div	Dist	School	City	St	Zip
1	1	BOSTON COLLEGE	CHESTNUT HILL	MA	02167
1	1	BROWN UNIVERSITY	PROVIDENCE	RI	02912
1	1	CENTRAL CONN. STATE UNIV.	NEW BRITAIN	CT	06050
1	1	UNIVERSITY OF CONNECTICUT	STORRS	CT	06268
1	1	DARTMOUTH COLLEGE	HANOVER	NH	03755
1	1	FAIRFIELD UNIVERSITY	FAIRFIELD	CT	06430
1	1	UNIVERSITY OF HARTFORD	WEST HARTFORD	CT	06117
1	1	HARVARD UNIVERSITY	CAMBRIDGE	MA	02138
1	1	UNIVERSITY OF MAINE	ORONO	ME	04469
1	1	UNIVERSITY OF NEW HAMPSHIRE	DURHAM	NH	03824
1	1	NORTHEASTERN UNIVERSITY	BOSTON	MA	02115
1	1	PROVIDENCE COLLEGE	PROVIDENCE	RI	02918
1	1	UNIVERSITY OF RHODE ISLAND	KINGSTON	RI	02881
1	1	UNIVERSITY OF VERMONT	BURLINGTON	VT	05405
1	1	YALE UNIVERSITY	NEW HAVEN	CT	06520
1	2	AMERICAN UNIVERSITY	WASHINGTON	DC	20016
1	2	BUCKNELL UNIVERSITY	LEWISBURG	PA	17837
1	2	CANISIUS COLLEGE	BUFFALO	NY	14208
1	2	COLGATE UNIVERSITY	HAMILTON	NY	13346
1	2	COLUMBIA UNIV.-BARNARD COLLEGE	NEW YORK	NY	10027
1	2	CORNELL UNIVERSITY	ITHACA	NY	14850
1	2	UNIVERSITY OF DELAWARE	NEWARK	DE	19711
1	2	DREXEL UNIVERSITY	PHILADELPHIA	PA	19104
1	2	DUQUESNE UNIVERSITY	PITTSBURGH	PA	15282
1	2	FAIRLEIGH DICKINSON UNIVERSITY	TEANECK	NJ	07666
1	2	FORDHAM UNIVERSITY	BRONX	NY	10458
1	2	GEORGE MASON UNIVERSITY	FAIRFAX	VA	22030
1	2	GEORGE WASHINGTON UNIVERSITY	WASHINGTON	DC	20052
1	2	GEORGETOWN UNIVERSITY	WASHINGTON	DC	20057
1	2	HOFSTRA UNIVERSITY	HEMPSTEAD	NY	11550
1	2	JAMES MADISON UNIVERSITY	HARRISONBURG	VA	22807
1	2	LA SALLE UNIVERSITY	PHILADELPHIA	PA	19141
1	2	LAFAYETTE COLLEGE	EASTON	PA	18042

NCAA SCHOOLS SPONSORING MEN'S GOLF TEAMS
1988–89 *(Continued)*

Div	Dist	School	City	St	Zip
1	2	LEHIGH UNIVERSITY	BETHLEHEM	PA	18015
1	2	LOYOLA COLLEGE	BALTIMORE	MD	21210
1	2	MANHATTAN COLLEGE	RIVERDALE	NY	10471
1	2	MONMOUTH COLLEGE	WEST LONG BRANCH	NJ	07764
1	2	MOUNT SAINT MARY'S COLLEGE	EMMITSBURG	MD	21727
1	2	NIAGARA UNIVERSITY	NIAGARA UNIV.	NY	14109
1	2	PENNSYLVANIA STATE UNIV.	UNIVERSITY PARK	PA	16802
1	2	PRINCETON UNIVERSITY	PRINCETON	NJ	08544
1	2	RIDER COLLEGE	LAWRENCEVILLE	NJ	08648
1	2	ROBERT MORRIS COLLEGE	CORAOPOLIS	PA	15108
1	2	RUTGERS UNIVERSITY	NEW BRUNSWICK	NJ	08903
1	2	SETON HALL UNIVERSITY	SOUTH ORANGE	NJ	07079
1	2	SIENA COLLEGE	LOUDONVILLE	NY	12211
1	2	ST. BONAVENTURE UNIVERSITY	ST. BONAVENTURE	NY	14778
1	2	ST. FRANCIS COLLEGE	LORETTO	PA	15940
1	2	ST. JOHN'S UNIVERSITY	JAMAICA	NY	11439
1	2	ST. JOSEPH'S UNIVERSITY	PHILADELPHIA	PA	19131
1	2	ST. PETER'S COLLEGE	JERSEY CITY	NJ	07306
1	2	TEMPLE UNIVERSITY	PHILADELPHIA	PA	19122
1	2	TOWSON STATE UNIVERSITY	TOWSON	MD	21204
1	2	U.S. MILITARY ACADEMY	WEST POINT	NY	10996
1	2	U.S. NAVAL ACADEMY	ANNAPOLIS	MD	21402
1	2	VILLANOVA UNIVERSITY	VILLANOVA	PA	19085
1	2	WAGNER COLLEGE	STATEN ISLAND	NY	10301
1	3	ALABAMA STATE UNIVERSITY	MONTGOMERY	AL	36195
1	3	UNIVERSITY OF ALABAMA	UNIVERSITY	AL	35486
1	3	UNIV. OF ALABAMA-BIRMINGHAM	BIRMINGHAM	AL	35294
1	3	APPALACHIAN STATE UNIVERSITY	BOONE	NC	28608
1	3	AUBURN UNIVERSITY	AUBURN UNIV.	AL	36849
1	3	AUGUSTA COLLEGE	AUGUSTA	GA	30910
1	3	AUSTIN PEAY STATE UNIVERSITY	CLARKSVILLE	TN	37044
1	3	BAPTIST COLLEGE	CHARLESTON	SC	29411
1	3	CAMPBELL UNIVERSITY	BUIES CREEK	NC	27506

NCAA SCHOOLS SPONSORING MEN'S GOLF TEAMS
1988–89 *(Continued)*

Div	Dist	School	City	St	Zip
1	3	UNIV. OF CENTRAL FLORIDA	ORLANDO	FL	32816
1	3	THE CITADEL	CHARLESTON	SC	29409
1	3	CLEMSON UNIVERSITY	CLEMSON	SC	29631
1	3	COASTAL CAROLINA COLL. OF USC	CONWAY	SC	29526
1	3	DAVIDSON COLLEGE	DAVIDSON	NC	28036
1	3	DUKE UNIVERSITY	DURHAM	NC	27706
1	3	EAST CAROLINA UNIVERSITY	GREENVILLE	NC	27858-4353
1	3	EAST TENNESSEE STATE UNIV.	JOHNSON CITY	TN	37614
1	3	EASTERN KENTUCKY UNIVERSITY	RICHMOND	KY	40475
1	3	FLORIDA A&M UNIVERSITY	TALLAHASSEE	FL	32307
1	3	FLORIDA INTERNATIONAL UNIV.	MIAMI	FL	33199
1	3	FLORIDA STATE UNIVERSITY	TALLAHASSEE	FL	32306
1	3	UNIVERSITY OF FLORIDA	GAINESVILLE	FL	32604
1	3	FURMAN UNIVERSITY	GREENVILLE	SC	29613
1	3	GEORGIA INSTITUTE OF TECH.	ATLANTA	GA	30332
1	3	GEORGIA SOUTHERN COLLEGE	STATESBORO	GA	30458
1	3	GEORGIA STATE UNIVERSITY	ATLANTA	GA	30303
1	3	UNIVERSITY OF GEORGIA	ATHENS	GA	30613
1	3	JACKSONVILLE UNIVERSITY	JACKSONVILLE	FL	32211
1	3	UNIVERSITY OF KENTUCKY	LEXINGTON	KY	40506
1	3	LIBERTY UNIVERSITY	LYNCHBURG	VA	24502
1	3	LOUISIANA STATE UNIVERSITY	BATON ROUGE	LA	70893
1	3	UNIVERSITY OF LOUISVILLE	LOUISVILLE	KY	40292
1	3	MARSHALL UNIVERSITY	HUNTINGTON	WV	25715
1	3	UNIVERSITY OF MARYLAND	COLLEGE PARK	MD	20740
1	3	MEMPHIS STATE UNIVERSITY	MEMPHIS	TN	38152
1	3	MERCER UNIVERSITY	MACON	GA	31207
1	3	UNIVERSITY OF MIAMI	CORAL GABLES	FL	33124
1	3	MISSISSIPPI STATE UNIVERSITY	MISS. STATE	MS	39762
1	3	UNIVERSITY OF MISSISSIPPI	UNIVERSITY	MS	38677
1	3	UNIVERSITY OF MISSISSIPPI	UNIVERSITY	MS	38677
1	3	MOREHEAD STATE UNIVERSITY	MOREHEAD	KY	40351
1	3	MURRAY STATE UNIVERSITY	MURRAY	KY	42071
1	3	UNIVERSITY OF NEW ORLEANS	NEW ORLEANS	LA	70148

NCAA SCHOOLS SPONSORING MEN'S GOLF TEAMS
1988–89 *(Continued)*

Div	Dist	School	City	St	Zip
1	3	NICHOLLS STATE UNIVERSITY	THIBODAUX	LA	70310
1	3	UNIVERSITY OF NORTH CAROLINA	ASHEVILLE	NC	28804
1	3	UNIVERSITY OF NORTH CAROLINA	CHAPEL HILL	NC	27514
1	3	UNIVERSITY OF NORTH CAROLINA	CHARLOTTE	NC	28223
1	3	UNIVERSITY OF NORTH CAROLINA	WILMINGTON	NC	28403
1	3	NORTH CAROLINA STATE UNIV.	RALEIGH	NC	27695
1	3	OLD DOMINION UNIVERSITY	NORFOLK	VA	23508
1	3	RADFORD UNIVERSITY	RADFORD	VA	24142
1	3	UNIVERSITY OF RICHMOND	RICHMOND	VA	23173
1	3	SAMFORD UNIVERSITY	BIRMINGHAM	AL	35229
1	3	UNIVERSITY OF SOUTH ALABAMA	MOBILE	AL	36688
1	3	SOUTH CAROLINA STATE COLLEGE	ORANGEBURG	SC	29117
1	3	UNIVERSITY OF SOUTH CAROLINA	COLUMBIA	SC	29208
1	3	UNIVERSITY OF SOUTH FLORIDA	TAMPA	FL	33620
1	3	SOUTHEASTERN LOUISIANA UNIV.	HAMMOND	LA	70402
1	3	UNIV. OF SOUTHERN MISSISSIPPI	HATTIESBURG	MS	39406
1	3	STETSON UNIVERSITY	DE LAND	FL	32720
1	3	TENNESSEE TECHNOLOGICAL UNIV.	COOKEVILLE	TN	38505
1	3	UNIVERSITY OF TENNESSEE	CHATTANOOGA	TN	37402
1	3	UNIVERSITY OF TENNESSEE	KNOXVILLE	TN	37901
1	3	TULANE UNIVERSITY	NEW ORLEANS	LA	70118
1	3	VANDERBILT UNIVERSITY	NASHVILLE	TN	37212
1	3	VIRGINIA MILITARY INSTITUTE	LEXINGTON	VA	24450
1	3	VIRGINIA POLYTECHNIC INSTITUTE	BLACKSBURG	VA	24061
1	3	UNIVERSITY OF VIRGINIA	CHARLOTTESVILLE	VA	22903
1	3	WAKE FOREST UNIVERSITY	WINSTON-SALEM	NC	27109
1	3	WESTERN CAROLINA UNIVERSITY	CULLOWHEE	NC	28723
1	3	WESTERN KENTUCKY UNIVERSITY	BOWLING GREEN	KY	42101
1	3	COLLEGE OF WILLIAM & MARY	WILLIAMSBURG	VA	23187
1	3	WINTHROP COLLEGE	ROCK HILL	SC	29733
1	4	UNIVERSITY OF AKRON	AKRON	OH	44325
1	4	BALL STATE UNIVERSITY	MUNCIE	IN	47306
1	4	BOWLING GREEN STATE UNIV.	BOWLING GREEN	OH	43403

NCAA SCHOOLS SPONSORING MEN'S GOLF TEAMS
1988–89 *(Continued)*

Div	Dist	School	City	St	Zip
1	4	UNIVERSITY OF CINCINNATI	CINCINNATI	OH	45221
1	4	CLEVELAND STATE UNIVERSITY	CLEVELAND	OH	44115
1	4	UNIVERSITY OF DAYTON	DAYTON	OH	45469
1	4	DE PAUL UNIVERSITY	CHICAGO	IL	60614
1	4	UNIVERSITY OF DETROIT	DETROIT	MI	48221
1	4	EASTERN ILLINOIS UNIVERSITY	CHARLESTON	IL	61920
1	4	EASTERN MICHIGAN UNIVERSITY	YPSILANTI	MI	48197
1	4	UNIVERSITY OF EVANSVILLE	EVANSVILLE	IN	47714
1	4	ILLINOIS STATE UNIVERSITY	NORMAL	IL	61761
1	4	UNIVERSITY OF ILLINOIS	CHAMPAIGN	IL	61820
1	4	INDIANA UNIVERSITY	BLOOMINGTON	IN	47405
1	4	UNIVERSITY OF IOWA	IOWA CITY	IA	52242
1	4	KENT STATE UNIVERSITY	KENT	OH	44242
1	4	LOYOLA UNIVERSITY	CHICAGO	IL	60626
1	4	MIAMI UNIVERSITY	OXFORD	OH	45056
1	4	MICHIGAN STATE UNIVERSITY	EAST LANSING	MI	48824
1	4	UNIVERSITY OF MICHIGAN	ANN ARBOR	MI	48109
1	4	UNIVERSITY OF MINNESOTA	MINNEAPOLIS	MN	55455
1	4	NORTHERN ILLINOIS UNIVERSITY	DE KALB	IL	60115
1	4	NORTHWESTERN UNIVERSITY	EVANSTON	IL	60201
1	4	UNIVERSITY OF NOTRE DAME	NOTRE DAME	IN	46556
1	4	OHIO STATE UNIVERSITY	COLUMBUS	OH	43210
1	4	OHIO UNIVERSITY	ATHENS	OH	45701
1	4	PURDUE UNIVERSITY	WEST LAFAYETTE	IN	47907
1	4	UNIVERSITY OF TOLEDO	TOLEDO	OH	43606
1	4	VALPARAISO UNIVERSITY	VALPARAISO	IN	46383
1	4	WESTERN ILLINOIS UNIVERSITY	MACOMB	IL	61455
1	4	UNIVERSITY OF WISCONSIN	GREEN BAY	WI	54311-7001
1	4	UNIVERSITY OF WISCONSIN	MADISON	WI	53711
1	4	WRIGHT STATE UNIVERSITY	DAYTON	OH	45435
1	4	XAVIER UNIVERSITY	CINCINNATI	OH	45207
1	4	YOUNGSTOWN STATE UNIVERSITY	YOUNGSTOWN	OH	44555
1	5	BRADLEY UNIVERSITY	PEORIA	IL	61625

NCAA SCHOOLS SPONSORING MEN'S GOLF TEAMS
1988–89 *(Continued)*

Div	Dist	School	City	St	Zip
1	5	UNIVERSITY OF COLORADO	BOULDER	CO	80309
1	5	CREIGHTON UNIVERSITY	OMAHA	NE	68178
1	5	IOWA STATE UNIVERSITY	AMES	IA	50011
1	5	KANSAS STATE UNIVERSITY	MANHATTAN	KS	66506
1	5	UNIVERSITY OF KANSAS	LAWRENCE	KS	66045
1	5	UNIVERSITY OF MISSOURI	COLUMBIA	MO	65211
1	5	UNIVERSITY OF NEBRASKA	LINCOLN	NE	68588
1	5	UNIVERSITY OF NORTHERN IOWA	CEDAR FALLS	IA	50614
1	5	OKLAHOMA STATE UNIVERSITY	STILLWATER	OK	74078
1	5	UNIVERSITY OF OKLAHOMA	NORMAN	OK	73019
1	5	SOUTHERN ILLINOIS UNIVERSITY	CARBONDALE	IL	62901
1	5	SOUTHWEST MISSOURI STATE UNIV.	SPRINGFIELD	MO	65804
1	5	ST. LOUIS UNIVERSITY	ST. LOUIS	MO	63108
1	5	UNIVERSITY OF TULSA	TULSA	OK	74104
1	5	WICHITA STATE UNIVERSITY	WICHITA	KS	67208
1	6	ALCORN STATE UNIVERSITY	LORMAN	MS	39096
1	6	ARKANSAS STATE UNIVERSITY	STATE UNIVERSITY	AR	72467
1	6	UNIVERSITY OF ARKANSAS	FAYETTEVILLE	AR	72701
1	6	BAYLOR UNIVERSITY	WACO	TX	76706
1	6	CENTENARY COLLEGE	SHREVEPORT	LA	71134
1	6	GRAMBLING STATE UNIVERSITY	GRAMBLING	LA	71245
1	6	HARDIN-SIMMONS UNIVERSITY	ABILENE	TX	79698
1	6	HOUSTON BAPTIST UNIVERSITY	HOUSTON	TX	77074
1	6	UNIVERSITY OF HOUSTON	HOUSTON	TX	77204
1	6	JACKSON STATE UNIVERSITY	JACKSON	MS	39217
1	6	LAMAR UNIVERSITY	BEAUMONT	TX	77710
1	6	LOUISIANA TECH UNIVERSITY	RUSTON	LA	71272
1	6	MC NEESE STATE UNIVERSITY	LAKE CHARLES	LA	70609
1	6	MISSISSIPPI VALLEY ST. UNIV.	ITTA BENA	MS	38941
1	6	UNIVERSITY OF NORTH TEXAS	DENTON	TX	76203
1	6	NORTHEAST LOUISIANA UNIVERSITY	MONROE	LA	71209
1	6	NORTHWESTERN STATE UNIVERSITY	NATCHITOCHES	LA	71497
1	6	PAN AMERICAN UNIVERSITY	EDINBURG	TX	78539

NCAA SCHOOLS SPONSORING MEN'S GOLF TEAMS
1988–89 *(Continued)*

Div	Dist	School	City	St	Zip
1	6	PRAIRIE VIEW A&M UNIVERSITY	PRAIRIE VIEW	TX	77446
1	6	RICE UNIVERSITY	HOUSTON	TX	77251
1	6	SAM HOUSTON STATE UNIVERSITY	HUNTSVILLE	TX	77341
1	6	SOUTHERN METHODIST UNIVERSITY	DALLAS	TX	75275
1	6	SOUTHERN UNIVERSITY	BATON ROUGE	LA	70813
1	6	SOUTHWEST TEXAS STATE UNIV.	SAN MARCOS	TX	78666
1	6	UNIV. OF SOUTHWESTERN LA.	LAFAYETTE	LA	70506
1	6	STEPHEN F. AUSTIN STATE UNIV.	NACOGDOCHES	TX	75962
1	6	UNIVERSITY OF TEXAS	ARLINGTON	TX	76019
1	6	UNIVERSITY OF TEXAS	AUSTIN	TX	78712
1	6	UNIVERSITY OF TEXAS	SAN ANTONIO	TX	78285
1	6	TEXAS A&M UNIVERSITY	COLLEGE STATION	TX	77843
1	6	TEXAS CHRISTIAN UNIVERSITY	FORT WORTH	TX	76129
1	6	TEXAS SOUTHERN UNIVERSITY	HOUSTON	TX	77004
1	6	TEXAS TECH UNIVERSITY	LUBBOCK	TX	79409
1	7	BOISE STATE UNIVERSITY	BOISE	ID	83725
1	7	BRIGHAM YOUNG UNIVERSITY	PROVO	UT	84602
1	7	COLORADO STATE UNIVERSITY	FORT COLLINS	CO	80523
1	7	GONZAGA UNIVERSITY	SPOKANE	WA	99258
1	7	UNIVERSITY OF IDAHO	MOSCOW	ID	83843
1	7	UNIVERSITY OF NEVADA	RENO	NV	89557
1	7	UNIVERSITY OF NEW MEXICO	ALBUQUERQUE	NM	87131
1	7	SAN DIEGO STATE UNIVERSITY	SAN DIEGO	CA	92182
1	7	SOUTHERN UTAH STATE COLLEGE	CEDAR CITY	UT	84720
1	7	UNIVERSITY OF TEXAS	EL PASO	TX	79968
1	7	U.S. AIR FORCE ACADEMY	COLORADO SPRINGS	CO	80840
1	7	UNIVERSITY OF UTAH	SALT LAKE CITY	UT	84112
1	7	WEBER STATE COLLEGE	OGDEN	UT	84408
1	7	UNIVERSITY OF WYOMING	LARAMIE	WY	82071
1	8	ARIZONA STATE UNIVERSITY	TEMPE	AZ	85287
1	8	UNIVERSITY OF ARIZONA	TUCSON	AZ	85721
1	8	UNIVERSITY OF CALIFORNIA	BERKELEY	CA	94720

NCAA SCHOOLS SPONSORING MEN'S GOLF TEAMS
1988–89 *(Continued)*

Div	Dist	School	City	St	Zip
1	8	UNIVERSITY OF CALIFORNIA	LOS ANGELES	CA	90024
1	8	UNIVERSITY OF CALIFORNIA	SANTA BARBARA	CA	93106
1	8	UNIVERSITY OF CALIFORNIA	IRVINE	CA	92717
1	8	CALIF. STATE UNIV.-FRESNO	FRESNO	CA	93740
1	8	CALIF. STATE UNIV.-LONG BEACH	LONG BEACH	CA	90840
1	8	LOYOLA MARYMOUNT UNIVERSITY	LOS ANGELES	CA	90045
1	8	UNIVERSITY OF NEVADA	LAS VEGAS	NV	89154
1	8	NEW MEXICO STATE UNIVERSITY	LAS CRUCES	NM	88003
1	8	OREGON STATE UNIVERSITY	CORVALLIS	OR	97331
1	8	UNIVERSITY OF OREGON	EUGENE	OR	97403
1	8	UNIVERSITY OF THE PACIFIC	STOCKTON	CA	95211
1	8	PEPPERDINE UNIVERSITY	MALIBU	CA	90265
1	8	UNIVERSITY OF PORTLAND	PORTLAND	OR	97203
1	8	UNIVERSITY OF SAN DIEGO	SAN DIEGO	CA	92110
1	8	UNIVERSITY OF SAN FRANCISCO	SAN FRANCISCO	CA	94117
1	8	SAN JOSE STATE UNIVERSITY	SAN JOSE	CA	95192
1	8	SANTA CLARA UNIVERSITY	SANTA CLARA	CA	95053
1	8	UNIV. OF SOUTHERN CALIFORNIA	LOS ANGELES	CA	90089
1	8	ST. MARY'S COLLEGE	MORAGA	CA	94575
1	8	STANFORD UNIVERSITY	STANFORD	CA	94305
1	8	U.S. INTERNATIONAL UNIVERSITY	SAN DIEGO	CA	92131
1	8	UTAH STATE UNIVERSITY	LOGAN	UT	84322
1	8	WASHINGTON STATE UNIVERSITY	PULLMAN	WA	99164
1	8	UNIVERSITY OF WASHINGTON	SEATTLE	WA	98195

NCAA MEMBERS SPONSORING MEN'S INTERCOLLEGIATE GOLF
1988–89

Div	Dist	School	City	St	Zip
2	1	AMERICAN INTERNATIONAL COLLEGE	SPRINGFIELD	MA	01109
2	1	ASSUMPTION COLLEGE	WORCESTER	MA	01609
2	1	BENTLEY COLLEGE	WALTHAM	MA	02254
2	1	UNIVERSITY OF BRIDGEPORT	BRIDGEPORT	CT	06602
2	1	BRYANT COLLEGE	SMITHFIELD	RI	02917
2	1	FRANKLIN PIERCE COLLEGE	RINDGE	NH	03461
2	1	UNIVERSITY OF LOWELL	LOWELL	MA	01854
2	1	MERRIMACK COLLEGE	NORTH ANDOVER	MA	01845
2	1	QUINNIPIAC COLLEGE	HAMDEN	CT	06518
2	1	SOUTHERN CONNECTICUT ST. UNIV.	NEW HAVEN	CT	06515
2	1	SPRINGFIELD COLLEGE	SPRINGFIELD	MA	01109
2	1	ST. ANSELM COLLEGE	MANCHESTER	NH	03102
2	1	ST. MICHAEL'S COLLEGE	WINOOSKI	VT	05404
2	1	STONEHILL COLLEGE	NORTH EASTON	MA	02357
2	2	CLARION UNIVERSITY	CLARION	PA	16214
2	2	DAVIS AND ELKINS COLLEGE	ELKINS	WV	26241
2	2	DOWLING COLLEGE	OAKDALE	NY	11769-1999
2	2	EAST STROUDSBURG UNIVERSITY	EAST STROUDSBURG	PA	18301
2	2	GANNON UNIVERSITY	ERIE	PA	16541
2	2	HAMPTON UNIVERSITY	HAMPTON	VA	23668
2	2	INDIANA UNIVERSITY	INDIANA	PA	15705
2	2	KUTZTOWN UNIVERSITY	KUTZTOWN	PA	19530
2	2	LE MOYNE COLLEGE	SYRACUSE	NY	13214
2	2	LOCK HAVEN UNIVERSITY	LOCK HAVEN	PA	17745
2	2	MERCY COLLEGE	DOBBS FERRY	NY	10522
2	2	MILLERSVILLE UNIVERSITY	MILLERSVILLE	PA	17551
2	2	NEW YORK INSTITUTE OF TECH.	OLD WESTBURY	NY	11568
2	2	PACE UNIVERSITY	PLEASANTVILLE	NY	10570
2	2	PHILA. COLLEGE OF TEXT. & SCI.	PHILADELPHIA	PA	19144
2	2	QUEENS COLLEGE	FLUSHING	NY	11367
2	2	SHIPPENSBURG UNIVERSITY	SHIPPENSBURG	PA	17257
2	2	SLIPPERY ROCK UNIVERSITY	SLIPPERY ROCK	PA	16057
2	2	WEST CHESTER UNIVERSITY	WEST CHESTER	PA	19383

NCAA MEMBERS SPONSORING MEN'S INTERCOLLEGIATE GOLF
1988–89 *(Continued)*

Div	Dist	School	City	St	Zip
2	3	BARRY UNIVERSITY	MIAMI SHORES	FL	33161
2	3	BELLARMINE COLLEGE	LOUISVILLE	KY	40205
2	3	COLUMBUS COLLEGE	COLUMBUS	GA	31993
2	3	DELTA STATE UNIVERSITY	CLEVELAND	MS	38733
2	3	ECKERD COLLEGE	ST. PETERSBURG	FL	33733
2	3	FAYETTEVILLE STATE UNIVERSITY	FAYETTEVILLE	NC	28301
2	3	FLORIDA ATLANTIC UNIVERSITY	BOCA RATON	FL	33431
2	3	FLORIDA SOUTHERN COLLEGE	LAKELAND	FL	33801-5698
2	3	JACKSONVILLE STATE UNIVERSITY	JACKSONVILLE	AL	36265
2	3	JOHNSON C. SMITH UNIVERSITY	CHARLOTTE	NC	28216
2	3	KENTUCKY STATE UNIVERSITY	FRANKFORT	KY	40601
2	3	KENTUCKY WESLEYAN COLLEGE	OWENSBORO	KY	42301
2	3	LIVINGSTONE COLLEGE	SALISBURY	NC	28144
2	3	LONGWOOD COLLEGE	FARMVILLE	VA	23901
2	3	MISSISSIPPI COLLEGE	CLINTON	MS	39058
2	3	UNIVERSITY OF NORTH ALABAMA	FLORENCE	AL	35632
2	3	UNIVERSITY OF NORTH CAROLINA	GREENSBORO	NC	27412
2	3	NORTHERN KENTUCKY UNIVERSITY	HIGHLAND HEIGHTS	KY	41076
2	3	PEMBROKE STATE UNIVERSITY	PEMBROKE	NC	28372
2	3	PFEIFFER COLLEGE	MISENHEIMER	NC	28109
2	3	RANDOLPH-MACON COLLEGE	ASHLAND	VA	23005
2	3	ROLLINS COLLEGE	WINTER PARK	FL	32789
2	3	ST. AUGUSTINE'S COLLEGE	RALEIGH	NC	27611
2	3	UNIVERSITY OF TAMPA	TAMPA	FL	33606
2	3	UNIVERSITY OF TENNESSEE	MARTIN	TN	38238
2	3	TROY STATE UNIVERSITY	TROY	AL	36081
2	3	VALDOSTA STATE COLLEGE	VALDOSTA	GA	31698
2	3	VIRGINIA UNION UNIVERSITY	RICHMOND	VA	23220
2	3	WEST GEORGIA COLLEGE	CARROLLTON	GA	30118
2	3	WOFFORD COLLEGE	SPARTANBURG	SC	29301-
2	4	ASHLAND COLLEGE	ASHLAND	OH	44805
2	4	BEMIDJI STATE UNIVERSITY	BEMIDJI	MN	56601

NCAA MEMBERS SPONSORING MEN'S INTERCOLLEGIATE GOLF
1988–89 *(Continued)*

Div	Dist	School	City	St	Zip
2	4	FERRIS STATE UNIVERSITY	BIG RAPIDS	MI	49307
2	4	HILLSDALE COLLEGE	HILLSDALE	MI	49242
2	4	INDIANA UNIV.-PURDUE UNIV.	FORT WAYNE	IN	46805
2	4	UNIVERSITY OF INDIANAPOLIS	INDIANAPOLIS	IN	46227
2	4	LAKE SUPERIOR STATE UNIVERSITY	SAULT STE. MARIE	MI	49783
2	4	LEWIS UNIVERSITY	ROMEOVILLE	IL	60441
2	4	UNIVERSITY OF MINNESOTA	DULUTH	MN	55812
2	4	OAKLAND UNIVERSITY	ROCHESTER	MI	48309
2	4	QUINCY COLLEGE	QUINCY	IL	62301
2	4	SAGINAW VALLEY STATE UNIV.	UNIV CENTER	MI	48710
2	4	SOUTHERN ILLINOIS UNIVERSITY	EDWARDSVILLE	IL	62026
2	4	UNIV. OF SOUTHERN INDIANA	EVANSVILLE	IN	47712
2	4	ST. JOSEPH'S COLLEGE	RENSSELAER	IN	47978
2	4	WAYNE STATE UNIVERSITY	DETROIT	MI	48202
2	4	WINONA STATE UNIVERSITY	WINONA	MN	55987
2	4	UNIV. OF WISCONSIN-PARKSIDE	KENOSHA	WI	53141-2000
2	5	AUGUSTANA COLLEGE	SIOUX FALLS	SD	57197
2	5	CENTRAL MISSOURI STATE UNIV.	WARRENSBURG	MO	64093
2	5	KEARNEY STATE COLLEGE	KEARNEY	NE	68849
2	5	LINCOLN UNIVERSITY	JEFFERSON CITY	MO	65101
2	5	MANKATO STATE UNIVERSITY	MANKATO	MN	56001
2	5	MISSOURI SOUTHERN ST. COLLEGE	JOPLIN	MO	64801
2	5	MISSOURI WESTERN ST. COLLEGE	ST. JOSEPH	MO	64507
2	5	UNIVERSITY OF MISSOURI	ROLLA	MO	65401
2	5	UNIVERSITY OF MISSOURI	ST. LOUIS	MO	63121
2	5	MORNINGSIDE COLLEGE	SIOUX CITY	IA	51106
2	5	NORTH DAKOTA STATE UNIVERSITY	FARGO	ND	58105
2	5	UNIVERSITY OF NORTH DAKOTA	GRAND FORKS	ND	58202
2	5	NORTHEAST MISSOURI STATE UNIV.	KIRKSVILLE	MO	63501
2	5	UNIV. OF NORTHERN COLORADO	GREELEY	CO	80639
2	5	PITTSBURG STATE UNIVERSITY	PITTSBURG	KS	66762
2	5	SOUTHWEST BAPTIST UNIVERSITY	BOLIVAR	MO	65613
2	5	ST. CLOUD STATE UNIVERSITY	ST. CLOUD	MN	56301

NCAA MEMBERS SPONSORING MEN'S INTERCOLLEGIATE GOLF
1988–89 *(Continued)*

Div	Dist	School	City	St	Zip
2	5	WASHBURN UNIVERSITY	TOPEKA	KS	66621
2	6	ABILENE CHRISTIAN UNIVERSITY	ABILENE	TX	79699
2	6	CAMERON UNIVERSITY	LAWTON	OK	73505
2	6	CENTRAL STATE UNIVERSITY	EDMOND	OK	73034
2	6	EAST TEXAS STATE UNIVERSITY	COMMERCE	TX	75428
2	6	EASTERN NEW MEXICO UNIVERSITY	PORTALES	NM	88130
2	7	COLORADO SCHOOL OF MINES	GOLDEN	CO	80401
2	7	REGIS COLLEGE	DENVER	CO	80221
2	8	UNIVERSITY OF CALIFORNIA	DAVIS	CA	95616
2	8	CALIFORNIA LUTHERAN UNIVERSITY	THOUSAND OAKS	CA	91359
2	8	CALIF. STATE U-DOMINGUEZ HILLS	CARSON	CA	90747
2	8	CALIF. STATE UNIV.-NORTHRIDGE	NORTHRIDGE	CA	91330
2	8	CALIF. STATE UNIV.-SACRAMENTO	SACRAMENTO	CA	95819
2	8	PORTLAND STATE UNIVERSITY	PORTLAND	OR	97207

Shinnecock Hills Golf Club, Southampton, New York. Site of the second U.S. Open in 1896. (Courtesy USGA)

NCAA MEMBERS SPONSORING MEN'S INTERCOLLEGIATE GOLF
1988–89

Div	Dist	School	City	St	Zip
3	1	AMHERST COLLEGE	AMHERST	MA	01002
3	1	BABSON COLLEGE	WELLESLEY	MA	02157
3	1	BRANDEIS UNIVERSITY	WALTHAM	MA	02254
3	1	CLARK UNIVERSITY	WORCESTER	MA	01610
3	1	COLBY COLLEGE	WATERVILLE	ME	04901
3	1	EMERSON COLLEGE	BOSTON	MA	02116
3	1	UNIVERSITY OF MAINE	FARMINGTON	ME	04938
3	1	MASS. INSTITUTE OF TECHNOLOGY	CAMBRIDGE	MA	02139
3	1	MIDDLEBURY COLLEGE	MIDDLEBURY	VT	05753
3	1	NEW ENGLAND COLLEGE	HENNIKER	NH	03242
3	1	NICHOLS COLLEGE	DUDLEY	MA	01570
3	1	ROGER WILLIAMS COLLEGE	BRISTOL	RI	02809
3	1	SALEM STATE COLLEGE	SALEM	MA	01970
3	1	SOUTHEASTERN MASS. UNIVERSITY	NORTH DARTMOUTH	MA	02747
3	1	UNIV. OF SOUTHERN MAINE	GORHAM	ME	04038
3	1	ST. JOSEPH'S COLLEGE	NORTH WINDHAM	ME	04062
3	1	SUFFOLK UNIVERSITY	BOSTON	MA	02114
3	1	THOMAS COLLEGE	WATERVILLE	ME	04901
3	1	TRINITY COLLEGE	HARTFORD	CT	06106
3	1	TUFTS UNIVERSITY	MEDFORD	MA	02155
3	1	WESLEYAN UNIVERSITY	MIDDLETOWN	CT	06457
3	1	WESTERN CONN. STATE UNIV.	DANBURY	CT	06810
3	1	WESTERN NEW ENGLAND COLLEGE	SPRINGFIELD	MA	01119
3	1	WESTFIELD STATE COLLEGE	WESTFIELD	MA	01085
3	1	WILLIAMS COLLEGE	WILLIAMSTOWN	MA	01267
3	1	WORCESTER POLYTECHNIC INST.	WORCESTER	MA	01609
3	1	WORCESTER STATE COLLEGE	WORCESTER	MA	01602
3	2	ALBRIGHT COLLEGE	READING	PA	19603
3	2	ALLEGHENY COLLEGE	MEADVILLE	PA	16335
3	2	ALLENTOWN COLLEGE	CENTER VALLEY	PA	18034
3	2	BUFFALO STATE COLLEGE	BUFFALO	NY	14222
3	2	CABRINI COLLEGE	RADNOR	PA	19087
3	2	CARNEGIE-MELLON UNIVERSITY	PITTSBURGH	PA	15213

NCAA MEMBERS SPONSORING MEN'S INTERCOLLEGIATE GOLF
1988–89 *(Continued)*

Div	Dist	School	City	St	Zip
3	2	CLARKSON UNIVERSITY	POTSDAM	NY	13676
3	2	DELAWARE VALLEY COLLEGE	DOYLESTOWN	PA	18901
3	2	DICKINSON COLLEGE	CARLISLE	PA	17013
3	2	ELIZABETHTOWN COLLEGE	ELIZABETHTOWN	PA	17022
3	2	ELMIRA COLLEGE	ELMIRA	NY	14901
3	2	FAIRLEIGH DICKINSON UNIVERSITY	MADISON	NJ	07940
3	2	GETTYSBURG COLLEGE	GETTYSBURG	PA	17325
3	2	GLASSBORO STATE COLLEGE	GLASSBORO	NJ	08028
3	2	GROVE CITY COLLEGE	GROVE CITY	PA	16127
3	2	HAMILTON COLLEGE	CLINTON	NY	13323
3	2	HARTWICK COLLEGE	ONEONTA	NY	13820
3	2	HOBART & WM. SMITH COLLEGES	GENEVA	NY	14456
3	2	JUNIATA COLLEGE	HUNTINGDON	PA	16652
3	2	KING'S COLLEGE	WILKES-BARRE	PA	18711
3	2	LEBANON VALLEY COLLEGE	ANNVILLE	PA	17003
3	2	LYCOMING COLLEGE	WILLIAMSPORT	PA	17701
3	2	MESSIAH COLLEGE	GRANTHAM	PA	17027
3	2	MONTCLAIR STATE COLLEGE	UPPER MONTCLAIR	NJ	07043
3	2	MORAVIAN COLLEGE	BETHLEHEM	PA	18018
3	2	MUHLENBERG COLLEGE	ALLENTOWN	PA	18104
3	2	NAZARETH COLLEGE	ROCHESTER	NY	14610
3	2	NEW JERSEY INSTITUTE OF TECH.	NEWARK	NJ	07102
3	2	NEW PALTZ STATE UNIV. COLLEGE	NEW PALTZ	NY	12562
3	2	NEW YORK UNIVERSITY	NEW YORK	NY	10012
3	2	OSWEGO STATE UNIV. COLLEGE	OSWEGO	NY	13126
3	2	RAMAPO COLLEGE	MAHWAH	NJ	07430
3	2	RENSSELAER POLYTECHNIC INST.	TROY	NY	12181
3	2	UNIVERSITY OF ROCHESTER	ROCHESTER	NY	14627
3	2	RUTGERS UNIVERSITY	CAMDEN	NJ	08102
3	2	UNIVERSITY OF SCRANTON	SCRANTON	PA	18510
3	2	SKIDMORE COLLEGE	SARATOGA SPRINGS	NY	12866
3	2	SPRING GARDEN COLLEGE	PHILADELPHIA	PA	19119
3	2	ST. JOHN FISHER COLLEGE	ROCHESTER	NY	14618
3	2	SUSQUEHANNA UNIVERSITY	SELINSGROVE	PA	17870

NCAA MEMBERS SPONSORING MEN'S INTERCOLLEGIATE GOLF
1988–89 *(Continued)*

Div	Dist	School	City	St	Zip
3	2	SWARTHMORE COLLEGE	SWARTHMORE	PA	19081
3	2	THIEL COLLEGE	GREENVILLE	PA	16125
3	2	TRENTON STATE COLLEGE	TRENTON	NJ	08625
3	2	U.S. MERCHANT MARINE ACADEMY	KINGS POINT	NY	11024-1699
3	2	UNION COLLEGE	SCHENECTADY	NY	12308
3	2	UPSALA COLLEGE	EAST ORANGE	NJ	07019
3	2	URSINUS COLLEGE	COLLEGEVILLE	PA	19426
3	2	UTICA COLLEGE	UTICA	NY	13502
3	2	WASHINGTON & JEFFERSON COLLEGE	WASHINGTON	PA	15301
3	2	WESLEY COLLEGE	DOVER	DE	19901
3	2	WIDENER UNIVERSITY	CHESTER	PA	19013
3	2	WILKES COLLEGE	WILKES-BARRE	PA	18704
3	2	WILLIAM PATERSON COLLEGE	WAYNE	NJ	07470
3	2	YESHIVA UNIVERSITY	NEW YORK	NY	10033
3	2	YORK COLLEGE	YORK	PA	17403
3	3	AVERETT COLLEGE	DANVILLE	VA	24541
3	3	BEREA COLLEGE	BEREA	KY	40404
3	3	BRIDGEWATER COLLEGE	BRIDGEWATER	VA	22812
3	3	CENTRE COLLEGE	DANVILLE	KY	40422
3	3	CHRISTOPHER NEWPORT COLLEGE	NEWPORT NEWS	VA	23606
3	3	EMORY UNIVERSITY	ATLANTA	GA	30322
3	3	FERRUM COLLEGE	FERRUM	VA	24088
3	3	GREENSBORO COLLEGE	GREENSBORO	NC	27401
3	3	HAMPDEN-SYDNEY COLLEGE	HAMPDEN-SYDNEY	VA	23943
3	3	JOHNS HOPKINS UNIVERSITY	BALTIMORE	MD	21218
3	3	LYNCHBURG COLLEGE	LYNCHBURG	VA	24501
3	3	MARYMOUNT UNIVERSITY	ARLINGTON	VA	22207
3	3	METHODIST COLLEGE	FAYETTEVILLE	NC	28311
3	3	MILLSAPS COLLEGE	JACKSON	MS	39210
3	3	NORTH CAROLINA WESLEYAN COLL.	ROCKY MOUNT	NC	27804
3	3	RHODES COLLEGE	MEMPHIS	TN	38112
3	3	ROANOKE COLLEGE	SALEM	VA	24153
3	3	SHENANDOAH COLLEGE	WINCHESTER	VA	22601

NCAA MEMBERS SPONSORING MEN'S INTERCOLLEGIATE GOLF
1988–89 *(Continued)*

Div	Dist	School	City	St	Zip
3	3	UNIVERSITY OF THE SOUTH	SEWANEE	TN	37375
3	3	VIRGINIA WESLEYAN COLLEGE	NORFOLK	VA	23502
3	3	WASHINGTON & LEE UNIVERSITY	LEXINGTON	VA	24450
3	4	ADRIAN COLLEGE	ADRIAN	MI	49221
3	4	ALBION COLLEGE	ALBION	MI	49224
3	4	ALMA COLLEGE	ALMA	MI	48801
3	4	AUGSBURG COLLEGE	MINNEAPOLIS	MN	55454
3	4	AUGUSTANA COLLEGE	ROCK ISLAND	IL	61201
3	4	AURORA UNIVERSITY	AURORA	IL	60506
3	4	BALDWIN-WALLACE COLLEGE	BEREA	OH	44017
3	4	BELOIT COLLEGE	BELOIT	WI	53511
3	4	BETHEL COLLEGE	ST. PAUL	MN	55112
3	4	BLACKBURN COLLEGE	CARLINVILLE	IL	62626
3	4	CALVIN COLLEGE	GRAND RAPIDS	MI	49506
3	4	CAPITAL UNIVERSITY	COLUMBUS	OH	43209
3	4	CARLETON COLLEGE	NORTHFIELD	MN	55057
3	4	CARROLL COLLEGE	WAUKESHA	WI	53186
3	4	CARTHAGE COLLEGE	KENOSHA	WI	53141
3	4	CASE WESTERN RESERVE UNIV.	CLEVELAND	OH	44106
3	4	CONCORDIA COLLEGE	MOORHEAD	MN	56560
3	4	DE PAUW UNIVERSITY	GREENCASTLE	IN	46135
3	4	DENISON UNIVERSITY	GRANVILLE	OH	43023
3	4	EARLHAM COLLEGE	RICHMOND	IN	47374
3	4	ELMHURST COLLEGE	ELMHURST	IL	60126
3	4	FINDLAY COLLEGE	FINDLAY	OH	45840
3	4	GUSTAVUS ADOLPHUS COLLEGE	ST. PETER	MN	56082
3	4	HAMLINE UNIVERSITY	ST. PAUL	MN	55104
3	4	HEIDELBERG COLLEGE	TIFFIN	OH	44883
3	4	HIRAM COLLEGE	HIRAM	OH	44234
3	4	HOPE COLLEGE	HOLLAND	MI	49423
3	4	ILLINOIS BENEDICTINE COLLEGE	LISLE	IL	60532
3	4	ILLINOIS COLLEGE	JACKSONVILLE	IL	62650
3	4	ILLINOIS WESLEYAN UNIVERSITY	BLOOMINGTON	IL	61701

NCAA MEMBERS SPONSORING MEN'S INTERCOLLEGIATE GOLF
1988–89 *(Continued)*

Div	Dist	School	City	St	Zip
3	4	JOHN CARROLL UNIVERSITY	UNIVERSITY HGTS.	OH	44118
3	4	KALAMAZOO COLLEGE	KALAMAZOO	MI	49007
3	4	KENYON COLLEGE	GAMBIER	OH	43022
3	4	KNOX COLLEGE	GALESBURG	IL	61401
3	4	LAWRENCE UNIVERSITY	APPLETON	WI	54912
3	4	MACALESTER COLLEGE	ST. PAUL	MN	55105
3	4	MAC MURRAY COLLEGE	JACKSONVILLE	IL	62650
3	4	MARIETTA COLLEGE	MARIETTA	OH	45750
3	4	MILLIKIN UNIVERSITY	DECATUR	IL	62522
3	4	MOUNT UNION COLLEGE	ALLIANCE	OH	44601
3	4	MUSKINGUM COLLEGE	NEW CONCORD	OH	43762
3	4	NORTH CENTRAL COLLEGE	NAPERVILLE	IL	60566
3	4	NORTH PARK COLLEGE	CHICAGO	IL	60625
3	4	OHIO NORTHERN UNIVERSITY	ADA	OH	45810
3	4	OHIO WESLEYAN UNIVERSITY	DELAWARE	OH	43015
3	4	OLIVET COLLEGE	OLIVET	MI	49076
3	4	OTTERBEIN COLLEGE	WESTERVILLE	OH	43081
3	4	RIPON COLLEGE	RIPON	WI	54971
3	4	ROCKFORD COLLEGE	ROCKFORD	IL	61101
3	4	ROSE-HULMAN INSTITUTE OF TECH.	TERRE HAUTE	IN	47803
3	4	ST. JOHN'S UNIVERSITY	COLLEGEVILLE	MN	56321
3	4	ST. MARY'S COLLEGE	WINONA	MN	55987
3	4	ST. OLAF COLLEGE	NORTHFIELD	MN	55057
3	4	COLLEGE OF SAINT THOMAS	ST. PAUL	MN	55105
3	4	TRINITY COLLEGE	DEERFIELD	IL	60015
3	4	WABASH COLLEGE	CRAWFORDSVILLE	IN	47933
3	4	WHEATON COLLEGE	WHEATON	IL	60187
3	4	UNIVERSITY OF WISCONSIN	EAU CLAIRE	WI	54702
3	4	UNIVERSITY OF WISCONSIN	LA CROSSE	WI	54601
3	4	UNIVERSITY OF WISCONSIN	OSHKOSH	WI	54901
3	4	UNIVERSITY OF WISCONSIN	PLATTEVILLE	WI	53818
3	4	UNIVERSITY OF WISCONSIN	RIVER FALLS	WI	54022
3	4	UNIVERSITY OF WISCONSIN	STEVENS POINT	WI	54481
3	4	UNIV. OF WISCONSIN-STOUT	MENOMONIE	WI	54751
3	4	UNIVERSITY OF WISCONSIN	SUPERIOR	WI	54880

NCAA MEMBERS SPONSORING MEN'S INTERCOLLEGIATE GOLF
1988–89 *(Continued)*

Div	Dist	School	City	St	Zip
3	4	UNIVERSITY OF WISCONSIN	WHITEWATER	WI	53190
3	4	WITTENBERG UNIVERSITY	SPRINGFIELD	OH	45501
3	4	COLLEGE OF WOOSTER	WOOSTER	OH	44691
3	5	BUENA VISTA COLLEGE	STORM LAKE	IA	50588
3	5	CENTRAL COLLEGE	PELLA	IA	50219
3	5	COE COLLEGE	CEDAR RAPIDS	IA	52402
3	5	CORNELL COLLEGE	MT. VERNON	IA	52314
3	5	UNIVERSITY OF DUBUQUE	DUBUQUE	IA	52001
3	5	GRINNELL COLLEGE	GRINNELL	IA	50112
3	5	LORAS COLLEGE	DUBUQUE	IA	52001
3	5	LUTHER COLLEGE	DECORAH	IA	52101
3	5	NEBRASKA WESLEYAN UNIVERSITY	LINCOLN	NE	68504
3	5	SIMPSON COLLEGE	INDIANOLA	IA	50125
3	5	UPPER IOWA UNIVERSITY	FAYETTE	IA	52142
3	5	WARTBURG COLLEGE	WAVERLY	IA	50677
3	5	WASHINGTON UNIVERSITY	ST. LOUIS	MO	63130
3	5	WILLIAM PENN COLLEGE	OSKALOOSA	IA	52577
3	6	TRINITY UNIVERSITY	SAN ANTONIO	TX	78284
3	7	COLORADO COLLEGE	COLORADO SPRINGS	CO	80903
3	8	UNIV OF CALIFORNIA-SAN DIEGO	LA JOLLA	CA	92093
3	8	CALIF. INSTITUTE OF TECHNOLOGY	PASADENA	CA	91125
3	8	CALIF. STATE U.-SAN BERNARDINO	SAN BERNARDINO	CA	92407
3	8	CALIF. STATE UNIV.-STANISLAUS	TURLOCK	CA	95380
3	8	UNIVERSITY OF LA VERNE	LA VERNE	CA	91750
3	8	LEWIS AND CLARK COLLEGE	PORTLAND	OR	97219
3	8	MENLO COLLEGE	ATHERTON	CA	94025
3	8	POMONA-PITZER COLLEGES	CLAREMONT	CA	91711
3	8	UNIVERSITY OF REDLANDS	REDLANDS	CA	92374
3	8	WHITTIER COLLEGE	WHITTIER	CA	90608
3	8	WILLAMETTE UNIVERSITY	SALEM	OR	97301

Totals Men's Golf		Dist1	Dist2	Dist3	Dist4	Dist5	Dist6	Dist7	Dist8
DIVISION I	254	15	42	72	35	16	33	14	27
DIVISION II	112	14	19	30	18	18	5	2	6
DIVISION III	198	27	55	21	68	14	1	1	11
TOTAL INST.	564	56	119	124	124	49	40	18	45

NCAA SCHOOLS SPONSORING WOMEN'S GOLF TEAMS
1988–89

Div.	Dist.	School	City	St.	Zip
1	1	BOSTON COLLEGE	CHESTNUT HILL	MA	02167
1	1	DARTMOUTH COLLEGE	HANOVER	NH	03755
1	1	UNIVERSITY OF HARTFORD	WEST HARTFORD	CT	06117
1	1	YALE UNIVERSITY	NEW HAVEN	CT	06520
1	2	JAMES MADISON UNIVERSITY	HARRISONBURG	VA	22807
1	2	PENNSYLVANIA STATE UNIV.	UNIVERSITY PARK	PA	16802
1	2	RUTGERS UNIVERSITY	NEW BRUNSWICK	NJ	08903
1	3	UNIVERSITY OF ALABAMA	UNIVERSITY	AL	35486
1	3	UNIV. OF ALABAMA-BIRMINGHAM	BIRMINGHAM	AL	35294
1	3	APPALACHIAN STATE UNIVERSITY	BOONE	NC	28608
1	3	AUBURN UNIVERSITY	AUBURN	AL	36849
1	3	AUSTIN PEAY STATE UNIVERSITY	CLARKSVILLE	TN	37044
1	3	UNIV. OF CENTRAL FLORIDA	ORLANDO	FL	32816
1	3	COASTAL CAROLINA COLL. OF USC	CONWAY	SC	29526
1	3	DUKE UNIVERSITY	DURHAM	NC	27706
1	3	FLORIDA INTERNATIONAL UNIV.	MIAMI	FL	33199
1	3	FLORIDA STATE UNIVERSITY	TALLAHASSEE	FL	32306
1	3	UNIVERSITY OF FLORIDA	GAINESVILLE	FL	32604
1	3	FURMAN UNIVERSITY	GREENVILLE	SC	29613
1	3	UNIVERSITY OF GEORGIA	ATHENS	GA	30613
1	3	JACKSONVILLE UNIVERSITY	JACKSONVILLE	FL	32211
1	3	UNIVERSITY OF KENTUCKY	LEXINGTON	KY	40506
1	3	LOUISIANA STATE UNIVERSITY	BATON ROUGE	LA	70893
1	3	MEMPHIS STATE UNIVERSITY	MEMPHIS	TN	38152

NCAA SCHOOLS SPONSORING WOMEN'S GOLF TEAMS
1988–89 *(Continued)*

Div.	Dist.	School	City	St.	Zip
1	3	UNIVERSITY OF MIAMI	CORAL GABLES	FL	33124
1	3	MISSISSIPPI STATE UNIVERSITY	MISS. STATE	MS	39762
1	3	UNIVERSITY OF MISSISSIPPI	UNIVERSITY	MS	38677
1	3	UNIVERSITY OF NORTH CAROLINA	CHAPEL HILL	NC	27514
1	3	UNIVERSITY OF NORTH CAROLINA	WILMINGTON	NC	28403
1	3	SAMFORD UNIVERSITY	BIRMINGHAM	AL	35229
1	3	UNIVERSITY OF SOUTH ALABAMA	MOBILE	AL	36688
1	3	UNIVERSITY OF SOUTH CAROLINA	COLUMBIA	SC	29208
1	3	UNIVERSITY OF SOUTH FLORIDA	TAMPA	FL	33620
1	3	STETSON UNIVERSITY	DE LAND	FL	32720
1	3	TENNESSEE TECHNOLOGICAL UNIV.	COOKEVILLE	TN	38505
1	3	VANDERBILT UNIVERSITY	NASHVILLE	TN	37212
1	3	WAKE FOREST UNIVERSITY	WINSTON-SALEM	NC	27109
1	3	WESTERN KENTUCKY UNIVERSITY	BOWLING GREEN	KY	42101
1	3	COLLEGE OF WILLIAM & MARY	WILLIAMSBURG	VA	23187
1	3	WINTHROP COLLEGE	ROCK HILL	SC	29733
1	4	BOWLING GREEN STATE UNIV.	BOWLING GREEN	OH	43403
1	4	UNIVERSITY OF CINCINNATI	CINCINNATI	OH	45221
1	4	ILLINOIS STATE UNIVERSITY	NORMAL	IL	61761
1	4	UNIVERSITY OF ILLINOIS	CHAMPAIGN	IL	61820
1	4	INDIANA UNIVERSITY	BLOOMINGTON	IN	47405
1	4	UNIVERSITY OF IOWA	IOWA CITY	IA	52242
1	4	MICHIGAN STATE UNIVERSITY	EAST LANSING	MI	48824
1	4	UNIVERSITY OF MICHIGAN	ANN ARBOR	MI	48109
1	4	UNIVERSITY OF MINNESOTA	MINNEAPOLIS	MN	55455
1	4	NORTHERN ILLINOIS UNIVERSITY	DE KALB	IL	60115
1	4	UNIVERSITY OF NOTRE DAME	NOTRE DAME	IN	46556
1	4	OHIO STATE UNIVERSITY	COLUMBUS	OH	43210
1	4	PURDUE UNIVERSITY	WEST LAFAYETTE	IN	47907
1	4	UNIVERSITY OF WISCONSIN	MADISON	WI	53711
1	5	CREIGHTON UNIVERSITY	OMAHA	NE	68178
1	5	IOWA STATE UNIVERSITY	AMES	IA	50011

NCAA SCHOOLS SPONSORING WOMEN'S GOLF TEAMS
1988–89 *(Continued)*

Div.	Dist.	School	City	St.	Zip
1	5	KANSAS STATE UNIVERSITY	MANHATTAN	KS	66506
1	5	UNIVERSITY OF KANSAS	LAWRENCE	KS	66045
1	5	UNIVERSITY OF MISSOURI	COLUMBIA	MO	65211
1	5	UNIVERSITY OF NORTHERN IOWA	CEDAR FALLS	IA	50614
1	5	OKLAHOMA STATE UNIVERSITY	STILLWATER	OK	74078
1	5	UNIVERSITY OF OKLAHOMA	NORMAN	OK	73019
1	5	SOUTHERN ILLINOIS UNIVERSITY	CARBONDALE	IL	62901
1	5	SOUTHWEST MISSOURI STATE UNIV.	SPRINGFIELD	MO	65804
1	5	UNIVERSITY OF TULSA	TULSA	OK	74104
1	5	WICHITA STATE UNIVERSITY	WICHITA	KS	67208
1	6	BAYLOR UNIVERSITY	WACO	TX	76706
1	6	HARDIN-SIMMONS UNIVERSITY	ABILENE	TX	79698
1	6	LAMAR UNIVERSITY	BEAUMONT	TX	77710
1	6	UNIVERSITY OF NORTH TEXAS	DENTON	TX	76203
1	6	SOUTHERN METHODIST UNIVERSITY	DALLAS	TX	75275
1	6	UNIVERSITY OF TEXAS	AUSTIN	TX	78712
1	6	TEXAS A&M UNIVERSITY	COLLEGE STATION	TX	77843
1	6	TEXAS CHRISTIAN UNIVERSITY	FORT WORTH	TX	76129
1	6	TEXAS TECH UNIVERSITY	LUBBOCK	TX	79409
1	7	BRIGHAM YOUNG UNIVERSITY	PROVO	UT	84602
1	7	COLORADO STATE UNIVERSITY	FORT COLLINS	CO	80523
1	7	UNIVERSITY OF HAWAII	HONOLULU	HI	96822
1	7	UNIVERSITY OF NEW MEXICO	ALBUQUERQUE	NM	87131
1	7	SAN DIEGO STATE UNIVERSITY	SAN DIEGO	CA	92182
1	7	UNIVERSITY OF TEXAS	EL PASO	TX	79968
1	7	UNIVERSITY OF WYOMING	LARAMIE	WY	82071
1	8	ARIZONA STATE UNIVERSITY	TEMPE	AZ	85287
1	8	UNIVERSITY OF ARIZONA	TUCSON	AZ	85721
1	8	UNIVERSITY OF CALIFORNIA	LOS ANGELES	CA	90024
1	8	CALIF. STATE UNIV.-LONG BEACH	LONG BEACH	CA	90840
1	8	NEW MEXICO STATE UNIVERSITY	LAS CRUCES	NM	88003

NCAA SCHOOLS SPONSORING WOMEN'S GOLF TEAMS
1988–89 *(Continued)*

Div.	Dist.	School	City	St.	Zip
1	8	OREGON STATE UNIVERSITY	CORVALLIS	OR	97331
1	8	UNIVERSITY OF OREGON	EUGENE	OR	97403
1	8	PEPPERDINE UNIVERSITY	MALIBU	CA	90265
1	8	SAN JOSE STATE UNIVERSITY	SAN JOSE	CA	95192
1	8	UNIV. OF SOUTHERN CALIFORNIA	LOS ANGELES	CA	90089
1	8	STANFORD UNIVERSITY	STANFORD	CA	94305
1	8	U.S. INTERNATIONAL UNIVERSITY	SAN DIEGO	CA	92131
1	8	WASHINGTON STATE UNIVERSITY	PULLMAN	WA	99164
1	8	UNIVERSITY OF WASHINGTON	SEATTLE	WA	98195

NCAA MEMBERS SPONSORING WOMEN'S
INTERCOLLEGIATE GOLF
1988–89

Div	Dist	School	City	St	Zip
2	1	SPRINGFIELD COLLEGE	SPRINGFIELD	MA	01109
2	3	LONGWOOD COLLEGE	FARMVILLE	VA	23901
2	3	ROLLINS COLLEGE	WINTER PARK	FL	32789
2	3	TROY STATE UNIVERSITY	TROY	AL	36081
2	4	FERRIS STATE UNIVERSITY	BIG RAPIDS	MI	49307
2	4	UNIVERSITY OF INDIANAPOLIS	INDIANAPOLIS	IN	46227
2	4	UNIVERSITY OF MINNESOTA	DULUTH	MN	55812
2	4	WINONA STATE UNIVERSITY	WINONA	MN	55987
2	5	MANKATO STATE UNIVERSITY	MANKATO	MN	56001
2	5	MORNINGSIDE COLLEGE	SIOUX CITY	IA	51106
2	5	UNIVERSITY OF NORTH DAKOTA	GRAND FORKS	ND	58202
2	5	NORTHEAST MISSOURI STATE UNIV.	KIRKSVILLE	MO	63501
2	5	SOUTH DAKOTA STATE UNIVERSITY	BROOKINGS	SD	57007
2	5	ST. CLOUD STATE UNIVERSITY	ST. CLOUD	MN	56301
2	7	U.S. AIR FORCE ACADEMY	COLORADO SPRINGS	CO	80840

NCAA MEMBERS SPONSORING WOMEN'S
INTERCOLLEGIATE GOLF
1988–89 (continued)

Div	Dist	School	City	St	Zip
3	1	AMHERST COLLEGE	AMHERST	MA	01002
3	1	MOUNT HOLYOKE COLLEGE	SOUTH HADLEY	MA	01075
3	3	MEREDITH COLLEGE	RALEIGH	NC	27611
3	3	METHODIST COLLEGE	FAYETTEVILLE	NC	28311
3	4	CONCORDIA COLLEGE	MOORHEAD	MN	56560
3	4	DE PAUW UNIVERSITY	GREENCASTLE	IN	46135
3	4	GUSTAVUS ADOLPHUS COLLEGE	ST. PETER	MN	56082
3	4	COLLEGE OF ST. BENEDICT	ST. JOSEPH	MN	56374
3	4	ST. OLAF COLLEGE	NORTHFIELD	MN	55057
3	4	COLLEGE OF SAINT THOMAS	ST. PAUL	MN	55105
3	4	UNIVERSITY OF WISCONSIN	WHITEWATER	WI	53190
3	5	BUENA VISTA COLLEGE	STORM LAKE	IA	50588
3	5	CENTRAL COLLEGE	PELLA	IA	50219
3	5	LORAS COLLEGE	DUBUQUE	IA	52001
3	5	LUTHER COLLEGE	DECORAH	IA	52101
3	5	NEBRASKA WESLEYAN UNIVERSITY	LINCOLN	NE	68504
3	5	SIMPSON COLLEGE	INDIANOLA	IA	50125
3	5	UPPER IOWA UNIVERSITY	FAYETTE	IA	52142
3	5	WARTBURG COLLEGE	WAVERLY	IA	50677
3	5	WILLIAM PENN COLLEGE	OSKALOOSA	IA	52577

Totals Women's Golf		Dist1	Dist2	Dist3	Dist4	Dist5	Dist6	Dist7	Dist8
DIVISION I	96	4	3	33	14	12	9	7	1
DIVISION II	15	1	0	3	4	6	0	1	0
DIVISION III	20	2	0	2	7	9	0	0	0
TOTAL INST.	131	7	3	38	27	28	9	8	1

10
CLOTHING

WHEN GOLF was becoming popularized in the late nineteenth century, men and women golfers were literally bound by fashion. They strove vainly to stretch their tee shots, all the while encumbered by early golf clothing.

Consider the plight of men golfers from 1875 to 1900. Weighed down by heavy tweed trousers and bulky, restrictive coats, they plodded down the fairways in clumsy shoes studded with hobnails, called "tackety boots." Atop their heads were bowlers and tams, an improvement over the top hats worn for matches at St. Andrews in 1850.

The more liberated men chose knickerbockers (which Americans call "knickers") and Norfolk jackets. The Norfolk jacket, originally designed for shooting, freed shoulder movement somewhat, but it was still a heavy, clumsy coat in which to swing a club. Long-sleeved shirts and knotted ties were standard golf wear.

Women golfers were even more encumbered. They sported stiff-collared white blouses with long muttonchop sleeves and pinned on straw boaters to hold their hair in place. Heavy, flowing skirts, often concealing a small bustle, were the fashion of the day. The long skirts posed a decided problem on a windy day so, with a little ingenuity, women devised a large elastic garter. The garter, called a "Miss Higgins," was worn around the waist, to be slipped down to knee level before hitting a shot to stop the skirt from billowing in the wind and obscuring the woman golfer's view of the ball.

By the 1920s and 1930s, most men played the game in knickerbockers and stockings. The long-sleeved shirts and ties remained, but sweaters offered greater swing freedom than the old jackets. Women of the era also adopted the sweater look. Their skirts, in length, were worn just below the mid-calf and were more formfitting, which eliminated the need for the graceless "Miss Higgins." Cloche hats were in fashion, or a brightly tasseled tam.

Golf fashions began to evolve into true sports clothes in the 1940s and 1950s. Short-sleeved shirts were accepted for both men and women. While men now wore pleated slacks, women at most clubs were required to wear skirts. Only in the late 1950s did country clubs begin to accept women striding off the tee in knee-length Bermuda shorts.

Two golfers helped hurry fashion evolution along: Jimmy Demaret, the flamboyant Texan, ordered slacks and shirts made of bright colors and lovely pastels previously suitable only for women. It wasn't long before other golfers caught on, and men soon stalked the fairway in brilliant yellows, pinks, and purples. Babe Zaharias, who had signed a contract with the Serbin clothing

> "Weighed down by heavy tweed trousers and bulky, restrictive coats, they plodded down the fairways in clumsy shoes studded with hobnails . . ."

Early golfers, like Walter Travis, played in heavy woven jackets, knickerbockers, and caps. (Courtesy Robert Kuntz)

company, helped design a golf dress for women featuring pleated sleeves and an elastic waistband for greater flexibility, with a good-sized detachable pocket in which to carry tees, markers, and balls.

And so, clothing manufacturers began to heed the requirements of the growing golf population for good-looking, flexible fashions designed of bright, durable fabrics that remained crisp, even after a round in the rain.

Today's golf-clothing companies offer a colorful array of clothing that never entered the dreams of early golfers. As we head into the 1990s, bright, bold fashions are the ticket. Men wear slacks or neatly constructed shorts. Women are decked out in all lengths of trousers—from shorts and knickers to finely tailored slacks. Shirts, sweatshirts, and sweaters are fashioned in a rainbow of hues and an assortment of bold patterns. Golf shoes are lighter, more durable, and better fitting. Stripes are big and bold, while cotton and cotton blends, cooler in summer weather, have made a comeback.

With the continued improvement in manufacturing and design, better golf fashions are ushering golfers into the twenty-first century and, no matter how high one's handicap, every golfer can look like a pro.

Golf Apparel Companies

A.M. Player
2322 Travers Avenue
Commerce, California 90040
(213) 888–2668

Men's apparel

Abel II Clothing
12785 S.W. Marie Court
Tigard, Oregon 97223
(503) 620–2070

Men's and women's apparel

Almorett, Inc.
1015 Baker Road
High Point, NC 27261
(919) 841–6777

Men's and women's apparel, rainwear, windbreakers

Antigua Sportswear, Inc.
9319 N. 94th Way
Scottsdale, Arizona 85258
(602) 860–1444

Men's and women's apparel, rainwear, windbreakers

Long skirts, long sleeves, and even bustles restricted the golf swing of early women players. (Courtesy Robert Kuntz)

Payne Stewart, winner of the 1989 PGA and noted for promoting National Football League licensed golf attire

The Apparel Group/Susan Carleton Golf
1309 N.W. 65th Pl.
Fort Lauderdale, FL 33309
(305) 968–7393

Women's apparel

Tommy Armour Golf Co.
8350 N. Lehigh Avenue
Morton Grove, IL 60053
(312) 966–6300

Men's and women's apparel

Ashworth Sportswear
2613 Temple Heights Dr. F
Oceanside, CA 92056
(619) 726–8924

Men's apparel

Aureus Ltd./Aureas-Ladies
P.O. Drawer A
W. Pittston, PA 18643
(800) 233–7100

Men's & women's apparel, hats, caps, visors

Areus Outerwear
Wiman Mfg. 2915 Niagara Ln.
Plymouth, MN 55441
(800) 522–5093

Rainwear and windbreakers

B.D. Baggies
1370 Avenue of the Americas
New York, NY 10019
(800) 223–6034

Men's Apparel

B.J. Designs Ltd.
136 Oak Drive
Syosset, NY 11791
(516) 496–8555

Men's and women's apparel, hats, caps, visors

Baja Activewear, Inc.
3012 Avenue E East
Arlington, TX 76011
(800) 367–2252

Men's apparel

Barrett Marketing
GOLF FANTASTIC INC.
6637 N. Sidney Place
Glendale, WI 53209
(414) 351–7070

Men's and women's apparel

Belding Sports
1621 Emerson Avenue
Oxnard, CA 93033
(800) 521–6197

Rainwear and windbreakers

Ben Hogan Co.
2912 West Pafford St.
Fort Worth, TX 76110
(817) 921–2661

Men's and women's apparel, hats, caps, visors

"Billie" Ross of the Palm Beaches
1981 Tenth Avenue North
Lake Worth, FL 33461
Mailing: P.O. Box 5678
Lake Worth, FL 33466
(407) 582–2853

Gloves, hats, caps, visors, oversize T-shirts

Boast, Inc.
5700 Columbia Circle
Mangonia Park, FL 33407
(800) 327–7666

Men's and women's apparel, rainwear, windbreakers, outerwear

Bobby Jones Sportswear by Hickey-Freeman
1290 Sixth Avenue
New York, NY 10104
(212) 237–1350

Men's apparel, rainwear

Bogner of America, Inc.
Bogner Drive
Newport, VT 05855
(800) 451–4417

Men's apparel, hats, caps, visors, rainwear, windbreakers

Braemar Sportswear
One San Jose Place, Suite 14
Jacksonville, FL 32257
(904) 262–1396

Men's and women's apparel

British American Golf Co.
11554 Salinaz Drive
Garden Grove, CA 92643
(714) 534–1200

Men's and women's apparel

CTI
17150 Newhope 607
Fountain Valley, CA 92708
(714) 557–2510

Men's and women's apparel, hats, caps, visors, shoes, children's apparel

Cagle Ltd.
2686 Dawson Ave.
Long Beach, CA 90806
(213) 426–7475

Men's and women's apparel

Cali-Fame of Los Angeles
2800 E. 11th St.
Los Angeles, CA 90023
(213) 268–3187

Hats, caps, visors, rainwear, windbreakers

Camp Hosiery
4503 Woodhaven
Marietta, GA 30067
(404) 977–2114

Men's Apparel

Darlyn Designs, Inc.
14345 Commerce Drive
Garden Grove, CA 92643
(714) 554–0254

Women's apparel

David Smith Co.
48 Main Street
North Reading, MA 01864
(508) 664–3600

Women's Apparel

Dee Lee's California Designs
13023 B Los Nietos Road
Santa Fe Springs, CA 90670

Hats, caps, visors

Derby Cap
P.O. Box 34220
Louisville, KY 40232
(502) 587–8495

Hats, caps, visors

Dexter Shoe Co.
1230 Washington Street
West Newton, MA 02165
(617) 332–4300

Shoes

Different Strokes
5244 E. Pine
Fresno, CA 93727
(209) 252–8881
(800)238–6335

Men's apparel, hats, caps, visors

Difini Ltd.
4 Eastern
Newport, VT 05855
(802) 334–7958

Men's and women's apparel

Divots Sportswear Co.
6900 Peachtree Ind. Boulevard
Norcross, GA 30071
(404) 447–4800

Men's and women's apparel

> *"Heavy, flowing skirts, often concealing a small bustle, were the fashion of the day."*

Elaine Benedict
3050 NW 40th St.
Miami, FL 33142
(305) 634–0463

Women's apparel

Etonic, Inc.
147 Centre Street
Brockton, MA 02403
(508) 583–9100

Men's and women's apparel, gloves, shoes

Evergood Lee Co.
9235 Greenleaf Ave.
Santa Fe Springs, CA 90670
(213) 946–5824

Men's apparel, hats, caps, visors, rainwear, windbreakers

FTM Sports/Cactus Golf
12118 SW 117 Court
Miami, FL 33186
(305) 225–2272
(800) 292–5589

Men's and women's apparel, rainwear, windbreakers

Foot-Joy, Inc.
144 Field Street
Brockton, MA 02402
(800) 333–4200

Gloves, shoes

Forrester's
1875 S.E. Belmont
Portland, OR 97214
(503) 230–9480

Rainwear, windbreakers

Gean-Edwards, Inc.
230 N. Mechanic St.
Princeton, WI 54968
(800) 558–6565

Men's and women's apparel

Golden Golf
9794 Forest Lane, Suite 726
Dallas, TX 75243
(214) 881–2662

Women's apparel, hats, caps, visors

Golf Bum by Innovation
3609 Thousand Oaks Boulevard 120
Westlake Village, CA 91362
(805) 373–5913

Men's & women's apparel, hats, caps, visors

Golf Couture
6550 Monero Drive
Rancho Palos Verdes, CA 90274
(213) 541–4425

Women's apparel

Golfaholics Anonymous
P.O. Box 222357
Carmel, CA 93922
(408) 624–4386
(800) 444–8813

Men's & women's apparel, hats, caps, visors

Haggar Golf Slacks
E. R. Fredricks Co. Inc.
4010 Morena Blvd., Suite 107
San Diego, CA 92117
(619) 272–6900

Men's apparel

Hamilton Tailoring Co.
490 E. McMillan St.
Cincinnati, Ohio 45206
(513) 961–0200

Men's and women's apparel

Harris Casuals
110 W. 11th
Los Angeles, CA 90015
(213) 749–5066

Men's apparel

Head Sportswear
9189 Red Branch Road
Columbia, MD 21045
(301) 730–8300

Men's & women's apparel

Imperial Headwear
5200 East Evans
Denver, CO 80222–5222
(303) 757–1166
(800) 432–3932

Hats, caps, visors

Izod Lacoste Golf & Tennis
Rt. 183, Airport Industrial Park
P.O. Box 15206
Reading, PA 19612–5206
(215) 374–4242

Men's and women's apparel, hats, caps, visors, rainwear, windbreakers

Jaccar of California
3001 South Croddy Way
Santa Ana, CA 92704
(714) 957–3300

Men's apparel

Jasper Classics by Jasper Textiles
One Classic Drive
Whiteville, NC 28472
(919) 642–0130
(800) 262–7408

Men's apparel

Jean Bell Collections
481 Shelton Ave.
Hamden, CT 06517
(203) 865–1137

Women's apparel

Jerri Sportswear
317 N. 11th Street, Suite 270
St. Louis, Missouri 63101
(314) 993–2902

Women's apparel

Johnston & Murphy Shoe Co. (Kasimatis Assoc.)
Nashville, TN 37202
(615) 367–8101

Shoes

Kangol Headwear Inc.
3 Westchester Plaza
Elmsford, NY 10523
(914) 592–2595

Hats, caps, visors

Karsten Mfg. Corp.—Ping
2201 West Desert Cove
Phoenix, AZ 85029
(602) 277–1300

Men's and women's apparel, hats, caps, visors

L & T Sales
42280 Beacon Hill, Suite D3
Palm Desert, CA 92260
(619) 341–4560

Men's apparel, hats, caps, visors, rainwear, windbreakers

La Mode
13301 South Main St.
Los Angeles, CA 90061
(213) 327–5188

Men's and women's apparel, hats, caps, visors, rainwear, windbreakers

Larlen-Dache, Inc.
3102 W. Alton Ave.
Santa Ana, CA 92704
(800) 322–4352

Men's and women's apparel

Lee Ann of California
1960 Peacock Blvd.
Oceanside, CA 92054
(619) 945–5366

Women's apparel

Leon Levin
1411 Broadway 32
New York, NY 10018
(212) 575–1900

Women's apparel

Lily's of Beverly Hills, Ltd.
12905 S. Spring Street
Los Angeles, CA 90061
(213) 770–0303
(800) 421–4474

Women's apparel

Line-up for Sport
15445-C Red Hill Avenue
Tustin, CA 92680
(714) 259–8155
(800) 654–6773

Men's and women's apparel

Lyle and Scott and Michael Thomas
101 County Avenue
Secaucus, NJ 07094
(201) 330–8122

Men's apparel

MacGregor Golf Co.
1601 South Slappey Boulevard
Albany, GA 31707
(912) 888–0001

Men's and women's apparel, hats, caps, visors, rainwear, windbreakers

Maggie R., Inc.
7701 East Gray A
Scottsdale, AZ 85260
(602) 951–3313

Men's and women's apparel

Magic Threads Inc.
292 4th St.
Oakland, CA 93607
(415) 465–5456

Men's and women's apparel

Marcia Originals
18324-3 Oxnard St.
Tarzana, CA 91356
(818) 881–3588

Women's apparel

Michele Palmer, Inc.
P.O. Box 1100
Greenville, NC 27834
(919) 756–1044

Women's apparel

Miller Golf Inc.
11 Commerce Road
Rockland, MA 02370
(617) 871–6400

Men's apparel, hats, caps, visors, rainwear, windbreakers

Mobile Pro Shop West
1116 Valencia Ave.
Fullerton, CA 92631
(714) 738–4673
(800) 241–2211

Men's and women's apparel, hats, caps, visors, rainwear, windbreakers

Natty
25111 Normandie
Harbor City, CA 90710
(213) 530–0222

Women's apparel

Needleworks Creations
453 E. Pine St.
Millersburg, PA 17061
(717) 692-2144

Men's and women's apparel

Nike, Inc.
9000 S.W. Nimbus
Beaverton, OR 97005
(503) 644-9000

Men's and women's apparel, hats, caps, visors, shoes

PGA Book & Gift Shop
100 Avenue of the Champions
Palm Beach Gardens, FL 33410
(407) 624-8535

Men's and women's apparel, hats, caps, visors, rainwear, windbreakers

Palm Springs Golf Co., Inc.
74-824 Lennon Place
Palm Desert, CA 92260
(619) 341-3220

Men's apparel, hats, caps, visors

Parcue, Inc. (Parcours)
849 S. Broadway
Los Angeles, CA 90014
(213) 612-0150

Women's apparel

Pickering/The Kimberton Co.
P.O. Box 599
Corner Lincoln/Walnut Sts.
Phoenixville, PA 19460
(215) 933-8985

Men's and women's apparel

Player's Design, Inc.
103 Kanawha St.
Fort Mill, SC 29715
(803) 547-5552

Pro Image
2086B Walsh Avenue
Santa Clara, CA 95050
(408) 986-1888
(800) 367-9698 Outside California

Women's apparel, hats, caps, visors

Property of Cora Lee Parsons
Box 2135, 1580 Monrovia Ave.
Newport Beach, CA 92663
(714) 642-2666

Men's and women's apparel

Quality Mills
P.O. Drawer 1107
Mount Airy, NC 27030
(919) 789-6161

Men's and women's apparel

Quantum Sportswear, Ltd.
10 East 32nd Street
New York, NY 10016
(212) 679-8060
(800) 232-8060, (800) 332-8060

Women's apparel

R.A.K. Enterprises
25 Tuna Puna
Coronado, CA 92118
(619) 424-7113

Women's apparel

Rainbow Sports/Silver Fox Sportswear
22500 S. Vermont Ave.
Torrance, CA 90502
(213) 328-8418

Men's and women's apparel, hats, caps, visors, rainwear, windbreakers

Ram Golf Corp.
2020 Indian Boundary Drive
Melrose Park, IL 60160
(312) 681-5800
(800) TEE-GOLF

Men's apparel, hats, caps, visors, rainwear, windbreakers

"Two golfers helped hurry fashion evolution along: Jimmy Demaret . . . and Babe Zaharias."

Reebok International
150 Royall Street
Canton, MA 02021
(617) 821–2800

Men's apparel, shoes

Resortowels, Inc.
4115 Silver Avenue S.E.
Albuquerque, NM 87108
(505) 265–4771
(800) 444–4771

*Men's and women's apparel, hats, caps, visors,
rainwear, windbreakers*

Ruff Hewn (Kasimatis Assoc.)
827 Herman Ct.
High Point, NC 27261
(919) 434–5111

Sahara Sportswear
241 Artcraft Road
El Paso, TX 79932
(915) 833–1145

*Men's and women's apparel, hats, caps, visors,
rainwear, windbreakers*

St. Croix
301 North Rampart, Suite E
Orange, CA 92668
(714) 634–9277

Men's apparel

Signature Tour Quality Footwear
1100 East Main Street
Endicott, NY 13760
(800) 321–2111

Shoes, socks

Sir Christopher Hatton
42 North Madison Avenue
Pasadena, CA 91101
(818) 304–0675

Men's and women's apparel

> *"Today's golf clothing companies offer a
> colorful array of clothing that never
> entered the dreams of early golfers."*

**Slazenger Golf USA/Davie Geoffrey &
Associates**
P.O. Box 7259
Greenville, SC 29610
(803) 295–4444

Men's apparel

Sporthomson
2 Ravinia Drive, Suite 1300
Atlanta, GA 30346
(404) 390–7480

Men's apparel

The Sporting House
P.O. Box 468
Vashon, WA 98070
(206) 463–2563

Women's apparel

Staco Enterprises, Inc.
P.O. Box 12511
Overland Park, KS 66212
(800) 282–0042

Men's and women's apparel, hats, caps, visors

Ste-Mak/United Golf Corp. of America
2110 South Ankeny Blvd.
Ankeny, Iowa 50021
(515) 964–6733

Men's and women's apparel

**Sun-Day Sports
(Imperial Headwear)**
5200 East Evans
Denver, CO 80222–5222
(602) 581–0091
(800) 345–8983

Hats, caps, visors

Sun-Daze By Nancy Haley
883 Parfet St. 3J
Golden, CO 80215
(303) 232–4647

Women's apparel

Tall Active Sportswear
3300 N.W. 41st Street
Miami, FL 33142
(305) 638–2650

Men's and women's apparel

Texaco Corp.
402 West Nueva
San Antonio, TX 78285–2800
(512) 227–7551

Hats, caps, visors

Tiger Shark Golf Co.
1682 Sabovich Street
Mojave, CA 93501
(800) 824–4551, (800) 654–9892
(800) 533–6294 in California.

Hats, caps, visors

Titleist Golf Division/Acushnet Co.
P.O. Box B 965
New Bedford, MA 02741
(508) 997–2811

Men's apparel, hats, caps, visors

Varela Slacks Inc.
1161 E. 12th St.
Los Angeles, CA 90021
(213) 627–0767

Men's and women's apparel

Virgin of Scottsdale
2115 East Cedar 4
Tempe, AZ 85281
(602) 966–6444

Men's and women's apparel

Whims by Natalie
121 E. 6th St. 101
Los Angeles, CA 90014
(213) 622–9412

Women's apparel, hats, caps, visors

Whitfield & Bridges
481 Shelton Avenue
Hamden, CT 06517
(203) 865–1137

Men's apparel

Whitney Lewis Golf Designs
4248 Sunset View Dr.
Salt Lake City, UT 84124
(801) 272–6304

Men's and women's apparel

Wilson Sporting Goods Co., Inc.
2233 West St.
Rivergrove, IL 60171
(312) 456–6100

Men's and women's apparel, hats, caps, visors

Yonex Corp.
350 Maple Avenue
Torrance, CA 90503
(213) 533–6014

Hats, caps, visors

11

EQUIPMENT

I N THE last decade, golf equipment companies have introduced a mind-boggling assortment of new products.

The results of space-age technology—brightly colored golf balls, metal "woods," composite shafts, and beryllium-copper club heads—have made their way to the pro-shop racks. The various properties of each are the subject of hot debate.

In golf, however, we might revise an old axiom to say that *very little* is new under the sun.

To protect the game and standards of play, the USGA and the Royal and Ancient, golf's custodians of equipment standards, have strict guidelines for the design of golf clubs and balls. Manufacturers have very little latitude in the physical design of equipment. Where they do have leeway is in the materials they use and in cosmetic design. A number of recent innovations, however, are simply recycled ideas.

Those orange or yellow golf balls, for example. They became so popular in the 1980s that by 1986 they made up about 40 percent of total golf ball sales. New? Not quite. Wilson Sporting Goods, which was then called Wilson-Western Sporting Goods Company, first introduced the brightly colored golf ball in 1928. Both the Hol-Hi and the Dura-Dist were available in "Oriole Orange" and "Canary Yellow."

"Color—means fewer lost golf balls," Wilson proclaimed in its advertising.

The idea didn't catch on in the late 1920s.

In 1981, however, Wilson reintroduced the rainbow-hued sphere and the rest is history.

Metal woods first came into the game nearly 100 years ago. In 1896, the Standard Golf Company of Sunderland, England, manufactured a popular line of aluminum-headed fairway woods. These old clubs today have nearly as much market value as that metal-headed driver you picked out last week in your pro shop—collectors will pay as much as $250 for a vintage aluminum wood. Because of their durability, aluminum-headed woods were also popular in the 1950s at driving ranges.

A number of today's top pros use composite shafts, like graphite over steel. This idea, of combining materials for club shafts of greater consistency and strength, was introduced in the late 1920s.

The U.S. Golf Manufacturing Company in Westfield, Massachusetts, produced a club shaft with an inner core of steel, a second layer of hickory, and an outer layer of bamboo.

U.S. Golf advertised, "We guarantee 10 to 25 yards more on your drive," when promoting the new shafts. Sound familiar?

Shafts made of fiberglass or aluminum appeared in the 1960s.

Today, beryllium copper irons retail for as much as $1,400 a set. Most manufacturers tout the softer "feel" of the copper club face. In 1955, MacGregor Golf Company introduced the copper-faced iron with pretty much the same sales pitch, claiming that the softer copper plating enabled "the club

One early golf ball was made of "maponite," a composition ball of gutta-percha and cork. Here, factory workers packed maponite balls for shipping in about 1900. (Courtesy Robert Kuntz)

head to literally 'grab' the ball and throw it accurately toward the cup."

While there are almost no differences in the basic design of golf clubs in the last century, improved technology and new, more durable, materials at least guarantee that today's golf equipment will last longer and be of more consistent quality.

Ben Hogan, a stickler for any small detail that would help his game, tested the uniformity of his golf balls by passing them through a ring. Today's golf balls get the ring test at the factory. Manufacturing techniques are much improved, and the golf balls you buy over the counter would have

passed the strictest criteria of tournament players thirty years ago.

The Shakespeare Golf Company was on to something with its fiberglass shafts in the 1960s. The shafts had good feel and sprang into the hitting area with a little extra kick. Today we have better materials for shafts. They can provide that kick, but the torque— the way the club head and shaft twist—is more consistent. *Timing* the kick of the club head into the ball is not the problem it once was with an exotic shaft.

Today's golf clubs are better balanced, and the changes in weight distribution on the club head are perhaps the most lasting

innovation in the modern game. Heel-toe-weighted putters have already proven their staying power. One of the most innovative designs is the relatively new perimeter weighting of club heads.

Traditional irons have compact clubheads with the weight massed behind the hitting area. Perimeter-weighted irons are cavity backed, with the weight distributed around the edges of the club head. This engineering technique is of great advantage to the high- and middle-range handicapper. The "sweet spot" is much larger, and it's much easier to get the ball consistently airborne.

Many of the younger playing profession-als now use perimeter-weighted irons. Some of the more established players, those who like to work the ball instead of hitting a consistently high shot right to the flagstick, say that perimeter weighting limits their variety of shots. They claim that it's more difficult to move the ball from left to right, or from right to left, with these irons. Because the irons are designed to get the ball airborne, it's also difficult to hit a low shot, some players claim.

Perimeter-weighted metal woods are also in favor. The larger sweet spot means less loss of distance on off-center hits.

Shaft consistency is another area of prog-

Early club making was primitive by today's standards. Here, an early Scottish "cleekmaker" pounds out an iron head on an anvil. (Courtesy Robert Kuntz)

ress. Improved technology means that tolerances are so closely matched that a player can get the same feel throughout an entire set of clubs. Better manufacturing techniques also mean that the flex point, that point of the shaft that provides the "kick," is consistently distributed throughout an entire set.

Today's great debate centers on whether the new equipment has made the game any easier. Do the new golf balls, which are now pushing the edge of the envelope of legal liveliness, fly farther? Do high-tech shafts and club heads yield greater distance than the traditional steel-and-persimmon combination? Will today's golf courses become obsolete? Will playing pros consistently break the scoring barriers?

In 1987, the United States Golf Association conducted driving-distance surveys at the U.S. Open and compared them to driving distances at the 1966 U.S. Open. What gives this test more credibility than most is that, in 1966 and 1987, the tests were conducted at the same U.S. Open site, the Olympic Club in San Francisco. Conditions were virtually identical: the game's top players, under championship pressure, trying to maneuver the golf ball around an Open course. The average driving distance of both groups—some twenty years apart—was the same.

In 1989 the USGA conducted a survey at the U.S. Open at Oak Hill Country Club to determine if players using metal woods drove the ball farther than players using persimmon woods. The survey included eighty-nine players who used metal drivers, and sixty-six using wood drivers. The drivers were measured on Oak Hill rain-soaked fairways, which provided almost no roll.

Drives were measured on two holes each day. Again, the average driving distance was 251.8 yards. Players using wood drivers hit the ball an average 252.5 yards.

The longest drive, incidentally, was 295 yards by Ian Woosnam, who used a wood driver.

Perhaps the only true test of golf equipment is finding a set of clubs and using a brand of ball, that "feels" right for you. That's why it's important to test a set of clubs before you buy them. If they're too heavy, or too light, you'll feel it and you'll be able to tell by the results you get.

In the end, perhaps the best innovation in golf equipment is the fact that we have many more models from which to choose. This variety and availability of equipment gives each golfer a better chance of finding the set of clubs that feels just right.

Golf Equipment: Products and Companies

Accuform Golf Ltd.
76 Fordhouse Boulevard
Toronto, Ontario, Canada, M8Z5X7
(800) 668–7873

Clubs and putters
Irons: Accuform PTM, Cavity Back
Woods: Original, Accuform

Modern golf equipment at a typical pro shop (Courtesy PGA of America)

Allied Golf Corp.
4538 W. Fullerton Ave.
Chicago, IL 60639
(312) 772–7710

Irons: Tour Model, Pro Design, Colonial, Reliant
Woods: Premium Series, Tour Grade
Women's Clubs: Regal Lady, Pro Tradition

Tommy Armour Golf Co.
8350 N. Lehigh Ave.
Morton Grove, IL 60053
(312) 966–6300

Irons: Silver Scot 986, Silver Scot 845, Golden Scot
845, T-Line, E.Q.L., Concept 2
Woods: Silver Scot 986, Concept 2, E.Q.L., Golden
Scot, Silver Scot 835, T-Line
Women's Clubs: Butterfly

Bel Air Golf Co.
235 East Gardena Blvd., Bldg. 8
Carson, CA 90746
(213) 373–8411

Irons: BE-CU 32, BAI-300
Woods: BASW-300D, BABW-300D, Cast Persimmon
Women's Clubs: TS-600, TML-100

Ben Hogan Co.
2912 West Pafford St.
Fort Worth, TX 76110
(817) 921–2661

Irons: Apex, Hogan Edge, Radial
Woods: Apex, Radial, Series 56
Women's Clubs: Lady Hogan

Cleveland Classics
14508 South Garfield Avenue
Paramount, CA 90723
(213) 630–6363

Irons: Tour Action 588T, Tour ActionP
Woods: TA588, AL44, TC15, DG43, RC85, Tour
Action Classic
Women's Clubs: Tour Action 588

Cobra Golf Inc. II
4645 North Avenue
Oceanside, CA 92056
(619) 941–9550
(800) /BAFFLER

Irons: Baffler Blade II, Aluminum Bronze, Super Senior
Woods: Persimmon, Baffler Steel Classics, Super
Senior, Traditional
Women's Clubs: Lady Cobra Baffler Blade, Lady
Cobra Steel, Lady Cobra Carbon

Compass Golf Products Inc.
17443 Mount Clifford Circle
Fountain Valley, CA 92708
(714) 557–6090
(800) 322–4653

Irons: Sensation, Tour Sight, Tour Preferred
Woods: Sensation, Tour Sight, Tour Preferred

Daiwa
7421 Chapman Avenue
Garden Grove, CA 92641
(714) 895–6689

Irons: Advisor 8601G, Advisor G.O.H., Hi-Trac,
Exceler II
Woods: DB 622, Hi-Trac, Exceler Whisker, Exceler
BPT
Women's Clubs: Cat's Eye

Dunlop Golf Division
P.O. Box 3070, 131 Fall St.
Greenville, SC 29602
(803) 241–2200
(800) 476–5400

Irons: Maxfli Pro Special, Maxfli Tour Ltd., Maxfli
Missile, Max 357
Woods: Maxfli Pro Special, Maxfli Tour Ltd., Maxfli
Missile, Max 357
Women's Clubs: Jan Stephenson

FTM Sports/Cactus Golf
12118 SW 117 Court
Miami, FL 33186
(305) 225–2272
(800) 292–5589 Outside Florida

Irons: Bronze Exclusive, CG 8840, Mastertrack
Woods: Cactus Blaster, Mastertrack, CG8840
Women's Clubs: Classic Edition

Karsten Mfg. Corp.—PING
2201 West Desert Cove
Phoenix, AZ 85029
(602) 277–1300

Irons: Ping Eye-2
Woods: Ping Eye-2

Langert Golf Co., Inc.
5115 Avenida Encinas
Carlsbad, CA 92008
(619) 438–4100

Woods: Tour De Force, Foiler Series

Louisville Golf Club Co., Inc.
2601 Grassland Drive
Louisville, KY 40299
(502) 491–1631

Irons: Select
Woods: Classic 50's, Wood Niblick, Select

Lynx Golf Inc.
16017 E. Valley Blvd.
City of Industry, CA 91749
(818) 961–0222

Irons: Parallax, Predator G
Woods: USA Tour, Parallax, Predator G
Women's Clubs: Tigress G, Tigress SP

MacGregor Golf Co.
1601 South Slappey Boulevard
Albany, GA 31707
(912) 888–0001

Irons: Nicklaus Muirfield, Tourney, RPM, CG1800
Woods: MacGregor M-88, CG1800, Muirfield 20th, Tourney
Women's Clubs: Lady CG1800, Lady Tourney, Lady MacGregor

Mizuno Golf
5125 Peachtree Industrial Blvd.
Norcross, GA 30092
(404) 441–5553

Irons: MS-7, MS-8, MS-9 Altron, MGC-35, Black Turbo II, Trump
Woods: MS-8, Altron, MST, MGC-35, Trump, Wings, Black Turbo, Turbo El, Black Turbo II, Turbo Pro, Turbo LX
Women's Clubs: MIZ

Oregon Golf International
100–8103 NE Killingsworth
Portland, OR 97218
(800) 262–8143

Irons: Phoenix Two, Phoenix Legend
Woods: Oregon Classic, Phoenix Classic, Phoenix Legend, Jumbo 7fore7, Phoenix Two

Pal Joey Golf
99 South Pine Street
Newark, Ohio 43055
(614) 334–6811
(800) 358–9881

Irons: Pal Joey, TD-1000, Tour Series
Woods: P.J. Collection, Tour Series, Copperhead

Palm Springs Golf Co.
74-824 Lennon Place
Palm Desert, CA 92260
(619) 341–3220

Irons: Forged, TRD, Diamond, Step Weighted, Gravity Balance, Desert Classic, Unique Standard
Woods: Laminated, Tour Series, Metal Woods
Women's Clubs: Lady Diamond, Desert Princess, Lady Unique Gold, Lady Unique

Penna Golf Co.
400 Toney Penna Drive
Jupiter, FL 33458
(407) 746–5146
(800) 327–1843

Irons: Penna Original, Penna Stainless
Woods: T.P. Model 88, T.P. Model 85, T.P. Cobalt, T.P.

Ram Golf Corp.
2020 Indian Boundary Drive
Melrose Park, IL 60160
(800) TEE GOLF

Irons: Golden Ram, Axial, Laser X-2
Woods: Golden Ram Tour, Axial, Tour Series, Laser X-2
Women's Clubs: Lady Laser, Golden Girl

Reflex Inc.
14435 N. Scottsdale Road, Suite 200
Scottsdale, AZ 85254
(602) 948–4295

Irons: Tourhawk-Raptor, Prohawk
Woods: Tourhawk-Raptor, Prohawk

Slazenger Golf USA/Davie Geoffrey & Assoc.
P.O. Box 7259
Greenville, SC 29610
(803) 295–4444

Irons: Crown Limited, Royal Panther, Panther B.C.
Woods: Crown Limited, Royal Panther, Crown Sterling

Slotline Golf
5252 McFadden Ave.
Huntington Beach, CA 92649
(714) 898–2888

Irons: Inertial E-Max
Woods: Inertial E-Max
Women's Clubs: Lady Rampant

Spalding Sports Worldwide
425 Meadow Street
Chicopee, MA 01021
(413) 536–1200

Irons: Tour Edition, Cannon Advance, Executive
Woods: Tour Edition, Executive, Top Flite XL,
Executive

Stan Thompson Golf Club Co.
2707 South Fairfax Ave.
Culver City, CA 90232
(213) 870–7228

Irons: Ginty II, ST-50, RC-20X, HT-431
Woods: RC-20X, Original Ginty, Top Gun, Ginty II,
HT-431, Ginty, ST-50
Women's Clubs: Lady Thompson

Taylor Made Golf Co.
2271 Cosmos Court
Carlsbad, CA 92009
(619) 931–1991

Irons: Tour Preferred
Woods: Tour Preferred, Pittsburgh Persimmon, Tour
Cleek Series

Tiger Shark Golf Co.
1682 Sabovich Street
Mojave, CA 93501
(800) 824–4551
(800) 654–9892
(800) 533–6294 in California

Irons: Great White
Woods: Tiger Shark, Great White

Titleist Golf Division
ACUSHNET CO.
P.O. Box B 965
New Bedford, MA 02741
(508) 997–2811

Irons: Tour Model, DTR
Woods: Tour Model, Titleist Metal

Ryobi-Toski Corp.
160 Essex St.
Newark, Ohio 43055
(800) 848–2975
(800) 824–6691 in Ohio

Irons: Target, Perfect Match, Unifix, Target B.C.,
Perfect Match, Swing Print
Woods: Target, Perfect Match, Unifix, Swing Print

Wilson Sporting Goods Co.
2233 West St.
River Grove, IL 60171
(312) 456–6100

Irons: Staff, 1200 Gear Effect, Staff Gooseneck, X31
Woods: Staff, 1200 Gear Effect, X31, 1200 LT, The
Whale, Ultra, 1200 LT, Aggressor
Women's Clubs: Patty Berg Cup Defender, Juli
Inkster

Yamaha Corp. of America
6722 Orangethorpe Ave.
Buena Park, CA 90602
(714) 522–9227

Irons: SX-25, Secret, Accurace
Woods: Hal Sutton, Accurace, X-200, EOS, Ex-Gold
Kevlar
Women's Clubs: X-101

Yonex Corp.
350 Maple Ave.
Torrance, CA 90503
(213) 533–6014

Irons: Tournament SP, Boroniron, Graphlex,
Carboniron, SX-25, Secret, Accurace
Woods: Boronwood, Graphlex, Carbonex II,
Carbonex 22, Hal Sutton, Accurace, X-200, EOS,
Ex-Gold Kevlar
Women's Clubs: Carboniron FL, Carbonex FL, X-101

12
GAMES AND SOFTWARE

COMPUTER SOFTWARE is rapidly finding a solid niche in the game of golf. There is software for the business of golf and software for golf services. For additional information on software for golf services, see Chapter 15, Services.

Of chief interest, naturally, is software that has been designed to help golfers analyze, and perhaps improve, their games.

This last development is a part of the golf handicapping software provided by a number of budding businesses. Smyth Business Systems of Canton, Ohio, for example, offers three computer software systems: a handicapping program, a pro shop program, and a club program. In the Smyth handicapping software program, golfers at a customer club turn in their scores and they are tabulated into handicaps, but the software system can provide a much more detailed profile of each golfer's game. Now any club can provide the same hole-by-hole stats that are analyzed in professional golf—the system records a golfer's number of birdies, percentage of fairways hit, percentage of greens in regulation, putting averages, and driving distance.

A number of software programs offer business systems for the club professional. Depending upon the sophistication of the system, software helps the club pro set up club tournaments, control inventory, do accounting and billing, and issue gift certificates. Software can also be a great aid to pro-shop sales. The Smyth system, for example, includes demographic profiles of a club's membership, recording clothing sizes for each member, their buying history, locker number, and even birthdays. The information can be invaluable to a professional. The club pro can notify a member that the shop's upcoming sale includes an overabundance of shirts in that member's size, or that a new shipment of the member's preferred D-2 swingweight irons with regular shafts will arrive the following week.

Another computer and software company, Logical Solutions of Carollton, Texas, spent eight years developing a software program for the PGA of America. Like the other companies, Logical Solutions offers a program that is a management system for country clubs. The program handles billing, payroll, food and beverage analysis, membership profiling for planning special events, general accounting, and other services.

Some club software programs can be tied into the pro shop system and handicapping system.

Video systems and tapes designed for golf instruction, like those produced by Sony and Golftek, have also become valuable teaching tools for golf professionals. Sources for professionals are listed below.

Not all video aids or computer software are designed for serious business. Accolade, of San Jose, California, has designed a computer golf game called "Jack Nicklaus' Greatest 18 Holes of Major Championship Golf."

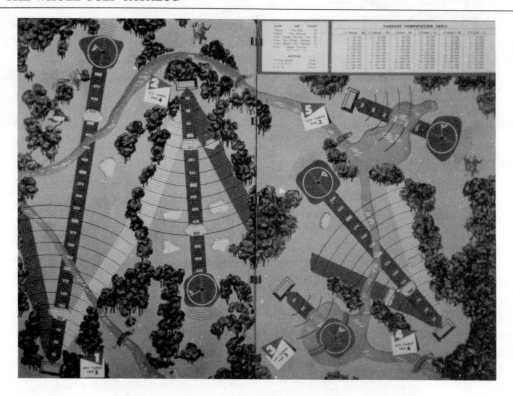

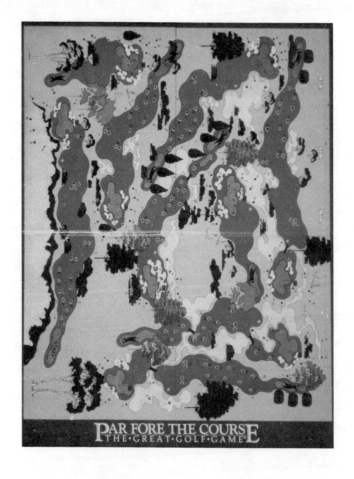

Nicklaus picked the eighteen most challenging holes from courses around the world on which he's played major championships. Two Nicklaus-designed layouts are included, giving the player three courses from which to choose.

In the game, Nicklaus is preprogrammed. You can tee it up against Jack, or take on your friends, or play in a foursome including Nicklaus.

The game includes a variety of weather and wind conditions. By pressing the computer key, the player controls distance and direction for every shot from the drive to the putts.

Hammacher Schlemmer has a Computer-Animated Hand-Held Golf Game, a smaller-scale course set up for one or two people. You determine club selection, the force and timing of the shot, and the ball is tracked on the viewing screen. Distance, strokes, player number, and hole number are on the readouts. Comes with a thirty-eight-page color course guide.

Golf-motif playing cards are a favorite gift item. The United States Golf Association offers classic sets of playing cards depicting traditional men and women golfers in early golf garb. The catalog service of the Ladies Professional Golf Association has a neat set of playing cards with the LPGA logo in green on white and white on green.

Another game/service is an aid for those who have trouble keeping score. To use the Links Computer Scorecard, sold by Hammacher Schlemmer of Fairfield, Ohio, the golfer logs the scorecard of the course to be played, including the stroke holes. The golfer then records the handicaps of playing companions. The Computer Scorecard keeps track of matches, scores in relation to par, birdies and bogeys, and net score. It's programmed in compliance with the USGA handicap system. Batteries are included.

Another company, U.S. Indoor Golf, of San Francisco, California, offers a coin-operated putting game.

The software industry and games companies have discovered golf but, although there's a wide assortment of new toys, the game is such that most golfers can still have a lot of fun putting on the living-room carpet.

Sources of Computer Software, Games, and Video Systems

Accolade
550 S. Winchester Blvd. Suite 200
San Jose, CA 95128

Nicklaus computer game

The Booklegger
13100 Grass Valley Avenue, Suite D
P.O. Box 2626
Grass Valley, CA 95945
(916) 272–1556
(800) 262–1556

Software, video systems, tapes

Country Club Systems
990 Fairport Office Park
Fairport, NY 14450
(716) 377–6730

Computer systems, software

Dunlop Golf Division
P.O. Box 3070, 131 Fall St.
Greenville, SC 29602
(803) 241–2200
(800) 476–5400

Video systems, tapes

Golftek
0203 3rd Street
Lewiston, Idaho 83501
(208) 743–9037

Video systems, tapes

"You determine club selection, the force and timing of the shot, and the ball is tracked on the viewing screen."

Hammacher Schlemmer
9180 LeSaint Drive
Fairfield, Ohio 45014
(800) 543–3366

Games

Logical Solutions
2217 Timberwood
Carrollton, TX 75006
(214) 387–8027

Software, computer systems

National Golf Foundation
1150 South U.S. Highway One
Jupiter, FL 33477
(407) 744–6006

Video systems, tapes

Smyth Business Systems
P.O. Box 8800
Canton, OH 44711
(800) 462–4372

Computer systems, software

Sony Corp. of America
One Sony Drive
Park Ridge, NJ 07656
(201) 930–7075

Video systems, tapes

Swing Check
12271 Monarch Street
Garden Grove, CA 92641
(714) 892–9000

Video systems, tapes

United States Golf Association Golf House
P.O. Box 2000
Far Hills, NJ 07931–9978
(800) 336–4446

Golf playing cards

U.S. Indoor Golf
229 Bush Street, Suite 660
San Francisco, CA 94104
(415) 781–1177

Golf simulation device, coin-operated putting games

Walker Direct Advertising Media
6008 Kirby Drive
Houston, TX 77005
(713) 666–8222

LPGA playing cards

"Now any club can provide the same hole-by-hole stats that are analyzed in professional golf—the system records a golfer's birdies, percentage of fairways hit, percentage of greens in regulation, putting averages, and driving distance."

13
KEY EVENTS

OVER THE years, golf fans as well as the great players have been enamored of golf's major events. In the Bob Jones era we became suddenly aware of the Grand Slam, Jones's combination of victories in the U.S. Open, the Open (more commonly called the British Open), the U.S. Amateur, and the British Amateur.

Later, when it was suspected that no amateur could ever again win those four championships in one lifetime, much less in one year, the players and press boosted the Masters, the U.S. Open, the Open, and the PGA Championship into major status and into the role of a modern grand slam. At this writing, no one has managed to win all four championships in one year. In fact, only four golfers—Jack Nicklaus, Ben Hogan, Gene Sarazen, and Gary Player—have captured all four titles during their careers.

On the women's side, the early majors were the U.S. Women's Open, the annual Titleholders' Championship (held at Augusta Country Club within hailing distance of Augusta National Golf Club, site of the Masters), and the Women's Western Open. When the Western Open folded after the 1967 event and the Titleholders was discontinued after 1972, the LPGA designated the rich Nabisco—Dinah Shore and the duMaurier Classic, a sort of Canadian women's open, as the third and fourth of the LPGA's majors.

These are all key championships, whether played among the graceful hills of Augusta,

the wave-thrashed cliffs of Pebble Beach, or under crystal-blue desert skies.

We remember them well. Who can forget Ben Hogan's dramatic 30 on Augusta's back nine? Or Jack Nicklaus's victory in the 1986 Masters, just when we thought the olden bear had ceased to roar? Or Tom Watson's

The four trophies of golf's major championships. At top, the trophies for the British Open, the PGA Championship, and the U.S. Open. The Masters trophy is in the foreground.

Mickey Wright, four-time U.S. Women's Open champion, is universally acclaimed for owning the game's greatest swing. (Courtesy LPGA)

Babe Didrickson Zaharias rose to fame as an Olympic track-and-field champion, then brought color and excitement to the fledgling LPGA Tour. (Courtesy Rhonda Glenn)

(Left to right) *Gene Sarazen, Ben Hogan, Gary Player, and Jack Nicklaus, the only four players to have won all four of golf's major championships: the U.S. Open, the British Open, the Masters, and the PGA Championship.*

holed chip shot at the Seventeenth at Pebble that clinched his U.S. Open title? Or Hollis Stacy's third Women's Open win at Salem? Or Laura Davies's pounding play at the 1987 Women's Open at Plainfield Country Club?

There is a special significance to these major championships. When Curtis Strange and Nick Faldo battled down over the final holes of the 1988 U.S. Open, ABC commentator Dave Marr expressed it so well when he said, "These are the afternoons you remember for the rest of your life."

Marr was speaking for the golfers. He might as well have been speaking for the fans.

As friends of the game, we glean stirring memories from these championships. As players, the winners claim a title that will belong to them forever. And yet, there are other majors, perhaps less heralded since they are so seldom televised, that put one player uniquely above the others. These are the national championships—the U.S. Amateur, the U.S. Women's Amateur, the amateur titles of Great Britain, and the national titles for the mid-amateurs, public links players, seniors, and juniors. There is no money here but these championships are

> ". . . only four golfers—Jack Nicklaus, Ben Hogan, Gene Sarazen, and Gary Player—have captured all four titles during their careers."

Liselotte Neumann, a graceful Swedish player, captured the championship cup at the 1988 U.S. Women's Open after a stirring final-round showdown with American Patty Sheehan. (Dost & Evans)

When Curtis Strange won his first U.S. Open title in 1988, he battled Nick Faldo over the final holes to go into a play-off. "These are the afternoons you remember for the rest of your life," said Dave Marr, ABC golf commentator, of that historic face-off. (Dost & Evans)

just as important as the Open. Win one of these, and the title is yours for life.

David Duval, seventeen, of Ponte Vedra Beach, Florida, summed it up after he won the 1989 U.S. Junior Boys Championship.

"It's like a British Open or a Masters," young Duval said. "Hey, when I'm dead, my name will still be in the record book. I guess it means I'm the best player under eighteen this year. It's just awesome to think about it."

While big championships yield great prestige, they also take a bigger toll in terms of emotional and physical endurance.

Golf writer Charles Price explained it by saying that while ordinary golf is like walking on the ground, tournament golf is like walking on a tightrope. Championship golf

is when they raise the rope sixty feet, Price said, and national championship golf is when they throw the net away.

In the last decade, there has been a startling boom in amateur competition. The number of traditional tournaments has remained fairly constant, but there has been great growth at both ends of the age spectrum—senior golf, mid-amateur golf (for those twenty-five and over), and junior golf.

"These are all key championships, whether played among the graceful hills of Augusta, the wave-thrashed cliffs of Pebble Beach, or under crystal-blue desert skies."

Fuzzy Zoeller captured the 1984 U.S. Open title after a playoff with Greg Norman. (Dost & Evans)

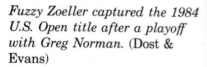

" 'These are the afternoons you remember for the rest of your life,' said ABC commentator Dave Marr."

According to the National Golf Foundation, which classifies as a senior any golfer age sixty or older, America boasts nearly 3.3 million senior players. The NGF also says that America has more than 2.4 million junior golfers. This growth in the number of players has triggered new tournaments for seniors, mid-amateurs, and juniors; golfers can tee it up competitively from ages eight to eighty.

One success story is the American Junior Golf Association tour. When the AJGA started in 1977, it sponsored two national junior events. In 1989, the AJGA scheduled twenty-seven tournaments in eighteen states and attracted more than 3,000 young golfers.

Another is the newest USGA-sponsored event, the U.S. Women's Mid-Amateur Championship for women twenty-five and older. The Women's Mid-Am kicked off in 1987 with 320 entries and drew 347 contestants in its second year in 1988.

And so, competitive golf, like the rest of the game, is booming. To recognize the best competitors, we've compiled charts of the men and women who have won the most major championships. Following that, you'll find a schedule with dates and playing sites for the key events of 1990. Two of the key LPGA events—the LPGA Championship and the duMaurier—are changing sites, and the golf courses for 1990 have yet to be determined.

Following the schedule are graphs showing the growth of senior and junior golf in the United States.

MEN'S VICTORIES IN MAJOR CHAMPIONSHIPS

Player	U.S. Open	U.S. Am.	Masters	British Open	Brit. Am.	PGA	Sr. Open	Mid Am.	Total
JACK NICKLAUS	4	2	6	3	0	5	0	0	20
BOB JONES	4	5	0	3	1	0	0	0	13
WALTER HAGEN	2	0	0	4	0	5	0	0	11
GARY PLAYER	1	0	3	3	0	2	2	0	11
JOHN BALL	0	0	0	1	8	0	0	0	9
BEN HOGAN	4	0	2	1	0	2	0	0	9
ARNOLD PALMER	1	1	4	2	0	0	1	0	9
TOM WATSON	1	0	2	5	0	0	0	0	8
HAROLD HILTON	0	1	0	2	4	0	0	0	7
GENE SARAZEN	2	0	1	1	0	3	0	0	7
SAM SNEAD	0	0	3	1	0	3	0	0	7
HARRY VARDON	1	0	0	6	0	0	0	0	7
LEE TREVINO	2	0	0	2	0	2	0	0	6
MICHAEL BONALLACK	0	0	0	0	5	0	0	0	5
JAMES BRAID	0	0	0	5	0	0	0	0	5
BYRON NELSON	1	0	2	0	0	2	0	0	5
JAY SIGEL	0	2	0	0	0	0	0	3	5
PETER THOMSON	0	0	0	5	0	0	0	0	5
JEROME TRAVERS	1	4	0	0	0	0	0	0	5
WILLIE ANDERSON	4	0	0	0	0	0	0	0	4
BILLY CASPER	2	0	1	0	0	0	1	0	4
LAWSON LITTLE	0	2	0	2	0	0	0	0	4
TOM MORRIS SR.	0	0	0	4	0	0	0	0	4
TOM MORRIS JR.	0	0	0	4	0	0	0	0	4
J.H. TAYLOR	0	0	0	4	0	0	0	0	4
WALTER TRAVIS	1	3	0	0	0	0	0	0	4

Schedule of Key Events: 1990

Event: The Masters
Date: April 5–8
Site: Augusta National Golf Club, Augusta, Georgia

Event: The U.S. Open Championship
Date: June 14–17
Site: Medinah Country Club, Medinah, Illinois

Event: The U.S. Women's Amateur Public Links Championship
Date: June 20–24
Site: Hyland Hills Golf Club, Westminster, Colorado

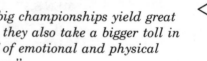

"While big championships yield great prestige, they also take a bigger toll in terms of of emotional and physical endurance."

JoAnne Carner has won more USGA Championships than any player except Bob Jones. Mrs. Carner won five U.S. Women's Amateur titles, two U.S. Women's Open Championships, and the U.S. Girls' Junior for eight victories in USGA events. Jones won nine. (Dost & Evans)

WOMEN'S VICTORIES IN MAJOR CHAMPIONSHIPS

	Player	U.S. Open	U.S. Am	LPGA	British Am	Dinah Shore	DuMarier	Title Holders	Western	Girls' Jr.	Sr. Am	Total
1.	PATTY BERG	1	1	0	0	0	0	7	7	0	0	16
2.	MICKEY WRIGHT	4	0	4	0	1	0	2	3	1	0	15
3.	LOUISE SUGGS	2	1	1	1	0	0	4	4	0	0	13
4.	BABE ZAHARIAS	3	1	0	1	0	0	3	4	0	0	12
5.	JOANNE CARNER	2	5	0	0	0	2	0	0	1	0	10
6.	BETSY RAWLS	4	0	2	0	0	0	0	2	0	0	8
7.	HOLLIS STACY	3	0	0	0	0	1	0	0	3	0	7
8.	KATHY WHITWORTH	0	0	3	0	1	0	2	1	0	0	7
9.	PAT BRADLEY	1	0	1	0	1	3	0	0	0	0	6
10.	JULI INKSTER	0	3	0	0	2	1	0	0	0	0	6
11.	NANCY LOPEZ	0	0	3	0	1	0	0	0	2	0	6
12.	GLENNA C. VARE	0	6	0	0	0	0	0	0	0	0	6
13.	AMY ALCOTT	1	0	0	0	2	1	0	0	1	0	5
14.	DONNA CAPONI	2	0	2	0	0	1	0	0	0	0	5
15.	CAROLYN CUDONE	0	0	0	0	0	0	0	0	0	5	5
16.	BETTY JAMESON	1	2	0	0	0	0	0	2	0	0	5
17.	DOROTHY PORTER	0	1	0	0	0	0	0	0	0	4	5
18.	ANN QUAST SANDER	0	3	0	1	0	0	0	0	0	1	5
19.	SUSIE M. BERNING	3	0	0	0	0	0	0	1	0	0	4
20.	SANDRA HAYNIE	1	0	2	0	0	1	0	0	0	0	4
21.	JOYCE WETHERED	0	0	0	4	0	0	0	0	0	0	4

" 'It's like a British Open or a Masters,' young Duval [a junior champion] said. 'Hey, when I'm dead, my name will still be in the record book. . . . It's just awesome to think about it.' "

Event: The duMaurier Classic
Date: June 25–July 1
Site: To be determined

Event: The U.S. Senior Open Championship
Date: June 28–July 1
Site: Ridgewood Country Club, Ridgewood, New Jersey

Event: The U.S. Women's Open Championship
Date: July 12–15
Site: Atlanta Athletic Club, Duluth, Georgia

Bobby Jones, winner of the 1930 United States Amateur (Courtesy USGA)

Event: The U.S. Amateur Public Links Championship
Date: July 16–21
Site: Eastmoreland Golf Club, Portland, Oregon

Event: The (British) Open
Date: July 19–22
Site: The Old Course, St. Andrews, Scotland

Event: The U.S. Junior Amateur Championship
Date: July 24–28
Site: Lake Merced Golf & Country Club, Daly City, California

Event: The Curtis Cup Match (U.S. vs. Great Britain & Ireland)
Date: July 28–29
Site: Somerset Hills Country Club, Bernardsville, New Jersey

Event: The LPGA Championship
Date: July 30–August 5
Site: To be determined

Event: The U.S. Women's Amateur Championship
Date: August 6–11
Site: Canoe Brook Country Club, Summit, New Jersey

Event: The PGA Championship
Date: August 9–12
Site: Shoal Creek Golf Club, Birmingham, Alabama

Event: The U.S. Girls' Junior Championship
Date: August 13–18
Site: Manasquan River Golf Club, Brielle, New Jersey

Event: The U.S. Amateur Championship
Date: August 21–26
Site: Cherry Hills Country Club, Englewood, Colorado

Event: The U.S. Senior Women's Amateur Championship
Date: September 19–21
Site: Del Rio Golf and Country Club, Modesto, California

Event: The U.S. Women's Mid-Amateur Championship
Date: September 29–October 4
Site: Allegheny Country Club, Sewickley, Pennsylvania

Event: The U.S. Mid-Amateur Championship
Date: October 6–11
Site: Troon Golf & Country Club, Scottsdale, Arizona

Event: The U.S. Senior Amateur Championship
Date: October 15–16
Site: Desert Forest Golf Club, Carefree, Arizona

Event: The Women's World Amateur Team Championship
Date: October 18–21
Site: Christchurch, New Zealand

Event: The Men's World Amateur Team Championship
Date: October 25–28
Site: Christchurch, New Zealand

"In the last decade, there has been a startling boom in amateur competition. The number of traditional tournaments has remained fairly constant, but there has been great growth at both ends of the age spectrum—senior golf, mid-amateur golf, and junior golf."

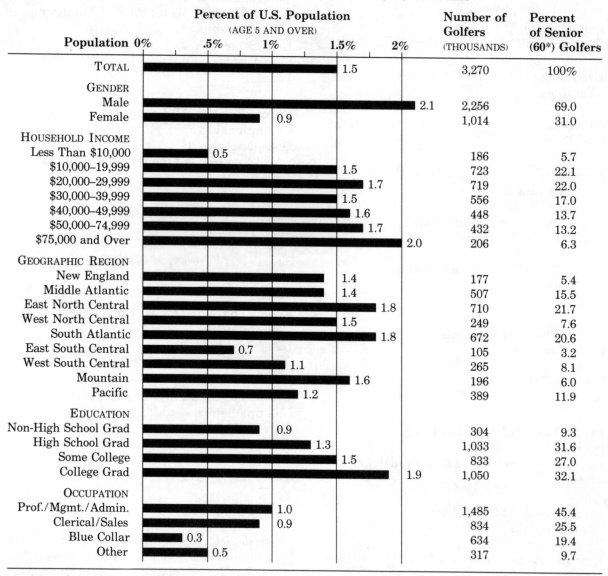

DEMOGRAPHIC PROFILE OF SENIOR (60*) GOLFERS

Population	Percent of U.S. Population (AGE 5 AND OVER)	Number of Golfers (THOUSANDS)	Percent of Senior (60*) Golfers
TOTAL	1.5	3,270	100%
GENDER			
Male	2.1	2,256	69.0
Female	0.9	1,014	31.0
HOUSEHOLD INCOME			
Less Than $10,000	0.5	186	5.7
$10,000–19,999	1.5	723	22.1
$20,000–29,999	1.7	719	22.0
$30,000–39,999	1.5	556	17.0
$40,000–49,999	1.6	448	13.7
$50,000–74,999	1.7	432	13.2
$75,000 and Over	2.0	206	6.3
GEOGRAPHIC REGION			
New England	1.4	177	5.4
Middle Atlantic	1.4	507	15.5
East North Central	1.8	710	21.7
West North Central	1.5	249	7.6
South Atlantic	1.8	672	20.6
East South Central	0.7	105	3.2
West South Central	1.1	265	8.1
Mountain	1.6	196	6.0
Pacific	1.2	389	11.9
EDUCATION			
Non-High School Grad	0.9	304	9.3
High School Grad	1.3	1,033	31.6
Some College	1.5	833	27.0
College Grad	1.9	1,050	32.1
OCCUPATION			
Prof./Mgmt./Admin.	1.0	1,485	45.4
Clerical/Sales	0.9	834	25.5
Blue Collar	0.3	634	19.4
Other	0.5	317	9.7

*Aged 60 and over.
Courtesy of The National Golf Foundation

DEMOGRAPHIC PROFILE OF JUNIOR GOLFERS

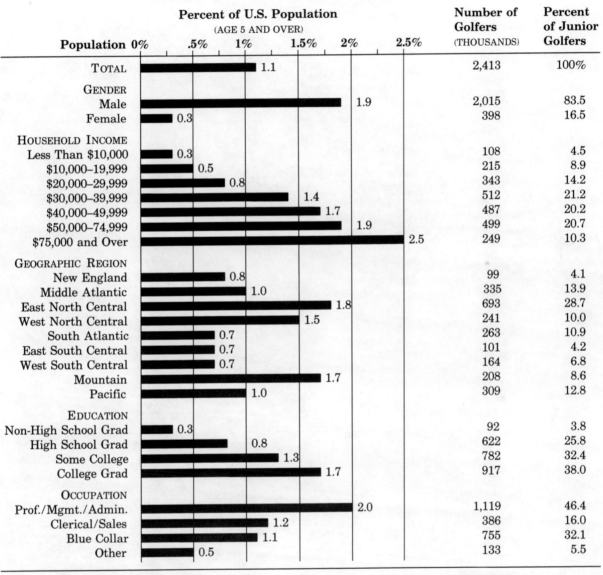

Population	Percent of U.S. Population (AGE 5 AND OVER)	Number of Golfers (THOUSANDS)	Percent of Junior Golfers
TOTAL	1.1	2,413	100%
GENDER			
Male	1.9	2,015	83.5
Female	0.3	398	16.5
HOUSEHOLD INCOME			
Less Than $10,000	0.3	108	4.5
$10,000–19,999	0.5	215	8.9
$20,000–29,999	0.8	343	14.2
$30,000–39,999	1.4	512	21.2
$40,000–49,999	1.7	487	20.2
$50,000–74,999	1.9	499	20.7
$75,000 and Over	2.5	249	10.3
GEOGRAPHIC REGION			
New England	0.8	99	4.1
Middle Atlantic	1.0	335	13.9
East North Central	1.8	693	28.7
West North Central	1.5	241	10.0
South Atlantic	0.7	263	10.9
East South Central	0.7	101	4.2
West South Central	0.7	164	6.8
Mountain	1.7	208	8.6
Pacific	1.0	309	12.8
EDUCATION			
Non-High School Grad	0.3	92	3.8
High School Grad	0.8	622	25.8
Some College	1.3	782	32.4
College Grad	1.7	917	38.0
OCCUPATION			
Prof./Mgmt./Admin.	2.0	1,119	46.4
Clerical/Sales	1.2	386	16.0
Blue Collar	1.1	755	32.1
Other	0.5	133	5.5

Courtesy of The National Golf Foundation

14
PUBLICATIONS

ALTHOUGH WE may live in the video-audio age, golfers have maintained a keen affection for the written word. To that end, the game supports dozens of regional golf magazines and newspapers in which golfers can keep up with the latest equipment trends, tournament results, and instruction. Golfers support no fewer than five major national magazines: *Golf Magazine, Golf World, Golf Digest, Golf Journal,* and the newest publication, *Golf Illustrated,* whose circulation has climbed from 35,000 to 400,000 since it was first published in 1985.

An example of the proclivity of golfers for information about their sport is the success of *Golf World,* America's oldest golf magazine. *Golf World* was founded by a former tour official, Robert Harlow, in 1947 in Southern Pines, North Carolina. Through four decades, the weekly magazine has offered "an insider's" view of the game and, for that reason, has been the bible for tournament players and golf professionals. Harlow believed that golfers shared a common bond and actually made up a "world" of their own. From the beginning, he sought to unify golfers by keeping them in touch with one another—a feat he accomplished by publishing amateur results, as well as pro tournament standings, from around the world.

Under Harlow, golfers became better known as people. In *Golf World,* a reader could follow men, women, and junior players, pros and amateurs from the birth of their competitive careers, literally to the grave, since the magazine published birth announcements, engagements, marriages, and even divorces.

Early *Golf World* covers had an innocent charm. They might show a famous woman amateur in her wedding dress, or Bing Crosby with his favorite foursome in Spain.

In 1962, Richard S. Taylor left his golf column at the Palm Beach *Post-Times* and became *Golf World's* editor. Under Taylor's leadership the magazine became even more of an opinion shaper. Taylor wrote pointed, sensible editorials. He put issues before the golfing public, and his close ties with a number of great players and industry leaders gave him keen insights into what was really happening in the game. For event coverage, Taylor often used local correspondents from tournament sites and, with his editing, *Golf World* stories were peppery and full of fun.

The magazine shrugged off instruction articles, the lifeblood of many golf magazines, and chose instead to be a source of information. In that role, it succeeded. Golfers who wanted to know what was truly going on in the game never missed an issue. The weekly "Bunker to Bunker" column was a must-

> *"Harlow believed that golfers shared a common bond and actually made up a 'world' of their own. From the beginning, he sought to unify golfers by keeping them in touch with one another..."*

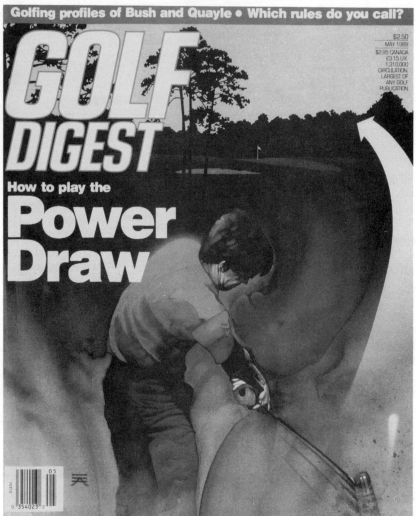

Golf Digest (Dost & Evans)

Richard S. Taylor

Golf World (Dost & Evans)

read for serious golfers. *Golf World* had a personality. Not only was the magazine highly informative, it also had charm and great readability.

In 1988, *Golf World* was sold to the *New York Times,* which also publishes the monthly *Golf Digest.* Under the new owners, Taylor stepped down as editor to become "editor at large," and continued to write his bright weekly column. The magazine moved from its home at Southern Pines to the *Golf Digest* headquarters in Trumbull, Connecticut. A couple of changes were instituted.

Golf World's look changed. With the new infusion of money, the weekly acquired slicker graphics, modern type styles, and better printing of photos. More space was devoted to the professional tours but less

> *"Early* Golf World *covers had an innocent charm. They might show a famous woman amateur in her wedding dress, or Bing Crosby with his favorite foursome in Spain."*

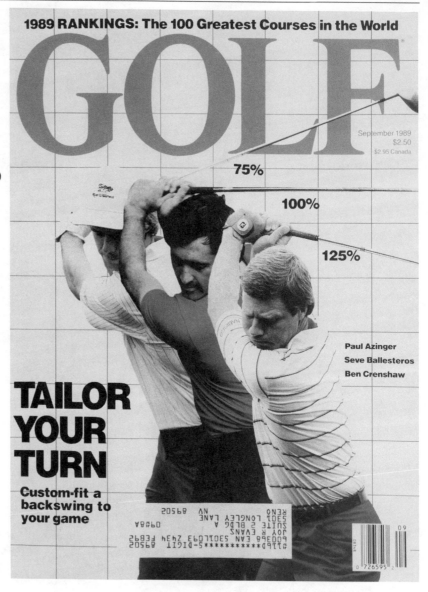

Golf Magazine (Dost & Evans)

space to amateur events and the insider tidbits that had given *Golf World* its unique place in the reading habits of serious players.

At this writing, *Golf World* is still getting on its feet under the new management.

Golf Magazine, established in 1959 in New York, has spawned a number of remarkable editors and writers: The pointed humor of Charles Price, who got his start at *Golf World,* blossomed further while he was on the *Golf Magazine* masthead. Al Barkow, who later became editor of the new *Golf Il-*

lustrated, is another *Golf Magazine* alumnus.

Golf Magazine has evolved, in recent years, into a sort of classicist publication. It's the "thinking golfer's" monthly. The magazine offers a literary slant on the game with the insights of fine columnists like Thomas Boswell and Frank Hannigan, former senior executive director of the United States Golf Association. Travel articles include the great international resorts, with stunning photographs.

Beginning in 1987, *Golf Magazine* scored

two coups under editor George Peper. Peper and senior editor Robin McMillan instituted monthly interviews with the game's major personalities, written versions of "up close and personal" visits with golf's movers and shakers. This series of "conversations" provided fascinating question-and-answer sessions with players of the caliber of Ben Hogan, Gene Sarazen, and Mickey Wright, and administrators like Deane Beman and Bill Blue, commissioners of the professional tours.

The series was prompted by *Golf Magazine*'s leap, in 1988, into a celebration of 100 years of American golf. The actual premise, that American golf was basically founded in 1888, stirred some controversy but when *Golf Magazine* celebrated the centennial in New York City in June, all was forgiven. In a glittering black-tie party at the Waldorf-Astoria, *Golf Magazine* editors managed to collect the American greats in one place, honoring a selected group called "golf's one hundred heroes." When the parade walked onto the dais—Ben Hogan, Byron Nelson, Sam Snead, Patty Berg, Arnold Palmer, Kathy Whitworth, Jack Nicklaus, and Tom Watson—it was goose-pimple time!

Golf Digest began life in 1950 in Evanston, Illinois, as a pamphlet-sized magazine called the *Arrowhead Golf Digest.* The book became a monthly in 1962. Under the umbrella of the *New York Times,* the magazine moved its headquarters to Norwalk, Connecticut, in the mid-1970s and now has a Trumbull, Connecticut, address.

The longtime circulation leader among golf publications, *Golf Digest* caught the attention of top players when the magazine instituted rankings of pros and amateurs and selected top performers to receive *Golf Digest* awards. The magazine branched out by sponsoring a sophisticated golf-instruction program in its *Golf Digest* schools and kept a number of top teaching pros on the masthead, including Jack Nicklaus, who was named Chief Playing Editor.

Over the years, *Golf Digest* captured some of the game's best writers: columnist Charles Price; Dave Anderson, the *New York Times* great; Peter Dobereiner, the British word guru; and Dan Jenkins, formerly of *Sports Illustrated.* Among golf authorities on the magazine's payroll are Joseph C. Dey, Jr., longtime USGA chief and former head of the PGA Tour; and Ron Whitten, golf course architecture expert.

Under Editorial Director Nick Seitz, the magazine became bigger, slicker, and flashier in the 1980s. Seitz and editor Jerry Tarde instituted frequent pointed critiques as part of the *Golf Digest* editorial policy. Sharply critical reviews and reader surveys pinpointed the best and worst golf personalities, books, broadcasts, videos, etc. The magazine stepped into previously unmapped territory when it asked readers to name their favorite and least-favorite touring professionals. The published results bruised feelings on both tours. *Golf Digest* editors also spearheaded trends, selecting periodical lists of what, and who, is "in" or "out."

Golf Digest boasts the slickest layouts and art of any of the golf magazines. Its person-

"Golf Magazine has evolved, in recent years, into a sort of classicist publication. It's the 'thinking golfer's' monthly. The magazine offers a literary slant on the game with the insights of fine columnists like Thomas Boswell and Frank Hannigan . . ."

"Golfers who wanted to know what was truly going on in the game never missed an issue. The weekly 'Bunker to Bunker' column was a must-read for serious golfers. Golf World *had a personality. Not only was the magazine highly informative, it also had charm and great readability."*

Golf Illustrated
(Dost & Evans)

ality profiles and equipment articles remain superior.

Golf Illustrated, which started publication in 1985, is a fast-growing and unique periodical. Stories are abbreviated, in-depth articles nonexistent, but *Golf Illustrated* offers a brief and trendy look at the game. While a golfer might include the other major magazines in a stack of bedside reading material, one can flip through *Golf Illustrated* on an airline flight. At fewer than 100 pages, the magazine doesn't offer the sheer bulk of *Golf Digest,* which boasts an "an-nual" edition of more than 250 pages. What it lacks in size and range, however, it makes up for in pep. Editor Al Barkow's column is colorful, instruction articles are simple and easy to read, and the magazine covers the small annoyances golfers must face—allergies, skin problems, and nutrition—in its Health & Fitness column. Like the others, *Golf Illustrated* covers new developments in the game: equipment, broadcasting, and videos. Its rise in circulation—twelve-fold in just four years—is a remarkable success story.

The magazine *Golf for Women,* marketed as *GFW,* began publication in 1988 in an effort to attract the game's growing number of distaff players. It is published by Debra and Woody Brummitt in Oxford, Mississippi.

GFW is heavy on instruction (the first issue included seven instruction articles) and boasts all-time leading tournament winner, Kathy Whitworth, as Playing Editor in Chief. Teaching professional, Sharon Miller, is Instruction Editor in Chief. The magazine includes news of state and regional women's golf associations, good coverage of amateurs as well as professionals, rules and equipment articles, health and fitness, profiles, and tournament coverage.

GFW is a first-class publication and as

> *"When the parade walked onto the dais—Ben Hogan, Byron Nelson, Sam Snead, Patty Berg, Arnold Palmer, Kathy Whitworth, Jack Nicklaus, and Tom Watson leading the way—it was goose-pimple time!"*

Golf for Women
(Dost & Evans)

Golf Journal
(Dost & Evans)

slick as any of the other golf periodicals, but women's golf has always been a tough market to crack.

Golf Journal, the official publication of the United States Golf Association, was first published in spring 1948. It's a subscription-only magazine and not available on newsstands. As the trumpet for the policies of the USGA, golf's ruling body in the United States, *Golf Journal* has always been at the forefront in terms of explaining changes in the game, from rules to equipment standards.

In recent years, the *Journal* has led all other publications in its focus on trends and issues. Readers have been presented with highly literate articles by publisher Robert Sommers and managing editor George Eberl on new concerns, environmental issues as they concern golf course maintenance and design, public golf, and women's golf. As the USGA goes, of course, so goes

Golf Journal, and the USGA's continuing concern for international play, history, artifacts, great old courses, and the game's integrity—such as the recent infamous bout over club grooves—is reflected in its pages.

The *Journal* is more than a serious tome: Eberl edits the notes at the beginning of the book with whimsy and finesse, and the magazine frequently runs funny little stories, well-edited, by addicted players of all ranks.

Current Publications

Arizona Golf Journal—Scottsdale, AZ
7124 E. 1st St.
Scottsdale, AZ 85251
(602) 949–8899
Published bimonthly

Back Nine magazine—Seattle, WA
Broadmoor Golf Club
2340 Broadmoor Drive E.
Seattle, WA 98112
(206) 325–5600

California Golf Journal—Palo Alto, CA
3790 El Camino Real, Ste. 164
Palo Alto, CA 94306
(415) 856–4775

Country Club—New Canaan, CT
(formerly The Golf Club)
16 Forest St.
New Canaan, CT 06840
(203) 972–3892
Issued bimonthly.

Eastern Golfer—New Jersey
P.O. Box 134
West End Station
West End, NJ 07740
(201) 222–4877
Issued eight times per year

Executive Golfer—Irvine, CA
2171 Campus Dr.
Irvine, CA 92715
(714) 752–6474
Issued bimonthly
Formerly *Country Club Golfer*
Published from 1971 to present

Fairway—New York
380 Madison Avenue
New York, NY 10017
(212) 687–3000
Issued annually

Fore—North Hollywood, CA
3740 Cahuenga Boulevard
North Hollywood, CA 91609
(213) 877–0901
Published from summer 1968 to present
Published bimonthly by the Southern
California Golf Association

> *"The magazine stepped into previously unmapped territory when it asked readers to name their favorite and least favorite touring professionals. The published results bruised feelings on both tours."*

George Eberl (Diane C. Becker)

Fore Golf—Wayne, Pennsylvania
2 Louella Court
Wayne, PA 19087
(215) 254–9619
Issued monthly

Golf Collectors' Society Bulletin—Lafayette Hill, PA
638 Wagner Road
Lafayette Hill, PA 19444
(215) 838–4492
Published from 1970 to present
Issued on an irregular basis
A bulletin for members of the Golf Collectors'
Society

Golf Course Management—Lawrence, KS
1617 St. Andrews Drive
Lawrence, Kansas 66046–9990
(913) 841–2240
Issued monthly
Formerly called *Golf Course Superintendent.*
Published by the Golf Course Superintendents'
Association of America

Golf Digest—Evanston, IL and Trumbull, CT
5520 Park Ave.
Trumbull, CT 06611
(203) 373–7000
First issue titled *Arrowhead Golf Digest.* They
moved to Connecticut in the mid 1970s. The
magazine became monthly in 1962.

Golf for Women (GFW)
426 S. Lamar Blvd.
Oxford, MS 38655
(601) 234–7570
Published from July 1988 to present

Golf Georgia—Atlanta
4200 Northside Parkway
Building 9, Suite 100
Atlanta, GA 30327
(404) 233–4742
Published quarterly
Publication of the Georgia State Golf
Association

Golf Illustrated—London
Published from June 1899 to present
A weekly, started as *Golf* in 1890

Golf Illustrated—New York
3 Park Ave.
New York, NY 10016
(212) 340–4805
Issued monthly
Published from 1985 to present

Golf Industry—Miami
915 NE 12th St., Suite 2C
N. Miami, FL 33161
(305) 893–8771
Issued nine times annually
Published from October 1975 to present
A trade journal for golf professionals,
retailers, etc.

Golf Journal—New York and Far Hills, NJ
USGA
Golf House
Far Hills, NJ 07931
(201) 234–2300
An official publication of the United States
Golf Association. Initially six issues, then
eight issues, then ten issues for a while in the
1970s, and now back to eight issues per year

Golf Magazine—New York
380 Madison Ave.
New York, NY 10017
(212) 687–3000
Issued monthly
Published from April 1959 to present
Frequency varied initially with twelve issues
per year starting 1963

Golf Market Today—Jupiter, FL
1150 South U.S. Highway 1
Jupiter, FL 33477
(407) 744–6107
Issued bimonthly
The official publication of the National Golf
Foundation

> *"GFW is a first-class publication and as
> slick as any of the other golf periodicals,
> but women's golf has, so far, been a
> tough market to crack."*

Golf Marketing North America, Inc.—New York
117 West 58th St., Suite 61
New York, NY 10019
(212) 956–2150
Issued as needed for professional tournaments, public and private golf courses. Spectator and yardage guides

Golf Monthly—Glasgow, Scotland
Published from 1910 to present

Golf News—Hove, England
Published from February 1979 to present
Formerly *Golf Club News*

Golf Pro Merchandiser—New York
7 East 12th Street
New York, NY 10003
(212) 741–5971
Issued four times annually

The Golf Reporter—Clinton, NC
Rt 6, Box 24
Clinton, NC 28328
(919) 592–3457

Golf Shop Operations—Norwalk, CT
5520 Park Ave.
Trumbull, CT 06611
(203) 340–7000
Issued 8 times annually
Supersedes Pro Shop Operations

Golf Traveler, The—Salt Lake City
1137 East 2100 South
Salt Lake City, UT 84106
(801) 486–9391
(800) 453–4260
Issued bimonthly
Published from 1976 to present

"As the USGA goes, of course, so goes Golf Journal, *and the USGA's continuing concern for international play, history, artifacts, great old courses, and the game's integrity—such as the recent infamous bout over grooves—is reflected in its pages."*

GolfWeek—Dundee, FL
P.O. Box 1808
Dundee, FL 33838
(813) 439–7424
Issued weekly

Golf World—Southern Pines, NC, and Trumbull, CT
5520 Park Ave.
Trumbull, CT 06611
(203) 373–7000
Formerly titled *Golf World Newsweekly.*
Moved to Southern Pines in 1968. Purchased by the *New York Times* in 1988. Moved to Trumbull, CT, in 1989. Published weekly, except bimonthly from October to December

Golf World—London
Published from 1962 to present
Absorbed *Golfing* in 1970

Golfer News Magazine, The
660 Rockside Road
Cleveland, OH 44131
(216) 749–4436
Issued monthly

Golfing in the Ohio Sun
660 Rockside Road
Cleveland, OH 44131
(216) 749–4436
Issued annually

Green Section Record—New York and Far Hills, NJ
USGA
Golf House
Far Hills, NJ 07931
(201) 234–2300
A United States Golf Association publication
Originally published until 1933 as the *Bulletin of the Green Section of the USGA.* Until this publication was revived in 1963, the USGA issued regional turf newsletters.

Grounds Maintenance Magazine's Golf Course Manual—Overland Park, KS
P.O. Box 12901
Overland Park, KS 66212
(913) 888–4664
Issued annually

Gulf Coast Golfer—Houston, Texas
9182 Old Katy Road, Ste 212
Houston, TX 77055
(713) 464–0308
Issued monthly
Published from February 1984 to present
A newspaper tabloid

Links Guide—Cleveland
1100 Superior Ave.
Cleveland, OH 44114
(216) 696–7000
Issued monthly

The Met Golfer—Norwalk, CT
17 North Ave.
Norwalk, CT 06851
(203) 849–5040
Published bimonthly

Michigan Golfer—Brighton, Michigan
7990 W. Grand River, Suite C
Brighton, MI 38116
(313) 227–4200
Published from April 1983 to present
Monthly April to September

North Texas Golfer—Houston
91820 Katy Road, Suite 212
Houston, TX 77055
(713) 464–0308
Issued monthly

Northern Texas PGA Professional Golfer—Plano, TX
500 N. Central #213
Plano, TX 75074
(214) 881–4653
Newsletter issued monthly
Annual issued yearly

> ". . . Golf Illustrated *covers new developments in the game: equipment, broadcasting, and videos. Its rise in circulation—twelve-fold in just four years—is a remarkable success story.*"

Ohio Golfer magazine—Columbus, OH
6290 Busch Blvd. Ste 20
Columbus, OH 43229
(614) 433–0393
Issued bimonthly

On the Green—Myrtle Beach
P.O. Box 1463
Myrtle Beach, SC 29582
(803) 272–8150
Issued quarterly
Published from 1977 to present
A South Carolina regional magazine

Palm Springs Golf News—Rancho Mirage, CA
P.O. Box 1040
Rancho Mirage, CA 92270

Par Excellence magazine—West Allis, WI
10401 W. Lincoln
West Allis, WI 53227

PGA Magazine—New York, then Palm Beach Gardens, FL
P.O. Box 109601
Palm Beach Gardens, FL 33410–9601
(407) 626–3600
Issued monthly
Published from 1920 to present
The official publication of the Professional Golfers Association of America

Score—Toronto
287 MacPherson Avenue
Toronto, Ontario, Canada M4V 1AY
Published from spring 1981 to present
Published quarterly

Senior Golf—Myrtle Beach
(No listed address, telephone only)
(803) 448–1569
Published from 1983 to present
Issued six times per year

Senior Golfer—Ft. Lauderdale
1323 S.E. 17th St., Suite 179
Ft. Lauderdale, FL 33316
(305) 527–0778
Issued bimonthly

Glenna Collett Vare, winner of six U.S. Women's Amateurs during the 1920s and 1930s. (Courtesy USGA)

Southern Golfer magazine—Winston-Salem
P.O. Box 11661
Winston-Salem, NC 27116
(919) 759312
Issued bimonthly

Southern Links—Hilton Head Island, SC
357 William Hilton Parkway
Hilton Head Island, SC 29926
(803) 681–7700
Issued bimonthly

Svensk Golf—Sweden
Published from 1975 to present

Tee Times—Orlando, FL
P.O. Box 561045
Orlando, FL 32856
(800) 833–7421
Issued monthly
Published from 1978 to present

Texas Golf—Austin, TX
Published from October 1978 to present

Tour—New York
380 Madison Ave.
New York, NY 10017
(212) 687–3000
Issued annually

South African Golf—Capetown
Published from June 1926 to present

15

SERVICES

NEW GOLFERS and old often find that there is a great deal more to being a golfer than simply playing the game. Whether in a country club or golf association, golfers sometimes discover that they are a part of running the game on a local and club level.

Green committees, handicap committees, and golf associations are full of board members who suddenly find they are faced with complex tasks in which they have little or no experience.

Does the green on the fourth hole have a fungus? Are members questioning their handicaps? What's the course rating and is it right? Do members want to take a golf trip? Does your junior program need a shot in the arm? Is your club hosting a big tournament? Perhaps new scorecards or yardage books are in demand.

Your golf professional, course superintendent, and club manager can be of great assistance in most of these tasks, but it's often up to club and association members to find new and better ways of running a golf operation.

Fortunately, a growing number of companies and organizations are devoting their efforts to the efficient and improved growth of the game.

One of the biggest assets in terms of problem solving is a club's membership in the United States Golf Association. The USGA offers member clubs, and golfers at large, invaluable assistance from the world's foremost golf experts.

For example, the USGA has assigned its Turf Advisory Service to help keep golf green. The USGA's experienced agronomists made nearly 1,400 personal visits to the nation's golf courses in 1988. Their goal is to help course superintendents and green committees develop the finest possible golf-course conditions. Thirteen such agronomists are on staff at the USGA for these consultations.

The Turf Advisory Service is available to any USGA member golf club or golf course.

Another service of the USGA Green Section, not readily apparent, will provide long-range benefits to the nation's golfers: the USGA funds turfgrass development at various colleges. The newest discovery is a turf-type buffalo grass developed with USGA funding at the University of Nebraska. Such hearty grasses will go a long way toward cutting down maintenance and watering costs.

The USGA is also releasing a videotape on how properly to construct a putting green, which may interest golfers who gaze at their own backyard and that nice level spot under the clothesline with a gleam in the eye!

Another available service is the rating of golf courses, now done with the USGA's

> "... it's often up to club and association members to find new and better ways of running a golf operation."

The USGA's handicapping service, GHIN, serves more than 900,000 golfers. (Courtesy USGA)

Slope System—a system that rates holes by their difficulty, taking all handicap groups into account.

The Slope System is complex. But trained course rating teams, certified by the USGA and available through your regional or state golf association, will be happy to rate your golf course.

While most of the nation's golf courses have already been "Sloped," this is an important step for any new layout.

The Slope System is a common denominator for golfers of differing abilities to play different courses with a legitimate handicap. Many of those handicaps are channeled through another USGA service, the Golf Handicap Information Network, commonly known as GHIN.

GHIN is the computerized clearinghouse for 900,000 golfers. Imagine what havoc this staggering number of golfers would have wreaked in the old days of handicap accounting! GHIN is now used by thirty-nine large regional golf associations.

Part of the service is the GHIN Electronic Option, an in-club terminal that communicates with the main GHIN computers at Golf House in Far Hills, New Jersey, through a modem using a toll-free number. More than 700 clubs use this option.

While the USGA runs GHIN as a nonprofit operation, a number of companies have entered the new field of computerized handicapping and offer excellent service. You'll find these companies in the listings at the end of the chapter. It's worth shopping around to find the best handicapping service for your club or local golf association.

The USGA handicap system is available to small groups as well as large golf associations. Recently the USGA specified that as few as ten people could make up a golf "club," if the group follows a few simple rules:

- The club must have a functioning handicap committee.
- Peer review must exist.
- A club must require the return of all attested scores made at home or away.
- Handicap committees must maintain the integrity of USGA Handicap Indexes.
- Club policies must abide by The Rules of Golf.

The National Golf Foundation is another service-oriented golf organization. The NGF offers valuable research material to members. For example, as a member, I recently requested and received the following booklets:

- Golf Market Today—chock full of information about growth in the golf industry.
- Golf Course Development Today—outlining the strategic planning of fulfilling the nation's needs for new golf courses, and tracking the latest golf course development projects.
- Golf Facilities in the United States—a survey of golf courses in each state.
- Senior Citizens and Golf—how to set up Senior organizations, using the successful programs in Tucson and Milwaukee as models.

If you're seeking to set up a good junior or senior golf program on any level, the National Golf Foundation—probably the premier information-gathering network in the game—will help you do it.

Private firms, oriented to the service side of the game, include companies that print scorecards and yardage books and companies to handle the chores of tournament management.

Golf travel is another growing industry, but the very fact that golf is growing worldwide gives those who deal in golf tours a unique set of problems. Through the early 1980s, it was relatively easy for American travel agencies to get tee times at the most desirable courses in Europe, most notably, in Scotland. Golf's popularity abroad, however, means that more international players are taking these same golf tours, and tee times are now at a premium. Many travel agencies are reluctant to guarantee starting times at the time-honored Scottish courses, like the Olde Course at St. Andrews. For that reason, many American tourists are discovering the pleasures of golf in Ireland and Spain. However, playing golf abroad remains a popular vacation choice.

Most travel agencies will be happy to provide information on foreign golf tours. A list of tour operators specializing in golf travel is included at the end of this chapter.

Another service organization is the PGA of America. The PGA offers a number of services for golf professionals and many aids for golfers as a group.

One of the most successful programs is the PGA's "First Swing" effort. First Swing is designed to promote junior golf. The program, which introduces children to golf, has been adopted by a number of school systems. The First Swing program is administered under the PGA of America's Junior Golf Foundation, which was founded in 1978.

Other junior golf programs run by the PGA of America include the very successful Clubs for Kids and School Golf Development.

The following organizations and companies are among those who can help you in these important behind-the-scenes phases of the game.

"The Slope System is a common denominator for golfers of differing abilities to play different courses with a legitimate handicap."

Golf Service Organizations and Companies

Country Club Systems
990 Fairport Office Park
Fairport, NY 14450
(716) 377–6730
Computerized handicapping

Golf Handicap Information Network (GHIN)
The United States Golf Association
Golf House
Far Hills, NJ 07931
(201) 234–2300
Computerized handicapping

Golf Marketing North America, Inc.
117 West 58th St., Suite 61
New York, NY 10019
(212) 956–2150
Yardage guides for public and private golf courses. Spectator guides for professional tournaments

Handicomp, Inc.
P.O. Box 87
60 Baldwin St.
Genison, MI 49428
(616) 457–9581
Computerized handicapping

Logical Solutions
2217 Timberwood
Carrollton, TX 75006
(214) 387–8027
Computerized handicapping

National Golf Foundation
1150 South U.S. Highway One
Jupiter, FL 33477
(407) 744–6006
Information, research on golf programs, golf-course development, related subjects

PGA of America
P.O. Box 109601
Palm Beach Gardens, FL 33410–9601
(407) 626–3600
Golf professional services, junior golf programs

Professional Tournament Management
3633 Talmadge Road
Toledo, O 43606
(419) 472–2317
Tournament management

Profile Publishing Inc.
441 5th Ave S.W., Suite 900
Calgary, Alberta, Canada T2P 2V1
(403) 233–8150
Scorecard publishing

Smyth Business Systems
P.O. Box 8800
Canton, O 44711
(800) 462–4372
Computerized handicapping, computerized tournament management

Turf Advisory Service
United States Golf Association
Golf House
Far Hills, NJ 07931
(201) 234–2300
Turf consultants, turfgrass research

Golf Travel

SCGA Travel
3740 Cahuenga Blvd.
North Hollywood, CA 91609
(818) 509–0662
International and domestic golf tours

GOLF IN ASIA

Eastquest
32 Pell St.
New York, NY 10013
(800) 638–3449

Speedtravel Destination Management Company
933 Pico Blvd.
Santa Monica, CA 90405
(800) 888–5898

GOLF IN AUSTRALIA

ITC Golf Tours
Box 5144
Long Beach, CA 90805
(800) 257–4981
(213) 595–6905 in California

SO/PAC
1448 15th St., Suite 105
Santa Monica, CA 90404
(800) 551–2012
(800) 445–0190 in California

South Pacific Travel Planners
25201 Paseo De Alicia
Suite 240
Laguna Hills, CA 92653
(800) 421–3197
(800) 624–7926 in California

Tourplan U.S.A.
P.O. Box 3739
New York, NY 10185
(718) 268–0285

GOLF IN AUSTRIA

International Golf Vacations
303 Radel Terrace
South Orange, NJ 07079
(201) 378–9170

Pego
A-6700 Bludenz
Sageweg 12, Austria
Telephone 5552–65666

Value Holidays
10224 N. Port Washington Road
Mequon, WI 53092
(800) 558–6850
(414) 241–6373 in Wisconsin

GOLF IN THE BAHAMAS

International Sports Council
P.O. Box 3071
Long Beach, CA 90803
(800) 523–1741
(213) 434–6741 in California

GOLF IN GREAT BRITAIN

Group Department
CIE Tours International
122 E. 42nd St.
New York, NY 10168
(212) 972–5604
(800) 223–6508

Especially Britain
P.O. Box 121398
Fort Worth, TX 76121
(817) 763–5754

Exclusive Golf Holidays
5925 Kirby Dr. #210
Houston, TX 77005
(800) 433–9386

Expeditions
72 Park St.
P.O. Box 998
New Canaan, CT 06840–0998
(800) 888–9400

Golf Tours
400 Esplanade Dr.
Suite 102
Oxnard, CA 93030
(800) PAR FIVE

International Golf Vacations
303 Radel Terrace
South Orange, NJ 07079
(201) 378–9170

International Sports Council
P.O. Box 3071
Long Beach, CA 90803
(800) 523–1741
(213) 434–6741 in California

"The GHIN handicap service is available to small groups as well as large. Recently the USGA specified that as few as ten people could make up a golf 'club,' if the group follows a few simple rules."

ITC Golf Tours
Box 5144
Long Beach, CA 90805
(800) 257–4981
(213) 595–6905 in California

Journeys Thru Scotland Co.
35 South Encino Rd.
South Laguna, CA 92677
(800) 521–1429
(714) 499–4410 in California

Scottish Golf Holidays
9403 Kenwood Road. Suite A205
Cincinnati, OH 45242
(800) 284–8884

Historic Homes of Britain
21 Pembroke Square
London W.8., England
Telephone 01–937 2402

Value Holidays
10224 N. Port Washington Road
Mequon, WI 53092
(800) 558–6850
(414) 241–6373 in Wisconsin

GOLF IN EUROPE

Expeditions
72 Park St.
P.O. Box 998
New Canaan, CT 06840–0998
(800) 888–9400

Value Holidays
10224 N. Port Washington Road
Mequon, WI 53092
(800) 558–6850
(414) 241–6373 in Wisconsin

> *"Private firms, oriented to the service side of the game, include companies that print scorecards and yardage books . . . handle the chores of tournament management . . . and set up golfing tours."*

Vantage
P.O. Box 5774
Greenville, SC 29606
(803) 233–7703
(800) 826–8268

GOLF IN IRELAND

Group Department
CIE Tours International
122 E. 42nd St.
New York, NY 10168
(212) 972–5604
(800) 223–6508

Exclusive Golf Holidays
5925 Kirby Dr. #210
Houston, TX 77005
(800) 433–9386

International Golf Vacations
303 Radel Terrace
South Orange, NJ 07079
(201) 378–9170

ITC Golf Tours
Box 5144
Long Beach, CA 90805
(800) 257–4981
(213) 595–6905 in California

Value Holidays
10224 N. Port Washington Road
Mequon, WI 53092
(800) 558–6850
(414) 241–6373 in Wisconsin

GOLF IN PORTUGAL

Exclusive Golf Holidays
5925 Kirby Dr. #210
Houston, TX 77005
(800) 433–9386

International Golf Vacations
303 Radel Terrace
South Orange, NJ 07079
(201) 378–9170

Robert T. Jones, the 1930 winner of the Grand Slam. The trophies (from left to right): the British Open, the U.S. Amateur, the British Amateur, and the U.S. Open. (Courtesy USGA).

Value Holidays
10224 N. Port Washington Road
Mequon, WI 53092
(800) 558–6850
(414) 241–6373 in Wisconsin

GOLF IN SPAIN

Exclusive Golf Holidays
5925 Kirby Dr. #210
Houston, TX 77005
(800) 433–9386

International Golf Vacations
303 Radel Terrace
South Orange, NJ 07079
(201) 378–9170

ITC Golf Tours
P.O. Box 5144
Long Beach, CA 90805
(800) 257–4981
(213) 595–6905

INDEX

Improve your game, find the reference material you need, and learn all the rules "officially," in these comprehensive Perigee golf guides.

Break 100 in 21 Days
A How-to Guide for the Weekend Golfer
by Walter Ostroske and John Devaney
illustrated with over 50 black-and-white photographs

The first easy-to-follow program for shooting in the 90s and 80s, aimed at the person who plays only ten to twenty times a year, mostly on weekends. Ostroske, a PGA teaching pro for over twenty years, teaches a swing that is the same for all clubs and ninety-nine percent of all shots. His 21-day program, geared to average men and women, has clear instructions and covers every important aspect of play.

Golf Rules in Pictures
An Official Publication of the United States Golf Association
Introduction by Arnold Palmer

Scores of clearly captioned pictures cover all the rules of golf: scoring, number of clubs allowed, procedure when a player's ball is hit accidentally, hazards, and penalty strokes. Included is the complete text of The Rules of Golf as approved by the United States Golf Association and the Royal and Ancient Golf Club of St. Andrews, Scotland.

These books are available at your local bookstore or wherever books are sold.

Also, ordering is easy and convenient. Just call 1-800-631-8571 or send your order to:

The Putnam Publishing Group
390 Murray Hill Parkway, Dept. B
East Rutherford, NJ 07073

- -

| | | PRICE | |
		U.S.	CANADA
_____ **Break 100 in 21 Days**	399-51600	$7.95	$10.50
_____ **Golf Rules in Pictures**	399-51438	6.95	9.25

Subtotal $ _____
*Postage & handling $ _____
Sales Tax $ _____
(CA, NJ, NY, PA)
Total Amouut Due $ _____
Payable in U.S. Funds
(No cash orders accepted)

*Postage & handling: $1.00
for 1 book, 25¢ for each
additional book up to a
maximum of $3.50

Please send me the titles I've checked above.
Enclosed is my   ☐ check   ☐ money order
Please charge my   ☐ Visa   ☐ MasterCard
Card # _____ Expiration date _____
Signature as on charge card _____
Name _____
Address _____
City _____ State _____ Zip _____

Please allow six weeks for delivery. Prices subject to change without notice.